PRECARIOUS
ACCUMULATION

PRECARIOUS ACCUMULATION

FAST FASHION BOSSES IN

TRANSNATIONAL GUANGZHOU

Nellie Chu

DUKE UNIVERSITY PRESS   DURHAM AND LONDON   2026

Project Editor: Ihsan Taylor
Designed by Matthew Tauch
Typeset in Alegreya and Retail by
Westchester Publishing Services

Library of Congress Cataloging-in-Publication Data
Names: Chu, Nellie, [date] author.
Title: Precarious accumulation : fast fashion bosses in
transnational Guangzhou / Nellie Chu.
Description: Durham : Duke University Press, 2026. |
Includes bibliographical references and index.
Identifiers: LCCN 2025026103 (print)
LCCN 2025026104 (ebook)
ISBN 9781478033097 (paperback)
ISBN 9781478029649 (hardcover)
ISBN 9781478061830 (ebook)
Subjects: LCSH: Ready-to-wear clothing industry—China—
Guangzhou—Management. | Ready-to-wear clothing
industry—China—Guangzhou. | Internal migrants—China. |
Capitalism—China.
Classification: LCC HD9940.C63 G83 2026 (print) |
LCC HD9940.C63 (ebook)
LC record available at https://lccn.loc.gov/2025026103
LC ebook record available at https://lccn.loc.gov/2025026104

Cover art: A typical *jiagongchang* household workshop
in Guangzhou, 2018. Photo by Nellie Chu.

I dedicate this book to my grandparents and parents,

Shirley and Louis Chu.

They have given me life, love, and hope.

Contents

Acknowledgments

They say that it takes a village to write a book. This book has been made possible by villages of mentors, friends, and colleagues scattered across the globe. I am indebted to them for the love, faith, trust, and support that they have provided me, from the early formulations of this project to the final version of the manuscript. Without them, I would not have had the courage and stamina to complete this book.

Lisa Rofel has provided me with generous guidance and unwavering support from my early years of graduate school training to today. A dedicated mentor and teacher, she has shown me what it means to be an exceptional scholar, one who remains committed to the work of promoting and advising younger generations of feminist scholars and writers. Without her guidance, I would not have been able to complete this project and publish this book. I hope to mirror her commitment to teaching, activism, and advising with my own students and mentees. I am also thankful to Gail Hershatter and Melissa Caldwell for their careful and attentive reading of the early drafts of this manuscript. Their honest and insightful feedback has helped me to develop my authorial voice and refine my arguments.

The scholarly training that I have received at the University of California, Santa Cruz, provided the foundational anthropological and historical training I needed to initiate this project. Instruction from Lisa Rofel, Gail Hershatter, Emily Honig, Melissa Caldwell, Anna Tsing, Carolyn Martin Shaw, Mark Anderson, Don Brennis, Triloki Pandey, Annapurna Pandey, Dan Linger, Susan Harding, James Clifford, Matthew Wolf-Meyer, and many others among the faculty in Santa Cruz has guided me through the delicate nuances of historical and ethnographic writing, while pushing me to remain intellectually open and curious about our world.

I remain thankful to my intellectual kin in Santa Cruz, who have nurtured my scholarly growth and development. I have fond memories of collectively working through complex ideas and readings while taking meditative walks in the forests by College Nine and along the beautiful beaches at West Cliff. Looking back, those days were crucial in helping me grow into the kind of scholar I wanted to be. Friends, including Micha Rahder, Patricia Alvarez Astacio, Kim Cameron-Dominguez, Conal Ho, Colin Hoag, Aimee Villareal, Ana Candela, Stephanie Chan, Sarah Chee, Carla Takaki-Richardson, Peter Leykam, J. Brent Crosson, Rosa Ficek, Xiaoping Sun, Amanda Schuman, Fang Yu Hu, Dustin Wright, Wenqing Kang, Jerry Chen, Daniel Allen Soloman, Xochitl Chavez, Michael Jin, Cassie Ambutter, Sarah Mak, Xiaobei Gao, Yajun Mo, Sara Smith-Silverman, Tim Yamamura, and Stephie McCallum made my time in Santa Cruz intellectually and personally meaningful. Special thanks to Jeremy Tai, Sarah Bakker Kellogg, Sarah Kelman, Noah Tamarkin, and Juno Parrenas, whose kindness and intellect have sustained me, especially in moments of self-defeat, impatience, and self-doubt. I feel truly loved and valued by their friendship and care. My memories shared with these special people are embedded in the pages of this book.

Field research in Guangzhou was made memorable by the inspiring conversations, city walks, and factory visits with the following friends and colleagues: Ellen Friedman, Eli Friedman, Florian Butello, May Bo Ching, Sujuan Huang, Boy Luethje, Kevin Carrico, Wenjuan Jia, Miao Tian, Guowei Liang, Xiang Zi, and Siqi Luo, and other friends I met at Sun Yatsen University in Guangzhou. They helped me to extend my scholarly interests to the realms of community engagement and social work. Damon Sit, Manon Diederich, Xiao Hu, Bintou Ndiaye Fall, Krystal Cheung, Ray Siu, and Arian Saghafi made my stay in Guangzhou fun and memorable. Peter Sharp Sack, Willa Dong, Hieu Pham, Jennifer S. Cheng, Rachel Core, Casey Miller, Annie Katsura Rollins, Haiyi Lu, Nathan Keltner, Janet Upton, and Tricia Wang, and other friends and colleagues whom I met through the US Department of State Fulbright Institute of International Education Dissertation Research Fellowship Program (Fulbright IIE) from Fall 2010 to Summer 2011 enhanced my field research experiences through unforgettable trips and exchanges. Conversations with Matthew Hale, Tu Hyunh, Jessica Wilczak, and Shayan Momin refined my knowledge of critical theory, particularly on the topics of class, labor, race, and social movements.

My days spent in the forests, cafes, and seminar rooms in Göttingen, Cologne, Berlin, and other cities in Germany and Switzerland allowed me to broaden my understanding of gender, Marxism, ethnology, religion, and Sinology. Katja Pessl, Tina Schilbach, Dietrich Homann, Saikat Maitra, Sarah Eaton, Daniel Fuchs, Leilah Vevaina, Tim Rosenkranz, Sabine

Mohamed, Scott Macloachlainn, Sajida Tuxun, Charlotte Bruckermann, Leonie Newhouse, Alanna Krolikowski, Liza Kam Wing Man, Nan Nan, Mario Becksteiner, Neena Mahadev, Malini Sur, Axel Schneider, Lisa Björkman, Angie Heo, Kristin Plys, Karolina Radon, Jean-Baptiste Pettier, Lena Kauffman, Michaela Pelican, Susanne Brandtstaedter, Sung Un, Heidi Ostbo Haugen, Peter Van der Veer, Tam Ngo, and Kenneth Dean were instrumental in the early years of my writing. They made my time in Europe meaningful, providing the support I needed to sharpen my skills in ethnographic writing, while I deepened my readings of migration, entrepreneurship, religion, and China. My postdoctoral position in Germany allowed me to expand my scholarly interests beyond an American-centric point of view. For that, I am truly thankful.

My colleagues at Duke University and at Duke Kunshan University (DKU) were critical in pushing me forward as I completed this marathon of book-writing. Mengqi Wang, Qian Zhu, Selina Lai-Henderson, Seth Henderson, Emily McWilliams, Lindsay Mahon Rathnam, Lincoln Rathnam, Zach Fredman, Yu Wang, Keping Wu, Robin Rodd, Megan Rogers, Titas Chakraborty, Jesse Olsavsky, Benjamin Anderson, Eric Chia-Chien Chen, Annemieke Van Dool, James Miller, Kim Hunter-Gordon, Yitzhak Lewis, James Miller, Kolleen Guy, Scott MacEachern, and other faculty members at DKU have provided wonderful collegiality and support. I am especially thankful to my friends and fellow coauthors Ralph Litzinger, Mengqi Wang, and Qian Zhu for working with me—in my early years at DKU—on our edited volume on China's urban villages in the journal *positions: asia critique*. Thanks to them, I found my joy for collaborative research and writing. I also thank Tani Barlow for making our edited volume possible.

The funding provided by the DKU Humanities Research Institute for a book manuscript workshop allowed me to transform early drafts of my work into a publication that I feel proud to present to the world. I am grateful to Lisa Rofel, Sylvia Yanagisako, Carlos Rojas, Ralph Litzinger, Noah Tamarkin, and Juno Parrenas for taking the time to carefully read and comment on my drafts. I am also grateful to Colin Hoag for his comments on my drafts. Editorial assistance by Micha Rahder was crucial to the final drafts of this book. Without her thoughtful and insightful comments on my writing, I would not have been able to complete this project.

Research support for this book was made possible by the DKU Center for Contemporary China Studies and the Humanities Research Institute; a postdoctoral fellowship provided by Cornell University School of Industrial and Labor Relations; the American Council for Learned Societies / Henry

Luce Foundation for China Studies; the National Endowment for the Humanities; a postdoctoral fellowship from the Center for Modern East Asian Studies (CeMEAS), University of Göttingen; and a postdoctoral fellowship from the Center for Transregional Research Network (CETREN) at the University of Göttingen, Germany. From April 2014 to April 2016, I collaborated with others under the project theme "Entrepreneurial Citizenship: New Economies and the Respatialization of Citizenship in China, India, and Europe," led by Srirupa Roy, Rupa Viswanath, Axel Schneider, and Peter van der Veer.

I also received financial support from the University of California Pacific Rim Research Program (Fall 2010–Summer 2011); an Advanced Graduate Research Fellowship for dissertation research in Guangzhou in 2010; the US Department of State Fulbright Institute of International Education (IIE) Dissertation Research Fellowship Program (Fall 2010–Summer 2011); the University of California Pacific Rim Research Program Mini-Grant in Summer of 2009; the National Science Foundation Graduate Research Supplementary Grant Research Fellowship in collaboration with principal investigator Lisa Rofel; the National Science Foundation Graduate Research Fellowship (Fall 2007–Summer 2009); the University of California, Santa Cruz Regents' Fellowship; and the University of California, Santa Cruz, Department of Anthropology, in summer of 2007. I am especially grateful to the city of Göttingen, Germany, for the state unemployment benefits that I received from 2016 to 2017. The financial support that I received during the gap year made my early publications possible.

I am also grateful to Li Zhang, Susan Mann, and G. William Skinner for their instruction and mentorship during my undergraduate years at the University of California, Davis. Their teaching and writing inspired me to set on this lifelong path of anthropological inquiry. I am especially thankful to Li Zhang for her encouragement and inspiration. As an undergraduate research assistant, I saw her passion and love for the discipline while I assisted her in putting the final touches on her first book. I am proud to present my first book to her in return.

I thank Ken Wissoker, Ryan Kendall, Ihsan Taylor, and the rest of the editorial team at Duke University Press—as well as copyeditor Steph Attia and indexer Nancy Zibman—for their unwavering enthusiasm and support during the review and publication process. I deeply appreciate the anonymous reviewers for their keen and insightful comments and feedback. Their attentive reviews helped me to refine and strengthen the conceptual framing and arguments of my manuscript beyond what I could possibly have imagined when I first submitted the draft.

Above all, I am thankful to my biological kin. Words cannot express the gratitude that I have, and will continue to have, for the unconditional love and support that they have entrusted upon me throughout my life journey. I am thankful to my bestie twin, Nelly Won Tinloy, and the Tinloy family for their kindness and care. I thank my brother, Lowell Chu, and his family, Conall and Lisa Chu, for their love and support. I am also grateful to my aunt Lily Mak; my paternal cousins in San Francisco, Sylvia Mark and Charlene Mak; and my maternal cousins Phyllis Chan and Iris Chan as well as the rest of my Chan family in Hong Kong, who have given me encouragement and support as I shuttled between Guangzhou, Hong Kong, and San Francisco over the course of my training and research.

My parents, Shirley and Louis Chu, gave me the love, care, and nurture that I needed to chart this scholarly life for myself. I dedicate this book to my parents and grandparents, particularly my mom and my grandmothers, whose life stories have spanned thousands of miles from Suzhou, Shanghai, Guangzhou, Macau, Hong Kong, and San Francisco. Their intergenerational experiences of war, transnational migration, and motherhood have shaped the contours of my family history. Even though I am, at present, not able to restitch my family history with any sense of finality or closure, their personal hardships and sacrifice have demonstrated to me what Chinese feminism looks like and how it is embodied through everyday practices of unconditional love and care. I hope that this book testifies to their personal strength and courage, and it is my wish that their spirits come alive through the stories told in this book for years and decades to come.

Introduction

On the evening of November 14, 2022, hundreds of migrants in Zhaocun and the surrounding urban villages of Guangzhou stormed out of their apartments and pushed down the tall, water-filled plastic barricades that lined one of the main thoroughfares of this garment district. The demonstrators, most of whom were migrants from Hubei Province who formed the informal *Hubeicun* (Hubei village), organized the collective action against stringent COVID restrictions, including daily mass testing and strict quarantine requirements. Most of the protesters included migrant bosses, the owners of small-scale household workshops that manufacture garments for fast fashion brands. Prior to the lockdowns, these migrant bosses and the laborers they hired had been frantically preparing garment production orders for November 11, or "Singles' Day," marketed by China's online corporate giants Taobao, Tianmall, and Alibaba as one of the biggest and most profitable shopping days of the year.

Here, in Guangzhou's largest garment district, migrants work across the global supply chains for low-cost fast fashion. Fast fashion is the "just in time" delivery of trendy and low-cost fashion garments and accessories, which are sold in low volumes. It relies critically on the transnational subcontracting of low-wage labor and manufacturing capabilities among rural-to-urban migrants in China and across the Global South. Globally recognized brands source their samples and accessories within these urban villages. Falling profits and dwindling production orders since the start of the COVID-19 pandemic in late 2019 made the flood of these production orders especially important to the economic survival of the small-scale businesses in Guangzhou and, along with them, to the financial livelihoods of the migrants who sustain them.

The lockdown mandates in the weeks and months prior to the protest event brought most, if not all, garment manufacturing activities to a halt. During the night of the protests, demonstrators cheered as they walked down the road in collective resistance against the long-standing lockdowns and other strict COVID measures in Guangzhou. Images of resistance and protest quickly circulated across social media channels in China and abroad, garnering international media attention for the scale and intensity of anger and discontent.

While observers and audiences across China and around the globe applauded the demonstrators, citing the collective action as rare direct resistance against state mandates, a deeper ethnographic analysis reveals the extent of exploitation and extraction that migrant bosses and laborers in these urban villages had already endured to keep up with fast fashion supply chains. Their experiences of ambivalent success and ongoing uncertainty had become structurally part of migrants' engagements with small-scale entrepreneurship and transnational capitalism, long before the COVID-19 pandemic. This book focuses on the market dynamics that shaped migrants' experiences of labor and livelihood as they worked across the transnational supply chains of fast fashion before and during the COVID-19 pandemic.

Mainstream critiques of fast fashion frequently center on problems related to climate change, sweatshop labor, unethical knockoffs, and cultural appropriation (Cline 2013; Klein 1999; Bravo 2020; The F Team 2021; Minney 2017; Siegle 2011; D. Thomas 2019).[1] While these criticisms highlight the nefarious effects of producing and consuming low-cost, disposable fashion characteristic of post-Fordist, "just in time" capitalism, this book lays out the stakes of fast fashion in a distinctive and unconventional light. It analyzes this sector of the global fashion industry as a historic movement in transnational capitalism that is specifically tied to China's postsocialist transformations of land, labor, and personhood.[2]

At the heart of these transformations is the emergence of the small-scale migrant entrepreneur, colloquially known as "boss," or *laoban*. Bosshood, I argue, is a transitional mode of personhood that migrants variously take on as they cross the threshold between labor and capital, attempting to convert their social statuses from working-class migrants to rightful entrepreneurs. Attention to migrant bosses therefore also shifts our analyses from fashion as a realm of consumption associated with cosmopolitanism and middle-class livelihood to migrant subcontractors in the worlds of production and distribution, whose own aspirations for these values compel them to take on various accumulative practices that are essential to the operation of fast fashion supply chains.[3] As a figure of capitalist accumulation, the migrant boss is characterized by the tension between the compulsion to accumulate capital and the various forms of dispossession that migrants experience in their pursuit of wealth and financial autonomy. I introduce the concept of *precarious accumulation* to bridge these structural conditions of precariousness with the intersubjective dimensions of aspiration and desire for bosshood. The figure of the migrant boss hovers on the knife-edge between boundless riches and merciless ruin in southern China's so-called workshop of the world.

While the title of "boss" implies control over stable and continuous accumulation, its juxtaposition with the position of the "migrant," as someone who embodies risk and economic instability, illustrates the ambivalence and contradictions that characterize precarious accumulation among migrant laborers and subcontractors in the world of fast fashion in Guangzhou. As a middle ground between freedom and constraint, bosshood enables migrants to negotiate the terms of their own exploitation so as to claim for themselves, albeit in limited terms, a sense of identity, autonomy, and respect. Migrants' aspirations and hopes tell us about more than the sense of hyperreality, false consciousness, or the manufactured reality of their experiences of labor and livelihood (as thinkers in the Frankfurt School might suggest, e.g., Horkheimer and Adorno [2002]). They lend insight into the structural violence that persists on a transnational scale and that remains deeply embedded within the promises of freedom through migratory self-enterprise.

In Guangzhou, rural migrants from China's countryside collaborate with South Korean jobbers and West African traders, two of the largest populations of transnational migrants in the city's fast fashion markets and urban villages, as they collectively bridge the transnational supply chains of low-cost garments and accessories via small-scale entrepreneurship. In their attempts to escape poverty, wage work, and unemployment in their home countries and native places, these migrant entrepreneurs aspire to become good, even godly, model entrepreneurs by improvising novel forms of subcontracted labor and cross-cultural collaboration.[4] While there is no single instantiation of bosshood, migrants' experiences of *laoban* are intimately shaped by these broader socioeconomic dynamics as well as by the employment and migration histories they bring into their divergent roles and positions along fast fashion supply chains.

By delving into the figure of the migrant "boss," this book takes the worlds of labor and capital not as separable entities. Rather, it examines the generative relations between these worlds, narrating how land, labor, and personhood in a postsocialist context are transformed into forces that are made ready and available for extraction. The migrant boss, as I show, is critically linked to deepening postsocialist China's engagements with global capitalism. The rise of this figure through small-scale subcontracting represents a historic moment in which productive energies that were once invested in Maoist projects of collectivization in China are now fragmented, individuated, and mobilized for profit: the main organizing principle of free market enterprise (Nitzan and Bichler 2009; Veblen 1904). Capital, in this sense, represents more than just an object or an ideology. It is a mode of power through which the dynamics of accumulation materialize via the extraction, exploitation, and extortion of the creative forces that undergird relations of class, industry, and labor (Nitzan and Bichler 2009). As a corollary, the "boss" is an agent of capital, an emergent mode of accumulative power.

An ethnographic analysis of the migrant boss reveals how this figure of labor and livelihood exceeds the notion of individual will or hard work. It exposes the underlying dynamics of power and inequality that entice vulnerable segments of society to engage in risky economic endeavors. Through their engagement with transnational fast fashion supply chains, migrant bosses enter a world of labor exploitation, racialized policing, and extortion in Guangzhou's urban villages across unequal relations of extraction and accumulation.[5] In this predatory "bust economy," peasant landlords, private officers, and market competitors extract fees and siphon profits from the migrant bosses. While the structural pressures of capitalist accumulation, including urbanization, low wages, debt, and discriminatory practices, continually operate against their best interests, the migrant bosses seek temporary gaps or market niches from which they can accumulate capital. In other words, my ethnographic analyses tell stories of broader relations of capitalization, inequality, and power (Marx 1857; Nitzan and Bichler 2009) whereby global supply chains for fast fashion accelerate and intensify the relations of accumulation among market participants in postsocialist China.

These experiences leave migrant bosses hovering in an ambiguous and ambivalent space somewhere in between the figure of the sweatshop laborer and the globe-trotting entrepreneur.[6] Their experiments in precarious accumulation demonstrate how vulnerable populations stake hope and better ways of living (more secure, less precarious, and less brutal) upon the rhythms of transnational capitalism. These life-generating projects paradoxically leave them with feelings of ongoing deferment, marked by ambivalence and vulnerability. Following this insight, this book asks: If entrepreneurship and self-enterprise are inherently risky, why do migrants and other vulnerable groups, who remain among the bottom segments of society, persistently aspire to achieve the perceived status and wealth associated with being an entrepreneur? What do they imagine are the promises of entrepreneurship? How do migrants' experiences of transnational and domestic rural-to-urban migration shape their cross-cultural encounters and experiments with bosshood? What does the rise of migrant bosshood tell us about China's postsocialist transformations and its position in global capitalism, particularly amid its intensified participation in transnational supply chains?

The stories that I present in these pages illustrate the spectrum of dilemmas and fantasies that make fast fashion and transnational capitalism possible. They also narrate how market liberalization leaves gaps through which state governance and neoliberal governmentality assert their influences upon migrant populations. Migrant bosses' actions shed light on the innovative work and imaginative possibilities that they forge for themselves to achieve some degree of wealth and accumulation while, at the same time, these novel practices leave them in conditions of precarity. Their experiences provide alternative perspectives to the notion of "freedom," whereby their experiences of market "freedom" leaves them vulnerable to divergent mechanisms of everyday regulation and governmentality delivered squarely via the market and not via direct policies of state control. As such, their stories demonstrate how capitalist concepts—including exploitation, extortion, racism, and expulsion—that are conventionally tied to waged labor play out through nonwage work across supply chains.[7] The chapters that follow show how capitalist accumulation materializes in cultural and relational practices. Ultimately, although migrants do not see their participation as "labor," this ethnography reveals the cultural labor that makes capitalist accumulation across transnational supply chains possible.

MIGRANT BOSSHOOD IN POSTSOCIALIST CHINA

"Our fate took a turn for the worst. The accident came at a time when we were financially struggling the most. Looking back, the short period of financial success we had turned out to actually be an omen, a curse," Xiao Ye, a thirty-year-old migrant and mother of two, confessed to me when I met her one afternoon in 2014. Earlier that day, I was wandering through the maze of factory workshops, pedicabs, and pedestrian traffic that stretched behind the towering accessories market in the garment district of Guangzhou. As I passed through the alleyways, I met Xiao Ye in her thread and yarn stall that served the fast fashion supply chains. During our conversation, Xiao Ye informed me that her brother had experienced a tragic hit-and-run motorcycle accident along one of the alleyways nearby that left him handicapped. Sadly, fires and vehicular accidents in these urban villages were quite common because traffic, fire, and other safety regulations were often neglected or, at best, infrequently enforced. The police never caught the driver, leaving Xiao Ye and her family to wonder why the accident befell them. Hospital bills left the family in financial hardship, but they were relieved that his life was spared.

Looking back ten years later, Xiao Ye acknowledged that those years of prosperity had, sadly, already passed. The family's initial enthusiasm for small-scale enterprise deteriorated over years of struggle and impermanent success. Xiao Ye explained that the prices of cotton and other raw materials had skyrocketed within a few years, making their business difficult to maintain. Private security officers had begun to exercise strict regulatory oversight over the flows of people, commodities, and money into and out of the urban villages. Oftentimes, these top-down pressures resulted in unexpected fines and threats that impinged upon the sense of security migrants once felt about living in the urban villages. "Right now," as she complained, "Business is no good, but there's not much else we can do. It's difficult to find workers [who are willing to work for us]. Factory jobs pay too little, and we don't have state security. We can't rely on anyone to take care of us. We need to rely on ourselves (kao ziji)." The financial burden that resulted from her brother's accident, compounded by the fall in profits of their small-scale business, led her to wonder whether they could ever reclaim their early successes. In a hushed tone, Xiao Ye said, "It's not good to make too much money. Having too much money brings bad luck."

As undocumented migrants from China's countryside, Xiao Ye and her family have no rights to the state-sponsored health and welfare benefits that city residents can access. This exclusion is due to the hukou household registration system, a policy that designates citizens as either rural or urban and agricultural and nonagricultural (Smart and Zhang 2006). It was initially enacted to contain the migration of peasants from the rural regions to the cities during the Maoist period, and it continues to be enforced in the present day. Migrants whose *hukou* remains tied to the countryside are excluded from state protections and benefits in the cities. As outsiders (*wai di ren*) and members of the "floating population" (*liudong renkou*), migrants are left without state protection and without a social safety net. Their status as migrants leaves them vulnerable to the exploitation associated with low-wage labor. They thus become exposed to the shadow economies of policing, extortion, and rent/fee extraction that often threaten the survival of their small-scale enterprises.

In Guangzhou's urban villages, for instance, rural migrants are often asked to show *hukou* identifications and business licenses to patrolling officers. Sometimes, officers order migrant bosses to shut down their vendor stalls or factories without notice. These examples show how rural migrants are compelled to navigate the entanglements of postsocialist urbanization in China, particularly the secondary extractive economies that have emerged as a result of urban renewal. In response to the uncertainties of livelihood and labor that they face in the cities, migrants like Xiao Ye take on the role of the "boss" to dictate the conditions of their precarity and exploitation.

To be sure, the *laoban*, as an illustrative figure of the entrepreneur in transnational Guangzhou, serves as an allegorical and culturally significant persona that underscores growing class-based inequalities and market uncertainties in a globalizing China built squarely on the backs of migrant laborers. The "boss" persona appropriates the trope of an American brand of rugged individualism, yet it is firmly rooted within the widening gender- and class-based disparities that characterize China's postsocialist transformation. Historically, since the introduction of market reforms, the "boss" as an aspirational figure embodies the Chinese counterpart to the American dream; the "boss" is publicly personified by a man, or by a similarly masculinist figure, who not only amasses wealth but also assumes *ownership* over his wealth by making deals, mediating requests, and acting as a provider among networks of personal dependents.

The demonstration of the "self-made" boss is dependent on one's ability to possess and assert control over one's wealth. As a self-made person, the boss attempts to defy administrative oversight and accountability by state powers while overcoming market crises through their attempts to gain access to global markets. More importantly, this figure mobilizes *aspirations* of entrepreneurial freedom among other bosses who have not quite secured their ranks in the globe-trotting elite classes. As Liu Xin (2002, 37) writes:

The person who pays is in charge; the person who is in charge owns; the person who owns takes responsibility for what happens; the person who takes responsibility for what happens is *laoban*. It does not mean that this term of address cannot be used, as a metaphor, by someone who addresses a person in charge, such as an official calling his superior, but in the story of (capitalist) development, particularly in South China, the word's connotations are determined by the emergence of an image of someone who is in charge by virtue of ownership.

In other words, the *laoban*, or "boss," takes charge of their fate in the face of increasing socioeconomic uncertainties, which are simultaneously marked by the retraction of state-sponsored welfare and by global market crises. At the same time, bosshood mobilizes people's dreams and aspirations for a better life despite these growing uncertainties.

The figure of the boss may be compared to other masculine risk-taking figures in the corporate world, such as stock market traders, Wall Street bankers, and the "salarymen" in Japan (Allison 1994; Hertz 1998; Ho 2009; Miyazaki 2013). In China, the biological reproduction of the family—upon which the Made in China model of low-wage, subcontracted labor power depends—is also gendered, since reproductive labor remains within the domain of women's work even though the family unit critically undergirds men's performances of entrepreneurial freedom (Federici 1975; Hochschild 1985, 2012; Prieto 1997; Pun 2005). While scholarly works tend to highlight the flexible strategies and disciplinary regimes associated with the crafting of gendered and class-based accumulative strategies around the world, many observers tend to overlook how migrants' involvement in these transnational modes of flexible accumulation, upon which their livelihoods depend, leads directly to precarious conditions. Indeed, one critical aspect of being economically "self-made"—assuming responsibility for and taking charge of one's financial future—also means taking on all the associated risks of becoming an entrepreneur.

For example, in recounting her story, Xiao Ye framed her experience of becoming her own boss (*zuo laoban*) in terms of misfortune, inexplicable tragedy, and state bias toward her and other working-class migrants, thus implicitly underscoring the social inequalities that have widened since Deng Xiaoping's introduction of market reforms in 1978. Such growing inequalities are exemplified by the prejudice and discrimination that local Guangzhou residents often display toward migrant workers who have taken up residence and low-wage employment in the city's urban villages.

Popular discourses of violence, danger, and crime that city residents project onto this garment district and its residents compel migrants like Xiao Ye to position themselves as aspirational bosses in relation to the post-Mao project of massive urbanization in the hope of escaping their former status as rural citizens. Her deep-seated feelings of personal loss, compounded by her struggles to sustain the family business, led her to reassess whether her family's entrepreneurial pursuits were worth the cost to the family's sense of security.

While the personification of the migrant boss in Guangzhou resembles other figures of entrepreneurial self-enterprise, bosshood in China, as I argue, is a uniquely postsocialist phenomenon. More specifically, it signifies a broader transformation of land, labor, and personhood as collective identities and senses of belonging fracture along class-based divisions of rural and urban designations. Displaced from their native places in the countryside and excluded by the *hukou* from state welfare benefits and protections offered by the cities (L. Zhang 2002; Yan 2008; Pun 2005; Siu 2007; Smart and Zhang 2015; Zhan 2015; Ling 2020), Chinese rural migrants have little recourse but to embrace the persona of the boss despite the precarious conditions of their labor. They take on the risks and rewards of small-scale, individual, and privatized experiments of capitalist accumulation—without the social safety nets needed to offset the losses entailed in risky self-enterprise (Y. Zhan 2022). Meanwhile, transnational migrants, particularly those from the Global South, especially West Africa and South Korea, are not part of the *hukou* system. Yet as noncitizens of China, they encounter similar exclusions and discrimination to Chinese rural migrants in Guangzhou (Lan 2016b; Castillo 2016; Wilzcak 2018; G. Huang 2019). For this reason, migrants retain their statuses as migrants, or *wai di ren* (domestic and transnational), regardless of the amount of wealth or social status they manage to accumulate.

The conditions of precarity and precariousness among migrants in China are especially apparent in the domain of property ownership (Lan 2016b; Castillo 2016; Wilzcak 2018; G. Huang 2019).[8] Although migrants can discursively declare, to a limited extent, ownership over the conditions of their labor and exploitation, they are able to claim only a very limited idea of ownership in practice, since the *hukou* and immigration policies legally and administratively constrain them from owning property while also excluding them from labor and business protections in the cities (Liao and Zhang 2020). The categorization of people as foreign and local as well as rural/urban and agricultural/nonagricultural, according to the *hukou*, critically determines migrants' access to sources of wealth and capital accumulation, including mortgage loans, fixed capital, property ownership, and state welfare benefits (Liao and Zhang 2020).[9] In turn, the *hukou* and immigration policies determine the spectrum of risks that domestic and foreign migrants must take on in order to accumulate or to build their wealth. In a broader sense, the exclusions of the *hukou* and other forms of policing transnational migrant populations create a migrant surplus, whose labor becomes available when the market needs them (Hillenbrand 2023). At the same time, the *hukou* and other migrant-regulation policies deny them claims to state protection and entitlements.

As Chinese rural migrants encounter transnational migrants in Guangzhou, both populations mutually realize the possibilities and limitations associated with the fragmentation of class collectivities across global supply chains. In light of the retreat of class as a source of political collectivization and personal identification, bosshood offers both domestic and transnational migrant subcontractors a social role through which they can invest their labor and social identifications in the worlds of fast fashion and capitalist accumulation. The societal valorization of individual control, autonomy, and risk-taking enterprise draws migrant bosses into the supply chains through which they must learn the ropes of small-scale subcontracting. However, they take on the role of the boss without the state and social protections that offset the risks of entrepreneurial self-enterprise. As subcontractors, domestic and transnational migrants in Guangzhou experience firsthand the consequences of large-scale divisions of class and labor as well as the increasingly unequal dynamics of accumulation that undergird them.

Upon their arrival in the urban villages, migrants encounter peasant landlords (*tu er dai*), whose accumulative interests rest upon the rental incomes they receive from migrants who have no formal claims to land or property in the cities. Indeed, the mushrooming of garment mass manufacture in the urban villages provides a lucrative income for the *tu er dai*, who paradoxically were once peasants themselves—and thus demonstrating the large-scale effects of the class-based fragmentation of former peasants along rural/urban divides. Moreover, as migrants learn the ropes of small-scale subcontracting, they encounter competitors and bigger bosses, whose profit-driven interests may put migrant bosses' attempts to accumulate capital at risk. Competition, debt, and bankruptcy color migrants' experiences of small-scale entrepreneurship in Guangzhou. The figure of the full-fledged entrepreneur thus remains aspirational for many migrant bosses in Guangzhou.

In tracing the accumulative practices of domestic and transnational migrant bosses, I do not approach class and labor as ahistorical or preconceived categories. Rather, I view the discourses of class and labor as critically linked to the changing dynamics of accumulation among various migrant groups amid large-scale societal transformations, whereby factory work is no longer recognized as labor, a source of class-based collectivization and political identification. Migrant bosshood emerges from these postsocialist transformations. As an administrative and legal category, the migrant signifies social abandonment by the state through the exclusion of welfare and social protection (via the *hukou*), on the one hand, and entrepreneurial hope, dignity, and possibility, on the other.

Bosshood, as I argue, offers an imaginative, albeit ambivalent, space for migrants to grapple with, negotiate, and reflect on the complexities and paradoxes of human freedom and dignity in the era of transnational capitalism. These values, though expressed in public discourse as universalist and equally achievable for all, remain implicated in broader dynamics of wealth and accumulation that are dictated by the interests of landlords, multinational corporations, state officials, and even God. These overlapping and competing worlds of accumulation comprise the global supply chains of commodity manufacture and exchange. The ethnographic analyses that I sketch in the following chapters illustrate the paradoxes and tensions embodied by the figure of the migrant boss, which has emerged from and continues to signify the postsocialist fragmentation of class as well as the retreat of labor as a political category in China and beyond.

Today, the migrant boss is a figure of precarity and possibility. As aspirations shift from low-wage labor to entrepreneurial self-enterprise, Chinese migrants, particularly youths, no longer desire to work in the factories as employees (Y. Zhan 2022; Rofel and Yanagisako 2018; Ling 2020). The decline of the welfare state, rural decollectivization, and the breakup of the so-called iron rice bowl have compelled migrants to strive for capitalist accumulation at the scale of the individual. In a segment of the global fast fashion industry that relies on market speed, flexibility, and temporariness, the risks of migrant bosshood become even more pronounced for small-scale subcontractors who must anchor their aspirations for freedom, hope, and mobility upon the whims of global supply chain capitalism (Tsing 2009).

China remains the largest source of fast fashion commodities in the world (Simpson 2020). In 2018, for example, sales in China's apparel market exceeded $322 billion USD with a growth rate at 7.8 percent, the fastest growth rate since 2014 (Daxue Consulting 2019). In Guangzhou, rural Chinese, West African, and South Korean migrant subcontractors become aspiring agents of capital. As "bosses," they are not solely figures of low-cost labor, mere victims of exploitation upon which capitalists or multinational corporations depend. Rather, they labor as mediators and facilitators of transnational subcontracting, who in their efforts to become bosses themselves, generate novel practices of capitalist accumulation while inadvertently intensifying the fracturing of the migrant classes and relations of inequality across global supply chains. As an analytical framework, *precarious accumulation* lends insights into these everyday practices of capitalist accumulation and into how global supply chains mobilize the desires for migrant bosshood, in all its unique and divergent forms.

Precarity and precariousness are useful conceptual lenses through which to examine the social fragilities and volatilities associated with China and global capitalism since the late 1970s (the post-reform period); they help reveal the socioeconomic effects of labor and livelihood when collective identities and senses of personhood are no longer defined through the discourses of labor and class (Rofel 1999; Butler 2004; Neilson and Rossiter 2005, 2008; Tsianos and Papadopoulos 2006; Ong and Zhang 2008). More specifically, I use precarity and precariousness to bridge the structural dynamics of postsocialism and neoliberalism with the paradoxical conditions of mobility and immobility characteristic of migrant bosshood.

In China, the dismantling of state-operated enterprises, urban work units (*danwei*), and Maoist rural collectives mirrored in many ways the gradual decline of the welfare state, Fordist factories, and stable employment after the enactment of free market and neoliberal policies in countries across Western Europe and the former Soviet bloc, from which the discourse of precarity historically emerged (Dirlik 1989; Solinger 2022; Hillenbrand 2023).[10] More specifically, in China, state-sponsored projects of decollectivization, including the household responsibility system and township and village enterprises (TVEs) in the countryside, left millions of former peasants with little choice but to migrate to the cities in search of employment and affordable housing (Anagnost 1997; Rofel 1999; L. Zhang 2002; Siu 2007; Yan 2008).[11] Since the 1980s, migrant laborers have found employment in export factories that have mushroomed in Special Economic Zones (SEZs) such as Shenzhen and Guangzhou, fueling foreign direct investments and industrial development (Lee 1998; Pun 2005; Chang 2009; Breznitz and Murphree 2011; Litzinger 2013; Pun and Chan 2012; Friedman 2014).[12] At the same time, foreign subcontractors have migrated to the SEZs to forge industrial and financial relations with Chinese factory owners, thereby creating the early socioeconomic links that help to sustain global supply chain capitalism in the present day.

The rise of migrant bosses and the associated Made in China model of globalized, low-cost production have been made possible by linking the postsocialist experiments of market liberalization in China with the global capitalist economy after the collapse of the Soviet Union and the end of the Cold War. Impoverished in the countryside and their native places, rural Chinese and transnational migrants have left their native places to seek better employment opportunities and higher wages in the cities (Gaetano and Jacka 2004; Yan 2008). The popular discourse of *chuang* (or going out) into the worlds of entrepreneurship and self-enterprise draws migrants to cities like Guangzhou. However, for rural Chinese migrants, the *hukou* policy of population control excludes them from claiming rights and benefits in urban areas. Meanwhile, transnational migrants arrive in Guangzhou in hopes of achieving wealth and entrepreneurial freedom, though their statuses as foreigners also leave them excluded from certain rights and protections in the city. The combination of the deregulation of rent-seeking, profit-making activities and increased regulation of the mobility of these low-waged migrant laborers creates an opening through which third-party agents, village landlords, and more powerful bosses compete alongside migrant entrepreneurs across the fast fashion commodity chains, leaving self-enterprising migrants vulnerable to extraction and exploitation.

These large-scale postsocialist transformations have compelled some scholars and observers to question the extent to which the Chinese economy can be appropriately deemed neoliberal (H. Wang and Karl 2004; Harvey 2005; Rofel 2007; Ong and Zhang 2008; Weber 2018a, 2018b, 2020, 2021; H.-M. L. Liu 2023). Some scholars have asserted that neoliberalism is not a one-size-fits-all package of economic reforms and policies prescribed by the International Monetary Fund, the World Bank, and the World Trade Organization and passively adopted in China (H. Wang and Karl 2004; Rofel 2007; Weber 2018b). They argue that the Chinese state has enacted its own policies of market reforms, restructuring society and the economy in ways that have diverged from neoliberal policies, or *shock therapy*, as had been prescribed by the capitalist nations of the Global North and experimented in regions across the Global South (Rofel 2007; Weber 2021). After all, the Chinese state, at various levels, continues to assert its ongoing control and regulation over market activities across divergent domains of economic life, both domestic and abroad, leading some scholars to describe China's political economy as a mixed economy, or as state capitalism (Ong and Zhang 2008; Hung 2009; Liebman and Milhaupt 2015; Weber 2021; H. Zhang 2021; Du 2023).

While the question of whether China's economic growth since Deng's introduction of market reforms entailed policies that should be legitimately deemed neoliberal exceeds the scope of this book, it is imperative to address *how* neoliberalism, as an analytical framework, is relevant to China, particularly those aspects of economic life and livelihood in which the retreat of the welfare state and the rise of market-based practices of governmentality have deeply affected migrant laborers there (Weber 2018b). My approach to the intersecting topics of neoliberalism, precarity, and China focuses on the low-waged domestic and transnational migrant populations in China as well as on the modes of market-based regulation and government regulation of their mobility that emerged following market reforms. I argue that the freeing of certain market controls, accompanied by the large-scale withdrawal of state welfare, leaves spaces through which officials, third-party agents, and bigger bosses compete with small-scale migrant entrepreneurs. These forms of regulation and governmentality do not fit solely into an authoritarian order of institutionalized state governance. They rely on everyday nonstate practices of capitalist accumulation among migrant entrepreneurs that draw upon market mechanisms of supply and demand.

The societal effects of market liberalization and the subsequent precaritization of life and livelihood, as I show, are most evident among the low-waged migrant populations in China. Since the 1990s, during which the central government dismantled collective enterprise and promoted the market economy, the state oversaw the retreat of its welfare programs as well as the decentralization of its planned economy. These moves critically signaled a gradual shift in its role from overseeing a centralized, planned economy during the Maoist period to regulating economic practices based on market mechanisms via the everyday rhythms of migratory life and labor. As I will show in the chapters that follow, state entities, third-party agents, and other competitors—whether at the central or local levels—enter the market as active participants rather than as merely passive facilitators

(Weber 2018b, 2021). Their market-based activities, in turn, determine the opportunities and chances for profit-making and accumulation that small-scale migrant bosses encounter. Furthermore, the state engages with techniques of neoliberal governance, which entails cultivating desirable citizen-subjects and which ideologically justifies the central state's move away from a socialist planned economy along with the promises once guaranteed by a socialist welfare system, or the iron rice bowl, while simultaneously maintaining controls over the flows of commodities, people, and capital (Rofel 2007; Ong and Zhang 2008).

The notion of the neoliberal self that is embodied through migrant subcontracting and self-enterprise thus converges with China's postsocialist transformations in Guangzhou's urban villages. More specifically, the desiring, entrepreneurial self, particularly the figure of the rational, self-interested, and risk-taking boss (*laoban*) exemplifies the ideal citizen-subject characteristic of the reform era. As Margaret Hillenbrand (2023) argues, postsocialism and neoliberalism in China are twin conditions, structural developments that mirror and reinforce one another.[13] Both are characterized by the fracturing of class collectivities as well as by the individualization and privatization of the self whereby work is no longer politically and socially valued as labor. Rather, work is seen as a platform for self-enterprise and entrepreneurial risk-taking endeavors, practices of capitalist accumulation that have been made privatized, modulated, and immediate (Amin 1994; Harvey 1987; Ong 2006; Rofel 2007; Ong and Zhang 2008; Tsing 2009; Yanagisako and Rofel 2018; Amin and Richaud 2020; G. Huang 2020; Kornbluh 2024; Nguyen et al. 2024).

This book provides ethnographic analyses of these socioeconomic transformations from the perspective of migrant laborers in China, demonstrating how small-scale self-enterprise does not spontaneously emerge from a privatized, autonomous self. Rather, it materializes out of historical and social relations of land, labor, and personhood that are anchored upon postsocialist transformations. For example, aspirations for entrepreneurial self-enterprise, or bosshood, have been promulgated in the state-sponsored projects of the "China Dream," serving as an alternative vision to the capitalist, accumulative aspirations of the "American Dream." This campaign aims to further flatten out the contradictions of free market practices and state regulation, that is, practices that do not fit strictly within a purely neoliberal or socialist ideology. As Lisa Rofel (2007) argues, the creation of desiring subjects across China's domains of public culture aims to remake the aspirations and desires of its subject-citizens in ways that reimagine the new world order and China's place in it in the aftermath of the Cold War. The figure of the migrant boss and the boss's entrepreneurial aspirations thereby signify a key moment whereby China's postsocialist transformations of land, labor, and personhood critically intersect with its intensified participation in the world's capitalist supply chains.

My ethnography thereby traces how migrant self-enterprise remains embedded in shared meanings and experiences of socioeconomic uncertainty, even if the language of class no longer holds the same social meaning and political force as it did during the Maoist period (Dirlik 1989; Pun 2005; Anagnost 2008; Smith and Pun 2018; K. Lin 2019; Chuang 2020; Hillenbrand 2023). This focus contributes to scholarly understandings of precarity and precariousness in several ways. First, I frame precarity and precariousness as not solely tied to waged employment, as conventionally defined, particularly with respect to economies of the Global North (Butler 2006; Standing 2011; Muehlebach 2011; Allison 2013; Swider 2015; Pang 2019; Driessen 2019; Hillenbrand 2023). Rather, I link precarity and precariousness with relations of accumulation and risk to flesh out the moments in which migrants are drawn into transnational supply chains through the aspirational forces of bosshood as well as the moments in which they are dispossessed and expelled from the chains. Precarity, in this sense, seems to mirror the notions of cruel optimism, anxious desire, and competing desires in the context of transnational capitalism (Berlant 2011; Millar 2018). Yet I view entrepreneurial aspiration, and the associated conditions of precarity and precariousness, as specifically tied to the movement of capital, particularly to the *dynamics of accumulation*, that fluctuate in unpredictable ways.

As I demonstrate, migrant bosshood (both domestic and transnational) emerges across fast fashion supply chains that continuously change according to variable market conditions on both national and transnational scales. As small-scale and self-employed subcontractors across the intermediary links of the commodity chains, migrant bosses become extremely vulnerable to fickle consumer demands that may change on a whim at one end of the production chain, while having to remain responsive to competing bosses and local manufacturers on the other end. In this way, migrant bosses must exploit their subcontractors and hired workers while at the same time learning to compete and evade exploitation by other, competing bosses in the industry.

Amid the proliferation of transnational subcontracting around the globe, the rise of the migrant boss illustrates what Silvio Lorusso (2019) describes as the emergence of the *entreprecariat*, a class of laboring subjects who have thrown off the shackles of wage labor and have embraced the spirit of entrepreneurship and self-employment. Free market enterprise taps into their dreams and imaginations, mobilizing their innate qualities of being human in the world.

The entreprecariat sheds critical light on entrepreneurship not only as an economic activity but also as a set of cultural values and particular ways of life that are becoming a defining aspect of labor and livelihood among workers around the world. This set of values champions the principles of rugged individualism, *race to the bottom* competition, masculine freedom, and risk-taking enterprise so as to marshal workers' human potential in pursuit of the universalistic ideals of autonomy and security (Lorusso 2019). Thus, in contrast to current framings in the anthropology of capitalism, the contradictory experiences of risk and reward, mobility and immobility, and freedom and exploitation show that precarity is produced out of aspirational entrepreneurialism through a combination of intersecting and contingent socioeconomic relations. These relations are intimately tied to forms of bosshood that remain fragmented and uneven.

Second, my book exposes how the notion of being self-made obscures the relational dimensions of precarity and precariousness, highlighting the relations of inequality that produce conditions of exclusion and dispossession in the first place. Migrants' experiences of bosshood shed light on precarity and precariousness as *uneven* relations of accumulation among various class groups. Scholars have cogently elaborated the creation of the migrant classes as a flexible reservoir of surplus workers, whose labor is mobilized and extracted when markets demand them and then subsequently disposed of when no longer needed (Solinger 1999; Zhang 2001; Pun 2005; Pun and Smith 2007; Siu 2007; Yan 2008; Swider 2015; I. Pang 2019; Evans 2020; Ling 2020; Y. Zhan 2022; Hillenbrand 2023).[14] This book contributes to these scholarly conversations by focusing not only on the labor practices of migrant groups but also on their accumulative practices and relations as they traverse the edges of labor and capital.

Across fast fashion supply chains, migrants move into and out of unemployment, wage work, and self-employment, thus blurring the boundaries between workers and entrepreneurs as well as between the conditions of wage work and those of self-employment. As aspirational entrepreneurs, migrant bosses are dispossessed and excluded from the legal statuses of legitimacy and security. Denied of labor protection, property ownership, and national citizenship in Guangzhou, they feel as if they are treading in place—a condition of *stalled mobility* that I return to below. As they experience the risks and rewards of bosshood, precarious accumulation highlights how transnational and domestic migrants become exposed to wider forces of extraction and dispossession by more powerful bosses who compete and seek to accumulate for themselves.

Finally, my work highlights the transnational dimensions of precarity and precariousness, challenging framings of these concepts within the boundaries of individual nation-states or solely within the Global North.[15] My stories of South Korean and West African migrant bosses in Guangzhou uncover the broader transnational and cross-regional dynamics of precarity and accumulation, which exceed national scales of analysis. Migrants' experiences of precarious accumulation unfold across both global and national scales, as they cross national boundaries and imagine China as a platform for religious and ethnic accumulation. While West African Christian traders echo the principles of the prosperity doctrine and attempt to accumulate God's graces of health and wealth as self-enterprising entrepreneurs in Guangzhou, South Koreans tap into the networks of ethnic accumulation by catching the global K-pop wave and operating as intermediary agents, colloquially known as jobbers, in the world of global Korean pop culture and fast fashion. The landscapes of precarity and precariousness weave together the cross-regional worlds of migrant uncertainty and dispossession across the global supply chains.

Furthermore, as transnational migrants, South Korean and West African migrants must bridge linguistic and cultural divides to settle and build their client bases in Guangzhou and to kickstart their businesses. While West Africans build relationships of trust, friendship, and romance with Chinese locals and migrants, South Koreans rely on the Korean Chinese (*Chaoxianzu*) ethnic community to serve as their cultural, linguistic, and market intermediaries. Thus, migrants' experiences of bosshood cast precariousness in a similar yet contrasting light from that which Lorusso (2019) proposes, linking it specifically to bosses' personal experiences of migration and mobility (domestic and transnational), which are themselves uniquely shaped by kin- and faith-based relationships as well as by migrants' aspirations for freedom, recognition, and distinction.

Accumulation is one of the foundational principles of free market enterprise. For migrants in Guangzhou who have emerged from unemployment, construction labor, and wage work in factories, urban legends of migrant bosses in the fast fashion industry unexpectedly tapping into a windfall of profits fuel their aspirational desires for wealth and security.

These aspirations for bosshood drive them to seek self-enterprising capitalist accumulation, while other means of fulfillment and manifestation of their desires for autonomy and dignity become foreclosed due to state-sponsored neoliberal projects and policies of privatization. Yet, many persist in their attempts to accumulate capital across the fast fashion supply chains, leaving them in conditions of ambivalence, uncertainty, and precariousness—stalled mobility.

STALLED MOBILITY

Scholars oftentimes approach aspiration and precariousness as separable facets of social life, placing the two ideas in a causal relationship such that aspiration leads the working class and vulnerable populations to conditions of precariousness or vice versa. Yet, the question remains as to whether the aspiration for wealth leads to precariousness, or whether the experience of precariousness leads to a deeper desire or need for capitalist accumulation. Taking this question as a stepping-stone, this book argues that in the current era of neoliberal transnational capitalism, accumulation and aspiration cannot be conceptually separated. More specifically, migrant bosshood bridges these concepts, grounding capitalism and accumulation in the everyday cultural practices of people who engage in and remake the meaning of entrepreneurship through their lived experiences.[16]

Accordingly, one aspect of precarious accumulation that migrant bosses experience when they encounter obstacles to accumulation is the experience of a treadmill-like effect of chasing after capital and social mobility, which I call *stalled mobility*. As migrant bosses move back and forth between the categories of worker, entrepreneur, and back again, their sense of stalled mobility instructs us that displacement is more than a condition that results from either mobility or immobility. Stalled mobility refers to a condition in which migratory bosses may be mobile yet feel that they are not going anywhere in life. They may also feel that their aspirations have been put on hold or are not aligned with their current circumstances and social positioning.[17]

My concept of stalled mobility draws inspiration from labor "in and of time" by framing the rhythms of migratory labor as sources of both fixity and mobility as well as of regulation and freedom (Bear 2014). For migrants, an itinerant life of uncertainty and precarious labor is the only recourse through which they can preserve their sense of human dignity and economic survival. Moving in and out wage and nonwage labor, migrants perceive time, specifically impermanence, as a source of constraint *and* as a source of autonomy. In this sense, stalled mobility differs from conditions of suspension (*xuanfu*) and involution (*neijuan*) among China's migrants and urban middle classes (Xiang 2021b; Q. Wang and Ge 2020). The notion of stalling underscores migrants' exclusion from meaningful accumulation and social mobility precisely through their market activities, not only through their exclusions from meaningful political participation. Migrants become vulnerable to the detrimental effects of free market enterprise, including debt, bankruptcy, and competition. Their aspirations remain *off*, that is, disjointed, led astray, and disconnected from the value of their labor across the supply chain. Even for those who are able to join the ranks of bosshood, contestations over their *legitimacy* as bosses are embedded within larger questions of claims to authenticity, land-owing power, the ability to extract rental income, and the state's legal authority to criminalize them as migrants.[18]

Recent studies of contemporary Chinese society have insightfully described the subjective dimensions of uncertainty, vulnerability, and insecurity that migrant populations grapple with as they face the large-scale retreat of state-sponsored welfare and protections. While Margaret Hillenbrand (2023) employs the notion of zombie citizenship to describe the dispossessive effects of creating a surplus labor population, Huwy-Min Lucia Liu (2023) describes funeral brokers in Shanghai as fragile to highlight migrants' demonstrations of personal agency as possibilities for political and civic participation are foreclosed in an increasingly authoritarian milieu.

This book draws from these insights and intervenes in them by approaching subjectivity not only as a singular role, persona, feeling, or state of being. Rather, I conceptualize bosshood as the ongoing tensions and paradoxes between the aspiration to accumulate capital and the forces of dispossession that leave migrants in conditions of stalled mobility, including authoritarian state surveillance, identification checks, bribery, and rent collection by landlords and competing bosses as well as by public and private security officers. As I demonstrate in the chapters that follow, local state agents operate as active competitors and regulators across the fast fashion supply chains in Guangzhou rather than as passive facilitators of the so-called free market. They regulate the physical movements of its migrant population via the *hukou* policy of population control. This form of neoliberal governmentality highlights how the role of the state seemingly diverges from the prescriptions of laissez-faire capitalism as promulgated by proponents of neoliberalism during the early decades of postsocialist market reform. State regulation and the free market, after all, are *not* mutually exclusive. The Chinese government continues to maintain control over economic life, but in ways that still allow market mechanisms of supply and demand to determine how capital, money, and limited resources are distributed across different areas of economic life in China, including its production chains.

Such forms of state regulation and neoliberal governmentality over market activities are evidenced in policies related to urban planning, land reform/property rights, the restructuring of the countryside via the household responsibility system, and most importantly, the *hukou* policy of population control. These policies may be thought of as aspects of market governance characteristic of so-called socialism with Chinese characteristics, whereby market liberalization is guided by a Party-state that maintains tight controls over political and civic lives of its migrants—but paradoxically without providing adequate welfare and economic safety nets for them in the cities where they live and work. This term, however, fails to fully capture migrants' experiences of bosshood or the ways in which regulatory practices within an authoritarian context operate *alongside* neoliberal and free market enterprise (Ong 2006; Rofel 2007; Ong and Zhang 2008). As my ethnographic analyses show, market forces operate together with the authoritarian state and quasi-state agents to produce dynamics of displacement and dispossession that leave migrants in conditions of stalled mobility. In fact, as I demonstrate, some migrant bosses describe the state as an invisible competitor in their attempts to accumulate capital. In chapter 3, for example, I show how the state furthers projects of capitalist accumulation within a globalized, neoliberal market economy in postsocialist China.[19] In my explication of *state effects*, the state may not be overtly present in the urban villages, but market forces *enable and intensify* state regulation over migrants' accumulative practices in Guangzhou. This is evidenced through the practices of *hukou* enforcement and what I call the *shenfen* economy: the collection of fees and rents, the regulation of counterfeit goods, and the enforcement of visas and citizenship.

Stalled mobility, in this sense, underscores the contradictions and ambivalences associated with the paradoxes of mobility and immobility characteristic of migrant bosshood. Though stalled mobility may be described as a type of cognitive dissonance that arises when the promises of free market enterprise directly clash with migrants' experiences of dispossession and exclusion (Hillenbrand 2023), I argue that it is more than a cognitive condition, whether shared or individual. It is a structure of feeling and a relational dynamic that shapes migrants' intersubjective experiences of bosshood, on the one hand, and the moments of collaboration and competition among migrant bosses, on the other (Williams 2014). While domestic and transnational migrants declare their work as "free," they paradoxically labor ten to twelve hours a day on the factory floor under the supervision of their clients. Meanwhile, their attempts to accumulate capital compel them to exploit other migrants further down the fast fashion supply chain as they learn to evade exploitation from other competing bosses.

Because domestic and transnational migrant bosses remain excluded from formal property ownership as well as from any legal claims to labor protection and state welfare in the cities, the *hukou* and other policing and regulatory practices make bosshood an all-or-nothing game of capital accumulation whereby migrants fall completely into and out of bosshood, and not in a partial or fractional sense. Their efforts to secure a rightful place in society as "boss" show how transnational subcontracting practices become zero-sum arrangements, in that one works either only for oneself or only for others, even if embeddedness in social obligations, reciprocity, and debt leave migrants dependent on kin-based or friendship relations. The worlds of migrant bosshood in Guangzhou and on the global stage thus demonstrate how the entrepreneurial self as a subject of capital accumulation is entangled in broader relations of dependency, competition, predation, and vulnerability. For these reasons, precarious accumulation cannot be taken out of larger contexts of exploitation, regulation, and competition within which it is situated.

At the same time, migrant bosses become exposed to the exploitative and unstable effects of global market forces. These various limitations compel migrant bosses to remain mobile, that is, in continual search of the next hub of capital accumulation (akin to David Harvey's spatial fix), even if this keeps them in conditions of precarity and precariousness (Harvey 1982). Migrants' experiences of bosshood in Guangzhou's fast fashion sector are directly affected by the fluctuations of global fashion exchange. Migrant bosses, for example, often complain about how rising prices in raw materials, climate change, and wars lead to downturns in the global fashion markets. Despite these challenges, many migrants continue to experiment with possibilities that embrace their aspirations and might lead them to what they perceive as freedom and prosperity. Transnational and domestic migrants' aspirations for bosshood and their attendant desires for freedom and prosperity compel them to leave conditions of poverty, war, exploitation, and debt in former socialist and colonial contexts. After their arrival in Guangzhou, however, their status as migrants, including the social exclusions and various forms of discrimination they face, place them in even more precarious circumstances.

Thus, migrants' affective investment into the figure of the entrepreneur is itself a political project, since it appropriates and reinforces state campaigns that publicize the Chinese Dream (Wielander 2018). In the current moment of market liberalization and the retrenchment of state-sponsored welfare, being boss, with its attendant risks and responsibilities, has taken on significant political meaning. For migrants in Guangzhou, laboring to become an entrepreneur has become an economic and social necessity. With the gradual erasure of the worker and the peasant as the vanguards of socialist transformation and the erosion of state-sponsored services and welfare, one of the most immediate spaces of economic and political hope for migrants remains market participation via entrepreneurship. Through this state-endorsed narrative, the entrepreneur embodies all that capitalist activities have to offer, though the role is devoid of meaningful improvements by the state to the lives and livelihoods of working-class migrants.

Teetering on the edges of boss/worker and employer/employee, migrant bosses experience a certain degree of mobility, but their attempts to fix and convert capital into a trajectory of progressive accumulation slip from under their feet. Their experiences of unemployment, debt, and violence lead them to realize that welfare services by the state do not benefit them. Instead, they must rely on their own labor and initiative, however risky their migratory routes and dreams of entrepreneurship may be. Along the way, migrants encounter competing bosses who hold similar dreams of wealth and financial security. They experience physical mobility as they move along the circuits of commodity and capital. However, the broader landscapes of factory discipline, racialized policing, real estate speculation, and even otherworldly divinity restrict their ability to embed and convert their economic gains to the authority and wealth necessary to elevate them into the ranks of rightful entrepreneurs.

UNKNOWING THE SUPPLY CHAIN

This ethnography presents accounts of fast fashion supply chains in Guangzhou that are anchored upon the everyday lives of domestic and foreign migrants who labor in postsocialist spaces that are critically linked to transregional chains of commodity manufacture and exchange via their accumulative practices. Rather than conceptualizing transnational capitalism as a top-down, homogeneous, and all-encompassing system of economic life, I remain committed to the experiences and perspectives of my interlocutors as they unfold on the ground. More specifically, I focus on the ways in which precarity, precariousness, and the entreprecariat are variously experienced by low-paid subcontractors across fast fashion supply chains—specifically, I look at domestic and transnational migrants in Guangzhou.

This ethnographic project grew out of my initial curiosity in migration, labor, and counterfeit culture in factory towns and other industrial zones in the Pearl River Delta region. In 2011, after a year of interviewing fashion designers, factory owners, and migrant laborers, I realized that these market participants were concerned not with fakes and counterfeits per se but rather with strategies that would sustain their small-scale businesses in light of cutthroat competition, extractive officials, and the rapid, unforgiving turnover of fast fashion trends for export.

Through ethnographic methods of participant observation, semistructured interviews, and personal conversations, I analyze migrants' personal reflections and how they articulate their experiences of precariousness. I also pay attention to their perceptions of social inequality as they intensify their accumulative activities via commodity production and exchange across the global supply chains for fast fashion. Remaining faithful to the experiential dimensions of my ethnographic subjects, I approach global supply chains as a heuristic device; these supply chains remain partially visible and imperfectly understood in their fragmented and incomplete forms. Through this, my analyses demonstrate how occluded aspects of the supply chains are, in fact, key to understanding how migrants navigate the fragmented and isolated worlds that sustain these fast fashion supply chains in Guangzhou. My conceptual framing of transnational capitalism as partial, fragmented, and situated in cultural practices informs the ethnographic approaches I have taken in this study of global supply chains.

As such, these accounts must necessarily be fragmented, partial, and incomplete. Indeed, migrant labor has been, for the most part, rendered invisible by the dictates of capital accumulation. For this reason, I highlight how migrants across the supply chains attempt to know or make visible other bosses and production sites further down the chains. This practice, as I demonstrate in chapter 2, involves creative guesswork among two or more bosses in a cross-cultural encounter, as well as improvisation and luck. This book draws inspiration from such practices among migrant bosses and laborers by narrating transnational supply chains as they are imagined and perceived by those who sustain them—in their incomplete and fragmented forms—through their everyday labor. This bottom-up perspective, as I assert, is no less empirical or scientific than other conceptualizations of commodity chains in other social science disciplines. In fact, representing global supply chains as diverse, partial, and fragmented reflects more closely the heterogeneous and particularistic worlds that come together as a supply chain.

While this project traces fast fashion commodities through the spheres of manufacture, exchange, and export, the human stories of migrants' successes and struggles—which breathe ethnographic life into the global commodity chains for fast fashion—are, at best, imaginations and interpretations that illuminate the affective nuances and rhythmic textures of migrant entrepreneurship. This partial, interpretative approach is critical to and reflective of this contemporary post-Fordist moment. The segmentation of processes through which commodities are mass manufactured and exchanged leaves spaces of production and labor that are incoherent, isolated, and fragmented from one another. The conjoining of spatially segmented sites of mass manufacture and exchange is akin to what Anna Tsing describes as the productive *friction* of dynamic cultural exchange—including coincidences, accidents, and misinterpretation—that comprises what she calls "supply chain capitalism" (Tsing 2005, 2009). The coming together of these disparate spheres of labor and exchange through a dynamic friction, as I elaborate in the chapters that follow, leaves openings or gaps where third-party agents or other market participants insert themselves to compete in their aspirations for capitalist accumulation.[20]

Moments of *unknowing* how supply chains operate thus become more concrete and revelatory than moments when observers and market participants assume with absolute certainty the organization of a supply chain. As scholars (Sontag 2001; Haraway 1988; Berger 2008; Lam 2019, 2020; E. Y. Huang 2021) have cogently explained, a distant and totalizing bird's-eye view of capitalist practice is a masculinist and artificial construct that not only flattens the cultural dynamics of economic activity but also privileges seeing as the primary mode of knowledge production and dissemination. Erasure, immobility, disconnection, uncertainty, and mistrust among bosses across the supply chain yield key ethnographic insights into how capitalism makes invisible the everyday rhythms of labor and livelihood upon which it depends.

This approach to ethnographic writing and analysis draws inspiration from feminist scholars (Rofel 1999; Ong and Collier 2004; Guyer 2004; Tsing 2005; Graham 2006a, 2006b; M. Zhan 2009; Bear et al. 2015; Rofel and Yanagisako 2018) who emphasize the diverse and particularistic lifeworlds that animate the affective and intimate contours of global commodity chains and other forms of commodity exchange. It also highlights how fast fashion operates precisely via the shadows, gaps, and partial linkages that are situated between these fragmented worlds.[21] Indeed, few if any individual subcontractors or corporate players, whether they are the movers and shakers of the fashion industry or the laborers at the bottom of the social ladder, truly see or understand the fast fashion supply chain in its entirety. There are no puppet masters, nor are there cogs in a grand machine. Like a house of mirrors, multiple moving parts enable these transnational supply chains. The blind spots and gaps make the ever-elusive mysteries of fast fashion and transnational supply chains critical mechanisms of capitalist accumulation.[22] At times, as Xiao Ye shows us, migrants confront unpredictable tragedies and inexplicable accidents threatening to eject them from the supply chains. Contending with the unknowable or the inexplicable becomes a way of life for many migrants who labor across the links of commodity production and exchange.

At the same time, my book pushes the limits of these feminist critiques of capitalism by exploring how migrants' aspirations for entrepreneurial freedom rub up against those of other market participants across the supply chains. The chains of commodity production that I describe are anchored upon land tenure, property relations, and worldly accumulative practices that overlap, compete, and clash in the life cycle of a fashion trend. Migrants' improvised and inventive practices include job hopping, reading clients, and flipping fashion objects as well as performing intersectional national, racial/ethnic, and religious identifications. Although migrants' access to relative mobility opens new horizons of aspiration and possibility, these horizons become co-opted by third-party agents of finance and real estate capital, who vigilantly police the boundaries between labor and capital. These third-party agents hold the migrant bosses back from realizing the wealth that they imagine should be possible given their entrepreneurial activities. The clashing as well as the conjoining of their profit-driven interests give rise to competing classes of laborers, bosses, landlords, officers, and other rent seekers in overlapping accumulative worlds.

Along this vein, my approach vis-à-vis globalization and transnational capitalism refuses predetermined logics of capitalist valuation and personhood along a spectrum of high- or low-end forms of globalization (Mathews 2011; Mathews et al. 2015) because the logics of market exchange are key to perpetuating the deleterious effects of global capital, including racial exclusion, poverty, climate change, and other forms of socioeconomic inequality. I pay particular attention to moments of contestation, competition, and ambivalence among market participants who personify and lend cultural meaning to entrepreneurship and other forms of capitalist exchange (Tsing 2009; Guyer 2004; Freeman 2014; Haugen 2018; Krause 2018; Rofel and Yanagisako 2018). This book thus argues for an intersectional approach to transnational capitalism, one that considers how class aspirations and belonging intersect with a spectrum of racial, ethnic, gendered, and nationalistic identifications.

The following chapters highlight different aspects of precarious accumulation as they manifest across the supply chains. The chapters take readers along the migratory pathways that are activated by fast fashion commodity chains, from small-scale household workshops to wholesale markets, underground churches, migrant neighborhoods, and into homes. They shadow processes ranging from mass manufacture in factories to commodity distribution in wholesale markets, to final export across transnational markets. Each chapter delves into a world of fast fashion in Guangzhou in ways that reveal how economic risks and uncertainties are passed along a network of domestic and transnational migrant bosses.

Throughout, my analyses show how migrants' personal sacrifices and family labors confront the accumulative interests of landlords, security agents, and bigger bosses who make the lives and livelihoods of these migrants more precarious. These dynamics highlight the tensions between mobility/immobility and freedom/unfreedom. The chapters unfold to show how migrant bosses encounter and negotiate the covert economies of fee collection, rent-seeking, and policing that are part and parcel of the fast fashion world. Ultimately, this book reconceptualizes migrants (both domestic and transnational) as aspiring agents who traverse and remake the boundaries between labor and capital. Yet in doing so, migrants' accumulative practices change the broader landscapes of power and inequality characteristic of transnational subcontracting. The migrants inadvertently reproduce social inequalities and structural violence in their drive for capital accumulation. Ultimately, they experience various forms of entrepreneurial deferment, namely stalled mobility, surveillance and regulation, flexible appropriation, and spatial imaginations of Guangzhou and China.

Chapter 1, "Made in China, Just in Time," details how Chinese, West African, and South Korean migratory pathways and global fast fashion supply chains are spatially mapped out across the postsocialist urban villages (*chengzhongcun*) and city districts of transnational Guangzhou. Specifically, I demonstrate how Guangzhou's postsocialist urban transformations articulate with the infrastructural organization of the global supply chains. The chapter introduces the specialized, family-based organization of life and work in household assembly workshops (*jiagongchang*), where migrants' low-wage piecework, low-volume production, and use of outmoded tools sustain the everyday rhythms of transnational subcontracting. The chapter also describes the transnational migrant districts of Guangzhou, where South Korean and West African migrants draw upon their national and religious identifications to carve out market niches in fast fashion supply chains. These same identifications, however, mark them as targets of ethnonationalist campaigns, forcing them to negotiate the risks and rewards of migrant entrepreneurship and possibly removing them from the supply chains altogether. The chapter's ethnographic accounts lay the foundation for understanding what the role of "the boss" means for different groups of people, how this role is differentially experienced and enacted, and what the risks are for migrants who take on this role.

Chapter 2, "Stalled Mobility," situates readers within the maze of dark alleyways of Guangzhou's urban villages, where small-scale, unregulated *jiagongchang* sustain the "just in time" delivery of fast fashion worldwide. With an ethnographic focus on the Wongs, a migrant family from neighboring Guangxi Province, the chapter elaborates the paradoxical condition of *stalled mobility*, whereby migrants describe their labor as "free" even though they struggle to keep up with the rapid pace of fast fashion production. As migrant bosses, the Wongs remain caught in the double bind of evading exploitation by clients and competitors while also exploiting other migrant laborers. Their experience demonstrates that accumulation by exploitation is a relational and dynamic practice that involves uncertain assertions of discipline and uneven power. Over time, the freedom of physical and social mobility they experience wears off and transforms into a sense of freedom deferred. Stalled mobility highlights how the Wongs and the temporary migrant workers they hire must negotiate the contradictory dynamics of mobility and immobility, as well as freedom and unfreedom.

Chapter 3, "Surveillance and Regulation in the *Shenfen* (Identification) Economy," moves from the narrow confines of migrants' household workshops (*jiagongchang*) into the wider context of Guangzhou's urban villages, tracing long-standing disputes over property relations between *tu er dai* village landlords, real estate corporations, and government officials, all of whom increasingly speculate on and contest the value of the land. It delves into the *shenfen* (identification) economy, whereby migrant bosses' everyday rhythms of life and livelihood are animated by racial criminalization, economic regulation, and extortion by local landlords, real estate speculators, and the police. While most studies on law enforcement consider the police the quintessential manifestation of state power, this chapter shows how nonstate actors like local landlords, property managers, and private security officers also take up violence to protect property rights and rental income. As such, the chapter shows how the market, and not only the state, serves as the impetus for (racialized) violence. The chapter explores how the everyday operations of fast fashion supply chains determine the kinds of surveillance and economic regulation that emerge in urban villages, how migrant bosses confront them, and how these regulatory constraints color migrants' gendered and racialized experiences of bosshood, including the deferment of their entrepreneurial aspirations.

Chapter 4, "Speculative Real Estate and Flexible Appropriation," moves into Guangzhou's wholesale markets to examine the boom-and-bust rhythms of the fast fashion sector that emerge from the intersection of commodity exchange and rampant real estate speculation. Amid the chaos of these markets, landlords and building managers carefully calculate and map the rhythms of fee collection and rent-seeking practices that govern the ways in which fast fashion commodities are produced and exchanged. Small-scale migrant bosses, in response, attempt to dodge predatory rent-seeking practices while struggling to catch up to the speedy turnover of fast fashion. The chapter shows how rent-seeking and fee extraction accelerate the relentless pursuit of profits among migrant bosses, compelling them to engage with the unique forms of fashion production that I call *flexible appropriation* that undergird Guangzhou's fast fashion markets. Flexible appropriation strategies include retagging garments, reassembling garment pieces, and "flipping" finished goods (*chao huo*) from one market to another. The chapter traces how the extractive economy of collusion and rent-seeking emerges like a shadow, deferring migrants' entrepreneurial dreams by following the creative and profit-seeking practices of migrant bosses who, in turn, seek to escape it. This dynamic intensifies the aura of "high stakes, high rewards" that entrepreneurship and fast fashion promise, thus highlighting the uncertainties and paradoxes embodied by the migrant entrepreneur.

Chapter 5, "Transnational Migrant Bosshood," brings the reader into the worlds of bosshood as experienced by West African and South Korean migrants in Guangzhou. Specifically, I present ethnographic analyses to illustrate how, in the years before the COVID-19 pandemic, these transnational migrant bosses were drawn into the supply chains in China based on their religious, ethnic, and nationalist identifications. West African and South Korean migrant bosses took and continue to take financial and social risks that are distinct from those faced by Chinese rural migrants, particularly through significant investment in bridging economic and cultural links to overseas markets. At the same time, these transnational migrants often lack the local connections and legal protections to offset the surveillance and other regulatory practices that they encounter based on their status as foreigners.

While rural Chinese migrants view Guangzhou as a platform for transnational capital and cross-cultural exchange, foreign migrants view China as a stage for worldly and otherworldly forms of ethnic and faith-based accumulation. Transnational migrants' religious faiths and ethnic identifications lead them to pursue precarious accumulation based on these affiliations: West African migrants bridge their religious faiths with desires for wealth via the prosperity doctrine, while South Korean migrants draw upon their ties to Korean Chinese (*Chaoxianzu*) ethnic communities in Guangzhou to accumulate capital that crosses ethnic and national boundaries. However, these very same religious and ethnic affiliations eventually lead to their departure from China. In effect, West African and South Korean migrant entrepreneurs demonstrate similar dynamics of stalled mobility as rural Chinese migrants, yet on different spatial scales of mobility/immobility.

Overall, the book shows that if the entrepreneurial self is never fully autonomous, it is also never fully realized. In light of China's postsocialist transformations of land, labor, and personhood, migrants' experiences of mobility and accumulation do not follow a linear path of future-driven, progressive growth. These migrants' experiences of small-scale entrepreneurship reveal how their entrepreneurial identities materialize in parts, or in gradients, as part of a longer nonlinear process of actualization and becoming. In the absence of state-sponsored protections for their risky endeavors, migrants' senses of entrepreneurial personhood become tied solely to their accumulative practices, which in turn are anchored to the fluctuations of global markets. Their claims to bosshood are possible only through their transactional engagements with the worlds of capitalist exchange, which occur unevenly in fits and starts. Migrants thereby view the actualization of their entrepreneurial agency and accumulative potential as possible only through relations of exchange, leaving them vulnerable to exploitation, extortion, and financial loss. They view entrepreneurship as a promise of prosperity, though not necessarily a delivery of that promise.

In their urgency to convert labor and subjectivity to the dictates of capital, migrants transgress the boundaries of nation-states as well as those of secular and spiritual worlds, along the crossroads of race, gender, class, and ethnonationalism. Their efforts to remake themselves into rightful entrepreneurs, however, are met with structural constraints that stem from debt, family obligations, predatory extortion, racial profiling, criminalization, and excessive regulation. Over time, migrants realize that working for oneself leads to their implication in the structural vulnerability that undermines their aspirations for entrepreneurial wealth and autonomy. These dynamics operate through cross-cultural encounters within webs of postsocialist profit-making and capitalist accumulation. They shed light on the delicate nuances, unexpected paradoxes, and contingent outcomes that make transnational supply chains possible. In short, precarity and the possibilities for overcoming it emerge from the practices and relationships of everyday labor and livelihood.

1 Made in China, Just in Time

Newly arrived migrants float among a sea of pedestrians as they slowly pass through the concrete arteries that lead to and from Guangzhou's main railway station. With luggage and babies in tow, these newcomers bump shoulders with migrant entrepreneurs from the Middle East, Eastern Europe, Southeast Asia, and Africa as they wander past the stifling traffic of pedestrians, buses, and cargo vans in search of the latest fashion and accessories. These migrant entrepreneurs drag behind them heavy bundles of clothing wrapped in black garbage bags while they scour through scores of multilevel wholesale markets for shoes, watches, and clothing. The inventory that they amass in these markets is often brought back to other wholesale markets and retail outlets in various regions across the Global South, thus forming the intermediary links along the longer transcontinental chains of commodity exchange. The global linkages for fast fashion, which intersect a diversity of places and people across the world's continents and oceans, converge precisely in this railway station.

In Guangzhou, the commodities, images, and discourses of fast fashion animate the city's colorful and cosmopolitan landscape, one that is distinctly linked to the transnational migratory chains and global supply chains of the Global South. Overlapping migratory chains and supply chains gather in areas of the city that are still undergoing postsocialist transformation. Guangzhou's railway station and neighboring provincial bus station serve symbolically as the ports of arrival for millions of migrants from across China's countryside, and many people's dreams of fast money begin and end there as well. This location serves as the original site of the historic and globally recognized Canton Fair, which traces its origins back to the Maoist period. Nearby, the famous Baima Market, the city's first fashion wholesale market that opened during the first years of the reform period, is situated not far from the station. Legends of fast money are conceived within this locale. The hordes of people and vehicles that flock upon this vicinity indicate the commercial opportunities that Guangzhou promises to its migrant population, both domestic and transnational.

While scholars have cogently examined the nuances and experiences of transnational migration, trade, and marriage across multiracial and ethnic groups in China (Mathews 2011; Bodomo 2012; Şaul and Pelican 2014; Mathews et al. 2015; Huynh 2015; Castillo 2016; Wilzcak 2018; Haugen 2018; Heila Sha 2020; Ibañez-Tirado and Marsden 2020; Xiang 2021b; M. Li et al. 2022; Osella 2022), fewer have taken as their analytical focus the ways in which different classes of domestic and transnational migrants construct competing imaginaries of "fashion" and "bosshood" across conjoining worlds of accumulation. As I show, the encounters and mutual negotiations of Chinese, West African, and South Korean migrant bosses across the fast fashion supply chains in Guangzhou are the results of histories of colonialism, national development projects, and memories of war amid large-scale austerity and privatization measures. Together, domestic and transnational migrant bosses bring into contact different experiences of migration and economic development while also shaping China's market liberalization efforts. The diversity of these migrant groups in the city are thus part and parcel of China's global capitalist expansion and postsocialist transition. The rhythms of precarious accumulation among these migrant groups in Guangzhou critically intersect with ongoing transformations of land, labor, and personhood, which collectively signify China's attempts to scrub, albeit unsuccessfully, its socialist legacy.

Historically, scholars have conceptualized postsocialism as a periodizing concept as well as an analytical tool to describe large-scale societal transformations in China and the post-Soviet bloc (Watson 1994; Berdahl 1999; Hann et al. 2001; Dunn 2004; Buyandelgeriyn 2007). Anthropologists of postsocialist societies have explored the multiscalar processes, historical particularities, and experiences of social transformation. The notion of transitionology for example, describes postsocialist transition as a collision of two differently constituted orders, namely the struggle among former socialist states to incorporate into the global capitalist economy (Verdery 1996, 2003).[1] Such analytical frameworks underscore the enduring relevance of postsocialism as an analytical tool that marks the distinction between its ideological significance and its actual existing condition. Caroline Humphrey (2002), for example, points out that Rudolf Bahro's (1978) notion of "actually existing socialism" persists as lived practices in everyday life and as ideological alternatives to capitalism. Katherine Verdery (1996) further argues that scholars have yet to work out the variegated meanings of *actually existing capitalism* before they can declare postsocialism an irrelevant category.

This book attempts to revive these debates in postsocialist literature by demonstrating the ways in which global supply chains and migrant entrepreneurship critically intersect with transnational migration, alongside postsocialist transformations of place-based property relations, national identity, and migration. These aspects of economic development and social life in China's cities, as I demonstrate, remain tied to Maoist legacies of land, labor, and industrialization. The "ghosts of Mao" leave their historical footprints in the material landscape of the home-based workshops and the urban villages upon which transnational supply chains critically rely (Barme 1996; Rojas and Litzinger 2016).

For Chinese rural migrants, for instance, the figure of the migrant boss symbolizes a further disavowal of the Maoist past as symbolized by the *peasant* as a political entity. Yet, the historical significance of the peasant (*nongmin*) in the post-reform era remains a topic of lively contestation and debate (Day 2013; Ou 2022). Scholars have debated the extent to which the privatization of collectivized land, particularly in urban villages, demonstrates an example of primitive accumulation in which peasants who once held or who continue to hold user-rights to the land have become completely dispossessed or depeasantized (Arrighi 2007; Andreas and Zhan 2015; Hayward and Jakimów 2022; P. C. C. Huang et al. 2012). While these scholarly debates have contributed invaluable insights into the complexities of class dynamics and urban accumulation in present-day China, they have tended to assume a linear rural-to-urban trajectory in the subjective and class-based identification of the Chinese rural migrant.

This ethnography offers a different approach to the debates by suggesting that the mobility and transformation of the former Chinese peasant and the migrant boss in contemporary China do not follow a linear rural-to-urban trajectory. Rather, as the industrialization of Guangzhou's urban villages demonstrates, former peasants who were once the vanguard of the Chinese Revolution have become fragmented into various classes of overnight landlords and migrant laborers. They experience varying degrees of dispossession and exploitation. Their accumulative interests rub up directly against each other, creating a secondary economy of policing, rent-seeking, and extortion. The peasant landlords, for instance, rely on rental income from their migrant tenants to assert their financial claims to the municipal government in the face of rapid urbanization and outright expropriation of the land. Meanwhile, migrant laborers who are the tenants become the most vulnerable group of the former peasant classes due to the *hukou* policy of population control, since they face not only exploitation of their labor but also extortion and policing based on their status as members of the floating population (*liudong renkou*).

At the same time, South Korean and West African migrants draw upon their nationalist and religious networks and identifications in Guangzhou to carve out market niches in city's fast fashion supply chains. These same identifications, however, become targets of ethno-nationalist campaigns that ultimately force them to leave China and, possibly, to remove themselves from the supply chains altogether. Their vulnerabilities and the uncertainties that they face as migrant bosses in Guangzhou demonstrate how the ethnic, racial, and religious identifications that drew them into the supply chains in the first place become the very same identifications that eventually lead to their expulsions from those chains, along with their departures from China.

Thus, migrant bosses who engage in transnational subcontracting across global supply chains in China provide other examples of the ways in which migrant bosshood is rife with contradictions and paradoxes for domestic and transnational migrant bosses. Bosshood, however, would not have been possible without the socialist legacies of the *hukou* policy of migratory control and the emergence of urban villages during the period of early market reforms. Amid these large-scale postsocialist transformations, Chinese officials at both the local and the centralized levels work out immigration laws and residence requirements for foreign traders from different regions of the world as migrants from the Global South begin to imagine China as a space of settlement and capitalist accumulation. In the following sections, I detail the ways in which Chinese, West African, and South Korean migratory pathways and the global supply chains for fast fashion are spatially mapped out across the postsocialist urban villages and city districts of transnational Guangzhou. I demonstrate the particular ways in which Guangzhou's postsocialist transformations of urban villages, household workshops, and multinational wholesale markets articulate with the infrastructural organization of the global supply chains for fast fashion.

THE RISE OF URBAN VILLAGES AND THE POLITICS OF
CAPITALIST ACCUMULATION FOR FORMER CHINESE
PEASANTS IN GUANGZHOU

Nestled within scattered pockets of the city, agricultural fields have given way to numerous urban villages across Guangzhou, where clusters of dense and low-lying factories, warehouses, and apartment buildings line the dark and musty alleyways. Colloquially known as "kissing buildings," these apartments are packed so closely that they seem to swallow up the sky, leaving only a narrow tunnel that leads up to the gray clouds above (Hsing 2010). Nearly all the long-standing members of former Maoist collectives, whose livelihoods once depended on crops grown on this land, have moved away from the area and into the fully urbanized districts of the city. They are colloquially referred to as the *tu er dai* 土二代 (peasant landlords). They are a group of former peasants who have been catapulted to the rentier class nearly overnight, thanks to their collective possession of use-rights to village land. As members these former Maoist collectives, the *tu er dai* peasant landlords seek to protect their accumulative interests via their possession of these use-rights.

Urban villages are spaces that are no longer agricultural villages. Yet according to the *hukou*, their residents and the surrounding land are not fully urban (Smart and Zhang 2006). Urban villages are the results of intensified urbanization over the past three decades. They differ from city neighborhoods that are constructed on state-owned land, since long-standing members of former agricultural collectives continue to possess the administrative use-rights to the land (Hsing 2010; Bach 2010; O'Donnell 2013; Al 2014; Bolchover 2018; N. Chu et al. 2022). Here, few people are concerned with land ownership per se; instead, they are more concerned with issues of administrative use-rights and fair redistribution of money based on land value (Hsing 2010). According to the *hukou* system, holders of the use-rights to the land are still considered rural citizens, even though some have become wealthy landlords who rent apartment spaces to rural migrants in search of jobs and affordable housing. For this reason, village collectives governed by the peasant landlords retain much of their administrative autonomy in regard to everyday business and security affairs.[2]

My project is situated within these urban villages in Guangzhou, with a particular focus on Zhaocun, Xiaobei, and Sunyuanli, urban villages where the city's largest wholesale markets and factories for fashion textiles and accessories are located. The linking of rural-to-urban migration and

1.1 Guangzhou's urban village, 2016. Photo by Nellie Chu.

transnational migrant flows in Guangzhou's urban villages results in competing demands and desires for accumulation among actors who are indirectly involved in the supply chains: landlords, police (private and state-run), and competing bosses. Their competing demands for profits emerge in pockets of the urban landscape where members of former Maoist collectives negotiate and protest land claims, namely the transfer of their land use-rights to the municipal government. Here, the place-based dynamics of postsocialist transformation of land, labor, and personhood link up with the cross-cultural experiences of transnational and rural migration among Chinese, South Korean, and West African bosses across uneven geographies of urbanization and capitalist accumulation.

Upon their arrival in the Guangzhou railway station, many Chinese migrants from the nation's countryside move into the city's Zhaocun garment district, which has historically served as the hub of low-cost garment manufacture and exchange since the early period of market reforms. Like many migrants who lived and worked in the urban villages of the southern capital of Guangdong Province, the Wongs, a migrant couple from the neighboring Guangxi Province, left their parents and children in her hometown of Guigang to try their luck at small-scale migrant entrepreneurship. Uncertain of the challenges that lay ahead, Mrs. Wong was at least minimally comforted by the accompaniment of her husband. Lured by the prospect of cosmopolitanism and wealth, the couple followed their fellow villagers to the outskirts of the sprawling city. There, low-lying garment factories, warehouses, and five-story apartment buildings were quickly transforming the lush, flat agricultural landscape, which was one of the city's largest collectively owned land area during the Maoist period, before the introduction of market reforms in 1978.

Mr. and Mrs. Wong quickly settled into the unfamiliar environs of the industrial enclave by taking up wage work in one of the hundreds of factories that were in operation there. At the time (1990), subcontractors from Hong Kong and Taiwan, who negotiated on behalf of the profit-driven interests of their American, Japanese, and European corporate fashion clients, converged on these factories in search of low-cost labor and manufacturing capabilities. With their modest savings, the Wongs aspired to capitalize on this financial opportunity, and they began to venture out on their own by opening a small-scale workshop directly behind the Wuchang Accessories Market. Over the ensuing decade, the migrant couple witnessed the fervor of market activity around them as township and village enterprises gave way to private real estate companies that had begun speculating on the value of the surrounding land (O'Donnell et al. 2017). Meanwhile, legends of migrants-turned-bosses striking it rich in Guangzhou's garment sector fueled their dreams of entrepreneurial wealth.

To be sure, the rise of the migrant bosses in Guangzhou would not have been possible without Deng Xiaoping's privatization of land and labor in 1978. The introduction of market reforms—marked by the designation of the Pearl River Delta area as a Special Economic Zone and Deng's famous "Southern Tour" in 1992—brought about intensified industrialization as well as the large-scale mushrooming of urban villages.[3] During the initial years of their operation, the Wongs joined in the fervor of entrepreneurial pursuit and unbounded possibility that characterized the early decades of market reform. Their business had remained steady and profitable. The Wongs recalled that their relative success enabled the entire family, including their children and the husband's aging parents, to relocate and settle in the garment district so that the family members could remain near one another. Their small-scale enterprise also enabled them to engage subcontractors from West Africa, South Korea, and the Middle East, allowing the Wongs to imagine themselves at the center of China's workshops of the world.

Today, the continued existence of urban villages illustrates the ways in which rapid urbanization and industrialization of a postsocialist city remain a double-edged sword. Although the shoddy, densely packed apartments are an eyesore, a reminder of the poverty and insecurities that migrants continue to endure despite the promises of economic development, the low barriers to market entry and to city living that urban villages provide enable low-cost manufacturing to sustain China's workshops of the world. Residents in these urban villages are members of the floating population, a population whose *hukou* administrative statuses keep them legally excluded from critical state benefits in the city, including housing, education, healthcare, and formal employment. Their social and material exclusions keep the migrants economically bound to low-paying jobs with oppressive labor conditions in the manufacturing and service industries, thereby creating one of the world's largest pools of exploitable low-wage labor while at the same time fueling desires for personal autonomy via entrepreneurship and bosshood.

Domestic and transnational migrants in Guangzhou's urban villages attempt to carve out alternative means of livelihood that keep them relatively autonomous and free from the oppressive conditions of industrial labor. Many migrant bosses who have traveled from China's countryside to

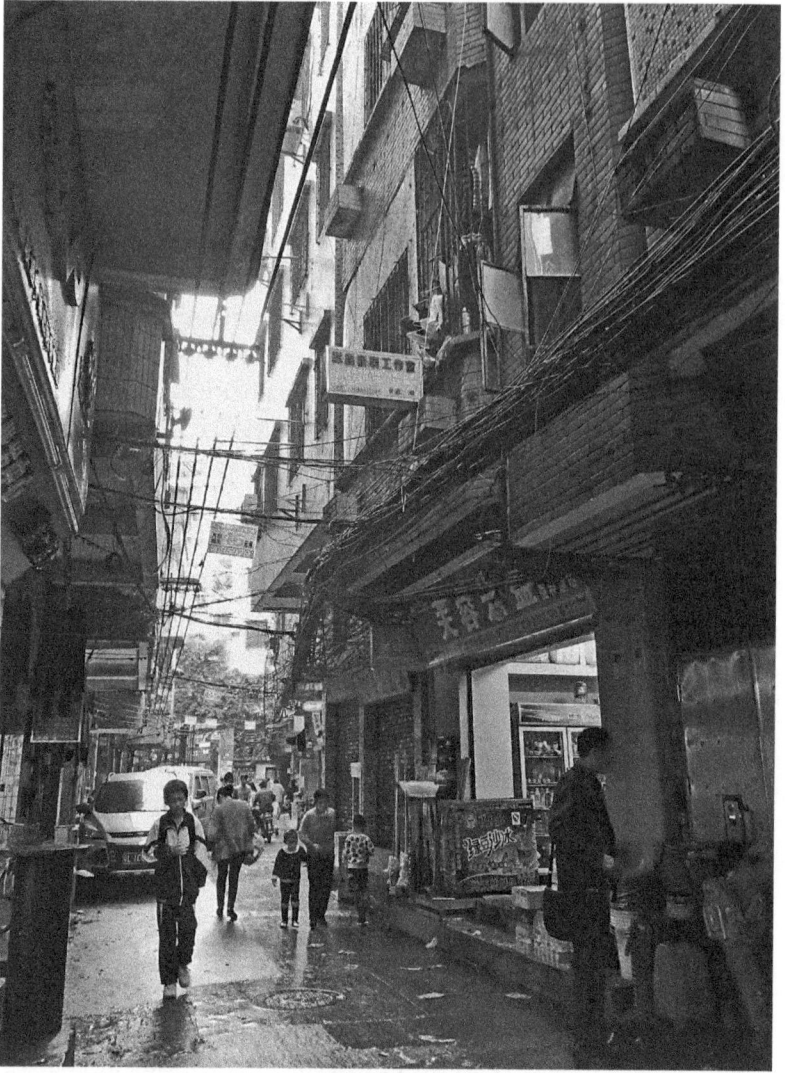

1.2 Guangzhou alleyway between densely packed apartment buildings, 2016. Photo by Nellie Chu.

seek employment in Guangzhou are older male and female migrants (thirty to fifty years old) who once served as the first generations of migrant laborers in the large-scale Fordist factories in Shenzhen. With a modest amount of starting capital, many Chinese migrant bosses follow in the footsteps of their relatives or close friends and open small-scale factories in urban villages across the Pearl River Delta region. Those who live in the urban villages can live with their families in apartments that are separate from their workplaces. They are no longer under the watchful eyes of their employers. Some move from one job to another when working conditions become unfavorable, while others juggle multiple part-time and temporary jobs as a means of stitching together sufficient income. Such freedom of mobility is otherwise not possible in larger, more centralized factories. These unstable conditions of temporary (self) employment among migrants who once worked in the Fordist-style export factories thus set the foundation for the emergence of migrant bosses and their practices of capitalist accumulation across the fast fashion supply chains in Guangzhou.

Key to migrants' accumulative efforts, as I will show in the chapters that follow, is the impetus to constantly reallocate and reinvest their labor power so as to secure long-term prospects for wealth and financial security. With the large-scale retrenchment of state protection since the early 1980s, migrant bosses had to learn to translate their abilities, wages, and possessions, however modest they were, into sources of future-led growth in order to secure the ongoing regeneration of wealth and surplus value in the long term. Chinese, West African, and South Korean migrants in Guangzhou achieved this by managing novel forms of labor and capital mobility. While some migrants moved in and out of self-employment, unemployment, and wage labor, others managed the ongoing circulation of fast fashions by flipping commodities from one market to another and by buying and reselling products in transnational markets through various practices of arbitrage.[4]

These improvised strategies, though constrained and limited, allowed rural and transnational migrant bosses to remain preemptive and responsive to the ever-changing dictates of capital. Much like the strategies of suspension, job-hopping, and contractual labor, these tactics of aspirational entrepreneurship and economic survival reflect a broader phenomenon of the casualization and informalization of labor and employment in China and around the globe (Standing 2011; X. Zhang 2008; Friedman and Lee 2010; Kuruvilla et al. 2011; Litzinger 2013; Mezzadri and Fan 2018; C. K. Chan et al. 2021).[5] After all, the long-term emphasis on work and livelihood no longer rests upon stable employment. Instead, the accumulative practices of these migrant entrepreneurs now mirror what Anna Tsing (2015) describes as "patchy," a mosaic of entangled ways of life that are open-ended, provisional, and uncertain. Migrant classes, particularly those of the '90s generation, anchor their entrepreneurial aspirations based on the long-term trajectory of capitalist accumulation rather than on long-term employment or wage labor.[6] For the migrants who labor across the supply chains for fast fashion in Guangzhou, the structural dynamics of fast fashion compel migrant laborers and small-scale entrepreneurs to perceive impermanence as the primary resource through which they can engage with and participate in the transnational chains of manufacture and exchange. With the foreclosure of possibilities that once rested upon the formalization of long-term and stable employment and the protection of fair working conditions and living wages, contingent accumulation and casualization of labor open temporary spaces of life, dignity, and hope for migrant bosses.[7]

At the same time, the accumulative practices of the migrant bosses in Zhaocun and other urban villages in Guangzhou dovetail with the profit-seeking schemes of the *tu er dai* peasant landlords. The intersection of their respective accumulative practices creates spatiotemporal gaps through which third-party agents, including private security officials, building managers, and competing bosses, exploit and extract fees and payments from the migrant bosses. While the emergence of the *tu er dai* peasant landlords is common throughout many urban villages across Guangzhou (including Xiaobei and Sanyuanli, which I introduce below), the articulation of the transnational fast fashion supply chains makes Zhaocun distinctive in that the histories of migrant entrepreneurship enable members of the *tu er dai* to delay the transfer of their use-rights to the land, while continuing to capitalize on their rent-seeking activities.

The *shenfen* economy or quite literally the "identification" economy serves as a case in point. It emerges as a secondary economy whereby those who are not directly involved in the fast fashion supply chains become implicated in them by shadowing the flows of migrants, people, money, and commodities into and out of factories and the urban villages. Their attempts to accumulate profits through the extralegal extraction of payments and fees operate alongside the rhythms and spaces of fast fashion manufacture and exchange. Indeed, the structural dynamics of fast fashion, the quick, just-in-time delivery of low-cost fashion commodities across small-scale and fragmented sites of mass production, enable opportunities for competing subcontractors, police, security officers, and real estate agents to extort capital, leaving migrant bosses even more vulnerable to the unstable conditions of labor and livelihoods across the supply chains.

JIAGONGCHANG HOUSEHOLD WORKSHOPS
AND THE RISE OF FAST FASHION

Another distinctive feature of Guangzhou's urban villages, and particularly Zhaocun village, are the thousands of small-scale household workshops that feed into the global supply chains for garment manufacturing and export, including those for globally recognized brands. Colloquially, they are known as cut-and-sew factories, or *jiagongchang*. Situated in makeshift kitchens, dilapidated garages, and abandoned ancestral halls, the organization of life and work in these assembly workshops is family-based and specialized. That is, temporary workers complete only one task in a longer chain of coordination, assembly, and manufacture. Transnational subcontracting practices are made possible by migrants' engagements with precarious labor and craft-based production that features low-wage piecework, low-volume production, modest technical skills, and outmoded tools.

In these *jiagongchang*, migrant laborers mass manufacture all types of garments at low prices. Many styles feature woven, lace, and knit fabrics with straight cuts, simple lines, and embellishments that feature the latest styles yet also allow for quick production. Because of the unforgiving demands of speed to market, fast fashion relies on the appropriation of exclusive runway looks, their mass manufacture, and their quick delivery at reduced prices, thus making high fashion ensembles accessible to middle-income consumers.[8] Multinational fast fashion corporations have out-competed retailers and fashion houses that have historically utilized a slower, more meticulous model of ready-to-wear clothing design and manufacture. Design practices that rest on long-standing claims to authenticity based on geography, cultural origins, and traditions in production are thereby being challenged by the speed with which fashions can now be brought to market (Reinach 2005; Park 2012, 2021; Thomas 2016; Moon 2014, 2016, 2020; Krause 2018; Rofel and Yanagisako 2018).

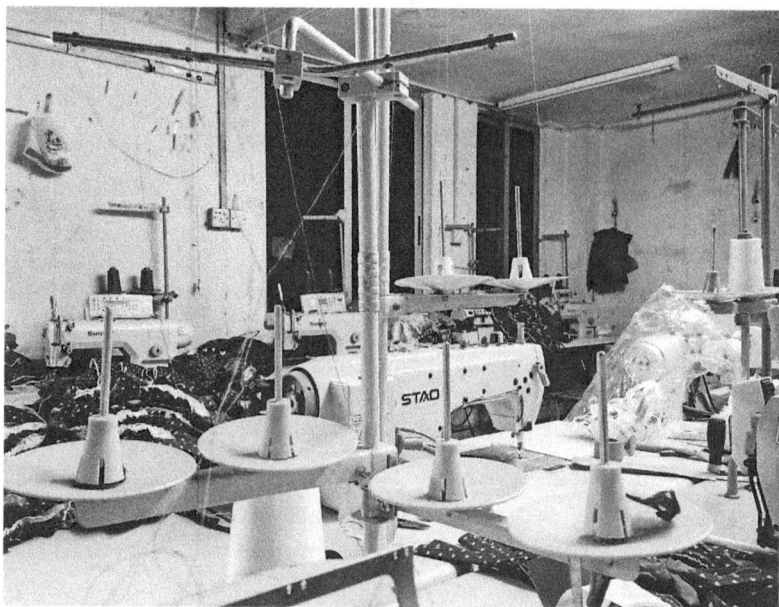

1.3 A typical *jiagongchang* household workshop in Guangzhou, 2018. Photo by Nellie Chu.

By offering high fashion looks at prices accessible to an average European or North American middle-class consumer, fast fashion companies territorialize an expansive market niche bridging low/high fashion with high and low technology and work practices. Global outsourcing and transnational subcontracting have led to an unprecedented drop in the worldwide prices for fashion clothing; and this drop in prices has been accompanied by transformations in consumer practices, particularly in markets across Europe and North America. Like other forms of fashion production, fast fashion emphasizes the ceaseless introduction of novel styles and trends. Its distinctiveness, however, lies in the speed with which the cycles of new fashions are designed, mass produced, and delivered.[9]

As the term *fast fashion* suggests, temporality plays a critical role in the constant remaking of this market niche as an end in itself (Horning 2011). Unlike couture fashion, the defining feature of fast fashion is the quick turnover of a diversity of styles, which intensifies the temporal cycles of market supply and demand (Horning 2011). Digital mass marketing and advertising techniques accentuate the quick, ongoing turnover of novel looks and designs such that consumers confront a barrage of new trends within ever-shorter intervals. The typical three-month cycle required to prepare a new seasonal collection fifteen years ago, for instance, has now been truncated to a mere two-week turnaround. The emphasis on the incessant, quick delivery of "new" fashions has reconfigured the boundaries of capital and labor across the realms of design, technology, consumption, and migrant labor at a worldwide scale (Horning 2011; Kornbluh 2024).

As a result, designers, agents, and manufacturers in Guangzhou's fast fashion sector constantly anticipate future trends in order to keep up with extreme market fluctuations. Fashion forecasting websites and fashion magazines from China and abroad have become engines of market information that enable various participants along the commodity chains to quickly identify future trends and compete to become the first to capitalize on the latest fads. Despite the technological advancements in photography, the internet, and design applications that enable consumers to dictate the terms and the scheduling of the production processes, business owners and migrant laborers struggle to keep up and maintain demanding production schedules.

The unprecedented speed by which commodities and capital travel has been attributed to the rise of the global e-platform economy, which has facilitated the growth of the digital economy, otherwise known as Industry 4.0. In this case, the Made in China model of low-wage mass manufacture based on migrant labor links up with nation's conversion from a low-tech base to a leader of the world's digital economy. This state-sponsored project of industrial upgrading has become a critical aspect of the evolving global fast fashion industry. Corporate giants on China's most successful digital platforms, such as Taobao, Shein, Tianmall, and Alibaba, achieve their multinational, monopolistic statuses primarily through the ongoing territorialization of a new kind of urban villages, otherwise known as "Taobao villages" or "Shein villages," as well as through the mobilization of transnational subcontracting (Lim 2015; Hao 2016; Fan and Luethje 2019). Present-day Taobao and Shein villages—where entire villages (not just urban villages) occupied by migrant laborers are organized to fulfill the demands of production and distribution of clothing and accessories via these e-platforms—exemplify their market successes and ubiquity. This multifaceted transformation of global outsourcing and intensified consumption would not have been possible without the on-the-ground mobilization of transnational subcontracting practices that comprise the intermediary links of the fast fashion supply chains in southern China.

Meanwhile, back at the Guangzhou railway station, young Chinese street
vendors showcase leather belts, pastel handbags, toys, and children's clothing on tarp mats spread out upon the concrete sidewalk. Down the street, a
clean and angular glass building towers above the bustling traffic. Here, the
Huimei fashion market beckons visitors from all corners of the world to in-
dulge in the latest trends. Window displays feature Korean script, exuding
an aura of foreignness and authenticity. Vibrant rainbows of pastel-colored
clothing and sparkling jewels adorn the white walls of the interior. Elec-
tronic pop music blasts through loudspeakers that are mounted to walls,
as young model-beautiful women strut past the narrow corridors that lead
to countless open-air showrooms and boutiques. The maze of countless
wholesale and retail outlets owned and operated by Chinese and Korean
investors, along with the crowds of cross-ethnic shoppers, extends another
seven levels, where offices and warehouses occupy the top floors. The fast-
moving escalators, air-conditioned spaces, and bright lighting tout the
market's contemporary, upper-class aesthetics.

As soon as one exits the building, however, visible contrasts between
the rich and the poor as well as the convergence of African, South Korean,
and Chinese people along the building's side streets are difficult to ignore.
Police cars blast their sirens and bus brakes screech in the distance. Older
men and women wait eagerly by the entrances of the building, as they informally solicit shoppers who need assistance in carrying their bundles
of merchandise to illegal pedicab drivers. Packs of brawny Chinese men
wearing neon-colored vests also wait by the front doors before they are assigned delivery tasks by young saleswomen and their patrons waiting inside the building. Along an avenue lined by makeshift market stalls selling
watches, shoes, and leather accessories, informal tents are set up by shipping and logistics companies that serve customers who wish to ship their
inventories to cities across China and around the world. In one tent, a
crowd of delivery men squat beside a massive metal scale, ready to weigh,
tape, and pack massive bundles of fashion merchandise for shipment out
of Guangzhou.

At around three o'clock in the afternoon, scores of male Nigerian street
vendors arrive along the side street. With suitcases and boxes in hand, they
lay out Louis Vuitton sneakers and handbags informally on top of parked
vehicles. These men stand side by side along the congested street as they

display jewelry, T-shirts, athletic wear, belts, watches, and leather bags to Chinese and African pedestrians who stroll by. Many of the men chat in groups of three or four as they conduct their business dealings with patrons from Poland, Russia, Singapore, Korea, and Senegal. Meanwhile, migrant street vendors who belong to China's various minority groups jostle alongside the crowds of African sellers who gather on the sidewalks in their attempts to make a living off the streets under the regulatory gaze of the police. Their informal activities link up with the intersecting links of commodity exchange that suffuse the surrounding cityscape.

In Guangzhou's fast fashion sector, West African and South Korean migrants embed their transnational market activities across the landscapes of postsocialist urban development, while Chinese rural migrants participate in the supply chains in order to expand their opportunities and hopes for wealth and financial security beyond the constraints of their statuses as migrants according to the *hukou* policy of population control. Collectively, their encounters demonstrate how precarious accumulation mobilizes divergent performances of personhood that emerge from the uneven worlds of labor and capital. Migrants animate figurations of labor by drawing upon an intersection of performances based on race, gender, class, nationality, and ethnicity across the supply chain. Indeed, fast fashion mobilizes people's intersubjective dimensions of identity and social relations—including gender, race, class, religion, and sexuality—to tap into their consumerist desires and aspirations for entrepreneurial autonomy (Hendrickson 1996; Lipovetsky 2002; Wilson 2003; Jones 2007; Woodward 2005; Woodward and Miller 2007; Miller 2009; Luvaas 2012; Moon 2020).[10] Likewise, in Guangzhou, fast fashion supply chains mobilize migrants' accumulative strategies based on the cultural dynamics of racism, ethnic nationalism, and faith-based enterprise.

The multifaceted transformation of global outsourcing and intensified consumption in Guangzhou has been critically facilitated by the labor of transnational migrants whose cross-cultural encounters constitute the links of distribution from southern China to the rest of the globe. Indeed, migrants' cross-cultural collaborations and intimate encounters retell the Made in China story as more than a singular narrative of Chinese migrant workers exporting the fruits of their exploited, low-wage labor to the rest of the world. Their migratory and economic activities show that development in China is not merely a state-driven project. It is made possible through capitalistic cross-cultural encounters among ordinary domestic and transnational migrants.

One scorching summer afternoon in 2015, Manuel, a thirty-five-year-old Algerian migrant entrepreneur from France, accompanied me on an exploration of Guangzhou's Xi Fang Hang, one of the world's largest wholesale markets for low-cost garments. Mesmerized by the immense scale of the markets and the flurry of entrepreneurial activities around us, Manuel raised his arms, took in a deep breath of air, and yelled, "I've come here at the right time and to the right place. This is where opportunity lies!" His determination and the eagerness of his entrepreneurial desires were infectious. The rhythms of his fast-paced walk as we passed by countless photos and displays of paisley-patterned shirts, polka dot shorts, and brightly colored hair ribbons mirrored the sense of urgency that pervaded the surrounding atmosphere. Later in the day, he described to me the chain of life events that led to his quest to become an entrepreneur in Guangzhou. He recalled:

> At that time, I was working part-time at the front desk of a small, dodgy hotel on the outskirts of Paris. There, I met countless numbers of businessmen coming and going with their luggage and packages in hand. Over time, I realized that they were carrying goods that were exported from China. They were in the business of bringing low-cost goods from China, often counterfeits, including small electronics and fashion wear, and selling them in places throughout Europe. One evening, I was casually surfing the internet when I came across the website of a language school in Shenzhen. Finally, it struck me that sitting at the front desk of a small hotel wasn't getting me anywhere. I could make much more money trading garments, small electronics, and household items between China and countries in Europe. The goods here (in China) are inexpensive, so all I needed was a small amount of capital. So, I obtained a tourist visa and decided to try my luck at running my own business.

Many migrant entrepreneurs from the Global South (most of whom are young men) echo the familiar tropes of risk, self-realization, opportunity, and enterprise that Manuel describes in his personal narrative. Indeed, the contemporary global capitalist economy, as characterized by low-wage factory labor and intensified consumption, has facilitated the availability of so-called cheap goods in China. This flood of inexpensive consumer items, has, in turn, opened pathways for many transnational migrants from Russia, Mali, Senegal, Nigeria, Malaysia, Singapore, Vietnam, and Korea to journey to China in search for quick profits, freedom, and social mobility. The lure of cheap stuff as a cultural category, as it is constructed in the world's consumerist and entrepreneurial imaginations, conjures the popular perception of China, particularly in cities such Shenzhen and Guangzhou, as a gateway for small-scale enterprise and economic opportunity.

As it did for Manuel, the popular notion of buying low and selling high does not merely reflect a rational and calculative engagement with capitalist pursuits for wealth and profit. Rather, the lure of cheap goods mobilizes entrepreneurial desires, drawing people across transoceanic boundaries to collectively converge upon the city streets of China and engage in the risks and rewards of small-scale enterprise. Their collaborative engagements, in turn, serve as the intermediary nodes through which global supply chains are formed. These small-scale entrepreneurial pursuits enable multinational wholesalers and retailers to subcontract from these migrants, thereby securing sources of low-priced Made in China exports. Though many consumers around the world often express disdain or distrust regarding personal health and safety when they see products that are made in China, small-scale traders and entrepreneurs who cross paths along the streets of Shenzhen and Guangzhou perceive the cultural categories of cheap and inexpensive goods as access to worlds of entrepreneurial freedom and economic opportunity.

Like Manuel, domestic and transnational migrants engage in the ongoing conversions of labor to capital, which take place along divergent pathways of mobility. These pathways, in turn, are defined by differences in class, gender, kinship, race, religion, ethnicity, and nationality. While Chinese manufacturers in the urban villages forge ties with West African Christian traders who sustain the transnational circulation of fast fashion commodities across Europe, the Middle East, and Africa via the prosperity doctrine, South Korean bosses collaborate with members of Chinese Korean ethnic groups to capitalize on the rise of K-pop trends and fashion around the globe.

Here, the transnational supply chains that these markets serve are variously marked by the everyday economic activities of these cross-racial and ethnic migrants as they jostle to occupy niches of capital accumulation (Lefebvre 1992). The cross-cultural dynamics of transnational mobility among the migrant bosses leave their material traces upon the urban

1.4 Delivery men sit among bags of cargo in front of a wholesale market for low-cost fast fashions, 2017. Photo by Nellie Chu.

landscape of the city, alongside a transnational mapping of the multiple supply chains that converge in Guangzhou's urban villages. An in-depth geographic tracing of the city's wholesale markets for fast fashion reveals how racism, ethnic nationalism, and faith-based accumulation shape the spatial mapping of the fast fashion supply chains in Guangzhou as well as the experiential dimensions of migrant bosshood for many who struggle to labor across these supply chains.

RACE-BASED ACCUMULATION AND PROFIT IN XIAOBEI

A walk through the district's intersecting boulevards and alleyways that lead directly to the city's ethnic enclaves unveils how the discourse of race articulates with the global supply chains for fashion via Guangzhou's African diaspora. In Guangzhou, traders from Africa, mostly young men and women from Senegal, Nigeria, Ghana, and the Congo, live and work in the city's African enclave, Xiaobei, racially dubbed the "chocolate city" by Chinese locals and denoting informality, illegality, and crime. Multi-storied glass buildings stand next to a kindergarten painted in pink, orange, green, and yellow, reflecting the visual vibrancy of the neighborhood. Handicapped beggars stand alongside young mothers of Uygur descent as they offer illegal currency exchange or sell calling cards to newly arrived migrants eager to conduct business in the district. Dressed in dark denim jeans, high-top tennis shoes, and light-colored headdresses, other young mothers from Xinjiang linger along street corners at night with their young children as they attempt to sell foreign currency to unknown clients on the street. Pairs of young women dressed in purple and azure blue African brocade and kente print skirt sets stroll through the streets pushing baby carriages as they purchase groceries for dinner.

As the densest, most ethnically diverse enclave in Guangzhou, Xiaobei sits approximately two miles south of the railway station. It is part of the larger Dengfeng district, a former agricultural area that now comprises a number of urban villages (Huang 2020). Restaurants, outdoor vendors, and storefronts animate the area's energetic street life. Residents' struggles with socioeconomic inequalities, however, become visceral as one meanders through its dark and congested alleyways.

Oftentimes, a police car waits patiently across the street from a pedestrian tunnel where vendors roast Halal-style chicken they sell to passersby and where older Chinese women offer eyebrow threading services to young fashionistas with small handheld mirrors resting on their laps. Officers wait as they plan another round of ID inspection checks among a large group of Nigerian men informally swapping currencies in front of an unmarked van. Along the bridge, a Chinese man offers to take photographs of wandering tourists against the backdrop of shiny high-rises and neon signposts. As a marketing ploy, he proudly holds up a massive collage of tourists from all over the world who have passed by this location along the bridge. Amid the pulsating traffic of cross-cultural people, food, and goods, the photographer's poster seems to declare this location in Xiaobei as the center of world.

With cash in hand, many of these migrant traders capitalize on the margins of China's budding cooperation with developing nations in Africa by venturing halfway across the world in hopes of realizing their entrepreneurial dreams. An estimated 20,000 documented migrants from Africa, at the time of my ethnographic research, live and work in Guangzhou's Xiaobei district; most of these migrants are men (Z. Li et al. 2009; Haugen 2012; Huynh 2015; Castillo 2016; Lan 2016a; Mathews et al. 2017). Countless others remain in the city, outside the purview of the municipal government.[11] The majority of residents in Xiaobei have migrated from countries in West Africa, including Mali, Senegal, Guinea (Conakry), Benin, Nigeria, and Côte d'Ivoire (Diederich 2013). Nearly half of these traders who eventually settle in Guangzhou work as brokers who mediate between Chinese producers and itinerant African importers who visit the city two to four times a year. Although importers purchase a range of China-made commodities—including kitchen appliances, motorcycles, electronics, and toys—distributors generally order copies of branded luxury items, including garments, bags, and accessories.

The informal and marginal exchanges among the Chinese exporters and African traders constitute transnational exchange networks, trading in commodities that span the global networks of other African diasporic communities across European metropolises, including Paris, Madrid, and Rome. Mediated through kin and native place networks, these traders constitute the commodity chains of branded items that radiate from Africa through Guangzhou to the boulevards and backstreets of Europe and the Middle East, where branded copies challenge the authenticity of their so-called original copies. In their attempts to appeal to the desires for branded fashion among tourists across Europe and the Middle East, these traders obscure the trail of commodity production back to China by capitalizing on the "Made in Italy" or "Made in France" labels of luxury logos. Thus, as in the case of these African migrants, the politics of authenticity and production origins critically shape the networks through which these branded goods travel.

Nearly half of the traders who eventually settle in Guangzhou work as brokers who serve as cultural bridges between Chinese producers and itinerant African importers. While some migrants manage to establish a relatively modest business for limited periods of time, others arrive in China only to find out that the snakeheads that brought them overseas have left them undocumented and penniless (Carling and Haugen 2020). Some of these unlucky migrants manage to leave China for Thailand, Cambodia, and other Southeast Asian countries, while others return to their home countries or struggle to establish their own business ventures elsewhere.

As for the lucky few who manage to settle in Guangzhou: Many of these traders establish their business establishments in a single high-rise in Xiaobei, the well-recognized Zhongnan building that towers over thirty floors.[12] Some members of this African community run licensed and unlicensed churches and other places of worship in this building, too; these churches are critically linked to their entrepreneurial endeavors in China. I describe their faith-based and entrepreneurial activities in more detail in chapter 5. Much like Hong Kong's Chungking Mansions, as Mathews (2011) describes in his ethnography, Zhongnan serves as the locus of cross-ethnic encounters among Xiaobei's migrant residents. The single tower houses guest houses, doctor's offices, salons, retail spaces, shipping outlets, restaurants, and apartment units. In fact, most commercial activity within Xiaobei remains confined to this single building, while older residential apartments crowd the district's side streets. The vibrancy of this building attests to the migrants' everyday attempts to sustain a sense of home and community despite the racism and other forms of exclusion they face in their business dealings (Castillo 2016).

Amid Xiaobei's signifiers of cosmopolitanism and urbanity, however, violent racism and visible poverty continue to mingle with the entrepreneurial fervor and colorful ethnic diversity that characterize this place. Indeed, the flourishing of fast fashion exchanges among the transnational migrant bosses in Guangzhou has engendered forms of regulation that materialize through practices of criminalization, racialization, and policing. The disparagement by local officials and urban residents of African and Chinese migrants as "criminals" and "counterfeiters" demonstrates the unequal access that aspiring entrepreneurs have to the state-sponsored welfare services and legal protections that are necessary for capital accumulation. In place of security and protection, ethno-nationalism, racism, and the policing of African migrants have fueled a secondary economy of predation, rent-seeking, and extraction in Xiaobei.

The migrants' worldly connections to Africa, the Middle East, Asia, and Europe seem to contradict their sense of racialized exclusion in Xiaobei and its neighboring ethnic enclaves in Guangzhou, including Sanyuanli and Tiyuxilu (Diederich 2013). As scholars (Bodomo 2011; Z. Li et al. 2012; Diederich 2013; Lan 2015, 2016a, 2016b; Haugen 2018) have noted, the majority of male and female traders from Africa remain confined within these enclaves, with the exception of occasional and short-term travel to factories and shipping docks outside of the city proper. Some migrants from Senegal and the Congo have complained on separate occasions that some passengers on the city bus would pinch their noses in front of them, indicating the prejudicial fallacy that Black people smell. To be sure, racism and linguistic barriers have become invisible walls around the district's geographic margins. Other race-based forms of regulatory surveillance and harassment materialize through the bodily presence of the municipal police, who attempt to govern the multiplicity of exchanges and practices of accumulation that take place within this district and out of the central state's regulatory control.

While studies often point to the police as the exemplary display of state power, the everyday rhythms of fast fashion exchange in Guangzhou's Xiaobei markets demonstrate how the transnational supply chains for fast fashion serve as platforms for market regulation and structural violence upon migrant groups and other vulnerable populations. Inside the wholesale markets, fast fashion exchange operates in sync with the daily forms of surveillance and harassment of African migrants by private security officers and the police. Migrant shopkeepers and shoppers unexpectedly encounter blackouts inside the markets during the day when uniformed inspectors pay a surprise visit to look for and fine "counterfeiters" or "criminals" whose business visas, licenses, and tax documents are missing or expired. Sometimes, these confrontations result in physical and emotional violence. Other officers pay unexpected visits to African tenants' private homes, resulting in the arrests of migrants and the fining of landlords. Such heavy-handed forms of inspection and policing lead many landlords to evict or refuse housing to Africans based solely on their race and migrant status.

In other cases, racism manifests in more covert and mundane ways. This becomes evident when Chinese migrants who trade fast fashion commodities to African migrants describe their everyday transactions with these transnational traders by using couched terms, such as cheap (*pianyi*), unprofitable, and low value along racialized hierarchies of human quality (*suzhi*). In this case, quality, whether it is used to describe people or commodities, is measured through determinations of high or low. In this way, Chinese migrant bosses confront their own precariousness through their market exchanges with their African clients. They describe consumer markets in Africa as offering the lowest margins of return. Yet, rather than confronting their structural vulnerabilities via their shared statuses as migrants, racism (namely Africans versus Chinese and vice versa, exacerbated by market fluctuation and competition) forces domestic and transnational migrants to compete and to negotiate for themselves the possibilities and risks of bosshood.

THE GEOGRAPHY OF GLOBAL FASHION THROUGH THE KOREAN DIASPORA IN GUANGZHOU

On the other side of the main Guangzhou railway station, the Sanyuanli district serves as a site of abode for many Nigerian and Korean migrants in Guangzhou. Much like Xiaobei, Sanyuanli is spatially marked by several apartment high-rises as well as by several central commercial buildings that serve as a multistoried wholesale markets for African and Euro-American branded fashions for adults and children. There, thousands of indoor stalls primarily owned and operated by South Korean and Chinese entrepreneurs serve clients from Russia, West Africa, and Singapore. One of these wholesale markets is Huimei, which, at the time of my ethnographic research, was one of the primary wholesale hubs for contemporary K-pop fashion in Guangzhou. This market is locally and internationally celebrated as the *hanban* (Korean) market, a counterpart to Seoul's internationally famous Dongdaemun district; Huimei features boutiques and wholesale stalls owned and operated by entrepreneurs from South Korea who have exported their fashion taste and expertise to Guangzhou. In fact, an advertisement for the market touts its global orientation by displaying its links to the transnational Korean diaspora: "After years of ceaseless hard work, Huimei Clothing Center has formed its distinctive characteristic that mainly engages in selling Korea-style clothes. Lots of people from Korea have flocked to Huimei and opened their own stores there." The advertisement thus paints a cultural representation of *hanban*, or "Koreanness," in Guangzhou that draws squarely upon global fashion and entrepreneurship.

Certainly, China's intensified economic collaboration with South Korea since the end of the Cold War has helped to develop fashion commodity chains in Guangzhou, which form critical transnational links across the globe via the South Korean diaspora. The international successes of the Korean American–owned retail chain Forever 21, which traces its supply links to Guangzhou, exemplify the prominence of these transnational business practices among other diasporic participants (Moon 2014, 2016, 2020; S. H. Lee et al. 2019).

Since the explosion of K-pop, or Korean pop culture, throughout East Asia and the world in the arenas of television, music, and film, many South Korean entrepreneurs in Guangzhou stage their economic successes as one of the world's Asian Tigers, asserting their ethnic and national identifications as the purveyors of *hanban* fashion upon a global platform (Moon 2020; Park 2021; Kwon 2023). Indeed, the emergence of Korean fashion in China intertwines with the history of state-sponsored capitalism in South Korea during the 1960s and 1970s. As Jaesok Kim (2013) explains, rising labor protests and increasing labor costs in South Korea have forced garment manufacturers to move their production facilities abroad, where manufacturing costs are relatively lower. These foreign direct investments were facilitated by state-partnerships that were negotiated through foreign trade councils and chambers of commerce.

In recent decades, many migrants from South Korea have become rightful entrepreneurs by establishing wholesale outlets for export fashion in cities across China. While some operate their own factories nearby, many South Korean entrepreneurs in Guangzhou collaborate closely with Chinese manufacturers by operating as contracted agents and as wholesalers. Many of these migrants work as expatriate employees of multinational fashion corporations in South Korea, while juggling their own business endeavors under their own labels. Lured by Guangdong's pool of low-wage migrant labor and relatively developed infrastructure, South Korean entrepreneurs work and reside in Guangzhou to take advantage of the city's proximity to one of the world's most expansive manufacturing hubs. Indeed, Guangzhou's infrastructural reach to various production hubs around the Pearl River Delta region enables these globe-trotters to emulate the business model of fast fashion, or *speed to market*, in Seoul, which is famously characterized by fast production responses to consumers' fickle demands (Park 2021). Through their entrepreneurial self-enterprise, migrant entrepreneurs capitalize on their diasporic ties by linking Guangzhou to other manufacturing and wholesale hubs in Latin America and Southeast Asia.

While members of the Korean diaspora contribute to Guangzhou's ethnic diversity by opening Korean restaurants, fashion boutiques, and wholesale outlets, their gathering spaces are fractured and dispersed. Like the West African migrant communities, they often attach their religious faith to their business enterprises. For example, members of several churches in Guangzhou serve South Korean religious communities that supply fashion commodities to consumers around the world (Moon 2014). One Christian community not far from the Zhaocun garment district, for example, includes South Korean designers and entrepreneurs who produce T-shirts in Guatemala; denim in Mexico; and knits in Argentina and Brazil. Yet unlike the African migrants in Guangzhou, the South Korean migrant population is not concentrated within a single, geographically prominent enclave. Most longtime residents speak Putonghua and reside in middle-class neighborhoods scattered across the metropolis. Young adults from South Korea live on university campuses and attend classes, juggling Chinese language classes with their small-scale business ventures in fashion.

In Huimei and Xi Fang Hang wholesale markets, which are predominantly owned and operated by entrepreneurs from South Korea (at the time of my research), migrant business owners mark their ownership of the coveted market spaces paradoxically through their physical absence. Many of Guangzhou's Korean or Korean Chinese (*Chaoxianzu*) designers, wholesalers, and boutique owners travel into and out of China and South Korea in order to source raw materials, including silks, leather, and other accessories. Others buy samples from the United States or countries in Europe before returning to China to organize their mass manufacture. Most of these bosses or company employees of South Korean fashion brands hire Korean Chinese translators as well as Chinese storekeepers, sales personnel, and brokers to mediate the cross-ethnic and linguistic gaps that exist between them and their China-based manufacturers and consumers.

In the years following the initial popularity of *hanban* or K-pop fashions in China, however, many South Korean migrant bosses encountered rising Han Chinese ethno-nationalism. While the cross-cultural performances and articulation of nationalistic and racialized identifications make fast fashion possible, these very same identifications leave many migrant bosses on the verge of expulsion from the supply chains. This countermovement eventually expelled South Koreans from the supply chains in Guangzhou. I address this topic in more detail in chapter 5. In 2017, the Korean-based retail giant, Lotte, signed a deal providing land for the American-based

Terminal High-Altitude Area Defense System (THAAD), sparking boycotts of Korean-owned businesses across China. This ethno-nationalist, consumerist movement led many Korean-owned business to close and forced many migrants out of the fast fashion supply chains across China, including in Guangzhou. Many South Korean bosses encountered difficulties selling their inventory and leasing commercial spaces for their businesses, even in Korean-dominated markets such as Huimei and Sanyuanli. These bosses eventually moved their businesses to countries in Southeast Asia, including Cambodia and Vietnam.

Although migrants' efforts in the ongoing conversion of labor to capital through the capitalization of the global K-pop wave led many South Korean bosses to stake their financial claims upon the fast fashion industry in Guangzhou, it was also their association with Koreanness that eventually expelled them from these supply chains. Their efforts in globalizing Korean pop fashion styles and distinction were ultimately met by ethno-nationalistic sentiments among consumers in China. To be sure, South Korean migrants' attempts to elevate and to globalize a certain stylistic flair based on ethnicity and culture failed to overcome nationalistic competition and resistance in China. Thus, the story of South Korean fast fashion in China shows how capitalist accumulation compels migrants to draw upon an intersection of performances based on nationality and ethnicity across the supply chain. Once migrants enter the world of capital, however, it is the very same performances that can undo their entrepreneurial aspirations, forcing them out of the supply chains. In the following chapters, this book elaborates on these push-pull dynamics by highlighting the ways in which cross-cultural encounters in the worlds of fast fashion destabilize subjectivities and social positionings which, in many cases, are already unstable and contingent.

EXPULSIONS FROM THE SUPPLY CHAINS

Accumulative dynamics reveal how the conditions that facilitate transnational supply chains paradoxically also set the stage for their eventual decoupling. Recent scholarship has shown that supply chains are made possible by unstable contractual relationships and contingent arrangements.[13] A growing number of scholars in the anthropological literature on precarious labor have noted the ways in which the "freedom" and mobility that migrant laborers are said to have experienced in recent decades (Deleuze

1990; Narotzky and Smith 2006; X. Zhang 2008; Y. Zhan 2022). Workers claim to feel free when they work flexible hours and move from one site to the next. Yet, they unintentionally contribute to the overall functioning and reproduction of the supply chain capitalism that ultimately excludes them.

The chapters that follow complicate this perspective by showing how the trajectories of migrant bosshood, upon which transnational subcontracting practices critically rely, are inherently risky and volatile. As migrant bosses adapt their labor power to the dictates of capital accumulation, they confront other intersecting hierarchies that disrupt the personifications of gender, nationality, ethnicity, and kinship that drew them into the supply chains in the first place. The crossing between labor and capital leads migrant bosses to confront ethnic and national divides, racialized and gendered separations, and conflictual rural-urban relations. On the one hand, these transnational and transregional divides embed global supply chains within China's postsocialist transformation. On the other hand, the intersection of these subjective and spatial divides destabilizes the gendered, ethnic, and kin-based hierarchies upon which labor mobilization across the supply chains depends.

As we have seen in the introduction to this book, Xiao Ye's rise and fall as a migrant compels her and her family to join the workforce as aspirational entrepreneurs in one of China's low-cost workshops of the world. Yet, once she elevates her status as boss, it is also her status as a rural migrant in the city of Guangzhou that excludes her from attaining the necessary state protections to become a legitimate entrepreneur. Similarly, South Korean and West African migrants became targets of various nationalist consumerist and eviction campaigns, forcing them to depart from the supply chains and eventually to depart from China altogether. As such, the rise of migrant bosshood demonstrates how the linking of supply chains through the mobilization of culture also lays the groundwork for their eventual fracture.

2　Stalled Mobility

Clustered within the city landscape, dense and low-lying factories, warehouses, and apartment buildings line the southeastern corner of Guangzhou. Here, several urban villages compose the city's long-standing garment district. When I walked through the Zhaocun urban village for the first time, a frenzy of commercial activity besieged me. A labyrinth of concrete buildings and twisted alleyways came into view as I passed through the front gate of the village. The elaborate gate, decorated with yellow and green stained ceramic tiles, marked the boundary between the village jungle and the rest of the urban terrain. I snaked through a long queue of vans delivering goods and people into and out of the factories. Thick clouds of pollution, combined with the blaring cacophony of ear-piercing honks from vehicles and the high-pitched chatter from crowds of pedestrians, left me feeling dizzy and disoriented.

Relieved to have escaped the bustle of fast-moving motorbikes, vans, and pedestrians, I wandered into a quiet alleyway with only the faint buzzing of sewing machines echoing from far away. A flicker of light danced against the shroud of evening darkness. The bright glow behind an iron gate led me into a musty garage that had been converted into a *jiagongchang* household workshop, an informal factory owned by Mr. and Mrs. Wong. Along these packed alleyways, thousands of migrant laborers from China's lower-tier cities and countryside live and work out of more than two hundred of these *jiagongchang* household workshops (or quite literally, the "site[s] of added labor"), where workers serve the transnational supply chains for fast fashion.

In contrast to large-scale factories that centralize garment mass manufacturing processes under a single roof, the arrangement of life and work in these assembly workshops is makeshift, fragmented, and family based. Situated in informal kitchens, dilapidated garages, and abandoned ancestral halls, the organization of mass production in these assembly workshops is specialized, so that temporary workers complete only one task in a longer chain of coordination, assembly, and manufacture.

I found Mrs. Wong alone in front of a large industrial worktable, gathering strips of pink ribbon into neat, orderly bundles. When I introduced myself to her as a Chinese American researcher interested in the garment industry in Guangzhou, she was as curious about me as I was about her. We were delighted that we could both speak Cantonese, even though we were both outsiders in a migrant neighborhood where residents primarily spoke Putonghua, which was the language of the state and of nonlocal people. We realized that our shared knowledge of Cantonese made us both partially local and partial outsiders to Guangzhou, even though we came from widely divergent backgrounds. Our interests in each other's life histories, bridged by our shared ability in Cantonese, enabled us to cultivate a deep friendship that allowed me to better understand the intricacies and nuances of her world.

The couple's journey into migrant entrepreneurship in Guangzhou's urban villages began when they met ten years ago as wage workers in a Hong Kong–owned garment factory in the nearby city of Dongguan. Both Mr. and Mrs. Wong traced their native places to the neighboring province of Guangxi, near the township of Guigang, where their parents resided and helped raise their two teenage sons. Mr. Wong was one of the senior managers who worked alongside the company head, and Mrs. Wong worked as a younger supervisor along the assembly line. After the couple married, Mr. and Mrs. Wong used their knowledge of garment export and manufacturing and invested a modest amount of their savings in a number of small business ventures. They experimented in several wholesale ventures, including the selling of plastic flowers, potpourri, ribbons, and toys. Over time, however, the couple realized that the cost of living in Shenzhen quickly outpaced the income they were able to scrape together every month. Luckily, Mr. Wong had learned that his older brother's garment factory in Guangzhou became profitable within a year of its opening. After spending a few months assisting in the brother's factory, the couple then decided to venture out on their own, with only a few months' salary in hand. They quickly rented a workspace directly behind a fabric wholesale market and rented second-hand sewing machines, an industrial iron, and a cutting table.

Like many of the migrant laborers whom I met in the *jiagongchang*, Mr. and Mrs. Wong openly express their preference for living in the urban villages, even though the *hukou* policy excludes them from property ownership as well as from critical state benefits including housing, employment, and healthcare in the cities. In contrast to the labor conditions within larger dormitory factories, migrants working in the urban villages could live and work with their families and loved ones and could enter or leave a job, mostly at will. By becoming the "bosses" of their own time and labor, migrants feel as though they can dictate the terms of their own exploitation. Their kin-based support allows them to juggle multiple jobs that hover between formal and informal employment, as well as self-enterprise and waged employment. Many workers, particularly young mothers and the elderly prefer to take up temporary work in the *jiagongchang* because the affordability of the urban villages enables them to live with their families, while they simultaneously provide financial support to other relatives in their home villages. Unlike the unmarried female migrants in China's large, centralized factories (Pun 2005; Pun and Smith 2007; Pun and Chan 2012), young parents in the urban villages are not confined and isolated in the factory dorms. They can return home to see their children after work, while grandparents can look after their grandchildren during the day and take up short-term work in the afternoons. Meanwhile, younger migrants, particularly male workers (married and unmarried), celebrate their mobility as so-called bosses of their labor by describing their work as free (*you zi you*), as they move in and out of their homes and neighboring factories.

Though Mr. and Mrs. Wong refer to themselves as "bosses," or *laoban*, I often see them work alongside their hired workers at least ten to twelve hours a day. Clients frequently request a single order and abscond without paying the Wongs for their labor, leaving the couple in debt. Workers sometimes storm off the factory floor in the middle of a production order when they disagree with the terms of their temporary employment. Such periods of sustained intensity are often followed by long intervals of idling or unemployment. The intensity of the couple's factory work, often punctuated by sudden lulls in production rhythms, leave the Wongs uncertain about the financial prospects for their small-scale business and their family life in Guangzhou.

As we will see in this chapter, the Wongs' life history illustrates the condition of what I call stalled mobility among rural migrant workers who are attempting to leverage their knowledge and skills of factory labor to claim a place for themselves as rightful members in the world of bosshood in Guangzhou. They do so in the hope of accumulating wealth and property in their home village, while they scale their labor capacities on the global supply chains for fast fashion. Stalled mobility, as I argue, emerges specifically from the conditions of self-enterprising labor that is characteristic of mass manufacture within Guangzhou's *jiagongchang* household factories. It refers to the condition in which migrants paradoxically declare their factory work as "free," despite the fact they struggle through long work-hours every day in order keep up with the rapid pace of fast fashion production, while also jumping from one low-wage factory job to another. It encapsulates, as I argue, the *mobility of labor* that is involved in making transnational subcontracting work, yet it prevents migrant workers from achieving upward mobility and accumulation of personal wealth.

Over time, migrants realize that the freedom of physical and social mobility they experience through their roles as self-enterprising contract workers and as small-scale bosses comes with a sense of stalling or deferment from achieving their ultimate desires for financial autonomy. Stalled mobility is a form of migratory entrapment specific to the structural limits and possibilities of migrant entrepreneurship and transnational subcontracting. Akin to what anthropologist Yang Zhan (2022) calls migratory "venturing," stalled mobility results from a precarious, just-in-time form of short-term accumulation made possible by being in the right place, at the right time. Eventually, however, the structural dynamics of transnational subcontracting prevent migrants like the Wongs from accumulating the necessary wealth to achieve financial security, thrusting them into an ambivalent bosshood devoid of meaningful autonomy despite their investments in money, time, and emotional labor.

Anthropological studies on labor and global supply chains have addressed the problems of universalizing freedom/unfreedom as an all-encompassing concept or analytic. Scholars have argued that this dichotomy falls short in capturing the full spectrum of experiences among vulnerable populations who participate in risky self-enterprise without deeply understanding the ethnographic contexts in which they are performed and articulated (Tsing 2009, 2015; Millar 2018). While freedom as a universal ideal and aspiration draws upon the notion of American-branded capitalism as defined by individual rational choice (dictated by laissez-faire markets) and movement/mobility on the one hand, and unfreedom with communal obligation/coercion and immobility, on the other, divergent experiences of labor across the supply chains lead participants to associate freedom with different values and different meanings.

To be sure, supply chains operate squarely through diverse performances and experiences of freedom since managerial discipline in the post-Fordist era has been redirected toward inventory across the supply chains rather than toward workers, as in the Fordist period (Tsing 2015: 25). In other words, entrepreneurship and subcontracting via participation in global supply chains are meant to feel "free." The promise of entrepreneurship in contemporary supply chain capitalism, as scholars point out, draws upon diverse meanings and performances of freedom (which include capitalist and noncapitalist performances) while simultaneously obscuring the risks and limitations of entrepreneurship, that is, the unfreedoms of market self-enterprise. This chapter finds inspiration from these ethnographies by moving beyond the universalizing freedom/unfreedom and mobility/immobility dichotomies by introducing the notion of stalled mobility, which highlights the tension between what migrants describe as freedom and unfreedom. In the ethnographic vignettes I narrate below, I emphasize that it is *the promise of* and *the aspiration for* financial freedom that enables migrants to temporarily experience freedom from the wage labor of the large-scale Fordist factories. In other words, it is the opportunity for accumulation and social mobility *beyond* what is promised by wage labor that migrants experience as "freedom."

At the same time, I push the scholarly discussions on entrepreneurial mobility and immobility as well as on freedom/unfreedom further by demonstrating how migrants experience these tensions as ongoing and sometimes conflicting dynamics between wage labor and nonwage labor. Migrants in Guangzhou forge practices of precarious accumulation through their movements into and out of industrial wage work and entrepreneurship, activities that are often associated with unfreedom and freedom, respectively. As a hallmark of lean production, the decentralized mode of commodity mass manufacture mobilizes migrant laborers when the market demands it, yet it expels the workers from its accounting systems when consumer demands dwindle. Unwilling to accept their losses and to forfeit their dreams, on the one hand, while determined to hold onto the investments in time, labor, and emotional energy they put into their entrepreneurial endeavors, on the other, migrants return to their experiments in self-enterprise, hopeful trying their luck again. Migrants' circular transitions from wage work to entrepreneurship and back again, as I argue, are key to the just-in-time delivery of finished products in the *jiagongchang* before commodities are transported across the supply chains to other regions of the world.

In China's urban villages, migrants who experience stalled mobility find that the ambiguous effects of this condition of migratory entrapment are difficult to undo. Though migrants often celebrate their ability to leave their temporary jobs in the factories at their discretion, their only options are to take on other exploitative, low-wage jobs or high-risk entrepreneurial ventures that might potentially leave them in debt or bankruptcy. In their view, however, wage labor in the larger factories, much like agricultural work in the countryside, is a subjective dead end, where there are no hopes or dreams for the future. Bosshood, by contrast, offers Chinese rural migrants a sense of direction as they attempt to accumulate capital. Because of their legal statuses as migrants based on the *hukou* household system of population control, migrants desire practices of accumulation that could potentially provide economic security and freedom back in their native places for their children and future generations of kin. They no longer desire agriculture jobs or low-paying wage labor, which for them is a form of accumulation that offers only temporal and financial cul-de-sacs. In this sense, their experiences as rural migrants in Guangzhou are key to understanding their desires for accumulation: one that presents a pathway, direction, and possibility of fulfillment and financial freedom.

Migrants' efforts to become socially mobile are made within the structural dynamics of transnational subcontracting in Guangzhou, in which the boundary between labor and capital is constantly blurred. Even those migrant bosses who can financially survive market fluctuations must labor alongside their temporary workers without clear boundaries of where authority and protection from exploitation reside. In the *jiagongchang*, for example, the techniques of discipline and rationalization combine with the contingent dynamics of encounter such that migrant factory bosses must constantly figure out what aspects of their makeshift assembly line they can and cannot control.

As such, migrant bosses are caught within the double bind of evading exploitation by clients and competitors while learning the necessity of exploiting *other* migrant laborers across the supply chain. Teetering on the edges of boss/worker and employer/employee, migrants may be mobile yet feel that they are not going anywhere in life. Their experiences instruct us that displacement is more than a result of either mobility or immobility. Migrant bosses feel that their aspirations are put on hold, are not aligned with their current circumstances and social positioning. Their contradictory experiences show that precarity is produced out of aspirational entrepreneurialism through a combination of intersecting and contingent socioeconomic relations.

GUANGZHOU'S HOUSEHOLD FACTORIES: THE SITES OF "ADDED LABOR"

The *jiagongchang* household factory in Guangzhou's urban villages is central in shaping migrants' experiences of stalled mobility, since it serves as a key node through which rural-urban migratory chains critically intersect with transnational supply chains. The *jiagongchang* serves as the primary link through which migrant laborers, who are normally excluded from legal claims to land in the cities, scale their kin-based, industrial production to the transnational supply chains of fast fashion. *Jiagongchang* are important sites of ethnographic analysis, since they bring together multiple social worlds that are constituted by overlapping spatiotemporal scales of the rural and the urban, the household and the factory, and the village and the "global."

Using secondhand machines and handheld tools, *jiagongchang* feature craft-based processes of industrial mass manufacture (N. Chu 2016). Each node of the clothing production process, such as dying fabric, cutting fabric, and adding embellishments, takes place within a separate *jiagongchang*. Each *jiagongchang* varies in size, organization, and composition of workers; but these small, subcontracted factories must operate alongside and synchronize with the rhythms of the bigger production sites. Some *jiagongchang* handle production orders subcontracted by larger factories, while others engage directly with foreign clients for export manufacture. This mode of household-based mass manufacture attempts to scale the low-tech capabilities of *jiagongchang* on the performance-driven and advanced technologies of fast fashion supply chains. Although these small-scale assembly workshops (*jiagongchang*) may be commonly described as cut and sew factories, the literal translation of *jiagong*—added (or supplementary) labor—better captures this historically specific and place-based form of garment mass manufacture.[1]

The notion of *jiagong* emphasizes the extent to which the human labor of cutting and sewing has been displaced and subsequently devalued in the contemporary era of just-in-time flexible production. Across the transnational supply chains, the Fordist figure of the waged worker has given way to non-living wages, intermittent work, and shifting spaces of mass production; features that once signaled the rise of Fordism have been relegated to the realm of informal labor in today's global economy. Such organizational segmentation of labor and garment production results in a division of profits rendering the financial gains from factory ownership increasingly low.

Many *jiagongchang* are owned and operated by migrants who served as the first generation of wage workers employed in larger export factories or on construction sites in Shenzhen, Dongguan, and Guangzhou. *Jiagongchang* rely primarily on temporary piecework among migrants who labor in one factory for no longer than eight to ten months at a time. These migrants consist primarily of those not comprised by the category of the *dagongmei*, including those who are not readily employable in the larger, more centralized garment factories. The *dagongmei* is a class of unmarried and female migrant workers, whose gendered and youthful bodies lend themselves easily exploitable in the large Fordist factories in the Pearl River Delta region (Pun 2005). They have constituted the largest demographic of factory workers in China since the introduction of market reforms.

By contrast, migrant laborers in Guangzhou's *jiagongchang* include older married women, elderly couples, younger female migrants (under sixteen years of age), and teenagers who wish to take up short-term piecework between waged employment in the service sector. They, like countless other migrant laborers in the region, perceive factory work either as a temporary stepping stone to employment in the service industry or as a dead end, a mere means of fulfilling their financial obligations. Younger migrant workers tend to favor more lucrative and favorable jobs in the service or business sectors. Service work and entrepreneurship are believed to offer opportunities for higher economic returns and greater freedom to dictate the terms of one's own labor.

Economist Michael J. Piore and sociologist Charles F. Sabel (1986) have described the rise of these small-scale, craft-based workshops as the "second industrial divide," whereby regional economies, including those across the Pacific Rim, mobilize mass manufacture techniques based on low-volume production, simple and nonspecialist technologies, and flexible labor. Flexible specialization, they argue, has replaced Fordist types of large-scale factories organized along vertically integrated lines (Piore and Sabel 1986; Amin 1994).[2] The main principles of just-in-time or flexible mass manufacture draw upon industrial approaches based on the ongoing movement or flow of various segments of the production process.

The uneven rhythms characteristic of industrial mobility echo those that were celebrated by industrial engineers in the early 1970s and 1980s. At that time, industrial engineers touted the cost-cutting and highly efficient potential of the lean, or kanban, approach to mass production—otherwise known as the Toyota Production System—as a profit-driven response to crises in capitalist accumulation (Shingō 1989). The minute synchronization of these moving parts is critical to shaving off excessive resources, labor, and time to complete the production process. To achieve this, the workers across the assembly line are organized so as to mimic the dynamic processes of just-in-time mass manufacture. The interface between the worker and the machines is seen as a vibrant, ever-changing series of interactions such that

workers are compelled to constantly reassess and reperfect the total operation of mass manufacture in a constant feedback loop.

Since the publication of Piore and Sabel's study in the early 1980s, some
scholars have questioned the extent to which the rise of flexible specialization based on craft-based production signals a radical and unique break
from Fordist forms of mass production, particularly as it relates to the
reorganization of labor and managerial control. More specifically, feminist
scholars have critiqued Piore and Sabel's comparisons between craft-based
workshops in postwar Italy and contemporary workshops along the Pacific
Rim by illustrating the gendered, generational, and class-based inequalities that color workers' relations of labor within these household factory
spaces (Hsiung 1994; Yanagisako 2002; Elyachar 2005; Narotzky and Smith
2006).[3] These anthropologists and industrial sociologists have analyzed
how craft-based practices of mass manufacture have long relied on enduring social relationships. They have questioned the ways in which the so-
called return to craft-based production has in practice successfully yielded
the emancipatory potential for laborers through processes of reskilling and
collaborative decision-making.[4]

One significant contribution within this set of feminist literature on
factory labor and industrial politics is the emphasis that mass production
and capitalist accumulation critically rely on contingencies, specifically
the instabilities of everyday life and labor of people who make transnational capitalist relations possible. Likewise, in the world of just-in-time
fast fashion production in Guangzhou, flexible mass production processes
are difficult to predict and assess. Yet, my analyses of the *jiagongchang* in
Guangzhou also departs from this set of literature by underscoring the
ways in which the disciplinary effects of mass production and assembly in
the *jiagongchang* are reconstructed *precisely through the tension between fixity
and mobility* of migrant labor in the assembly factories.[5] In other words,
the everyday operation of the fast fashion supply chains in Guangzhou relies on the ongoing recalibration and reassessment of the production processes. The physical processes of workers cutting and sewing fabric pieces
into finished garments entail both the meticulous calculation of time and
the disciplining of workers such that they remain fixed on the shop floor.
At first glance, these processes mimic Frederick Taylor's (1997) principle
of Scientific Management, whereby the paces of garment assembly must
be carefully synchronized with the minutiae of workers' bodily rhythms to
achieve the upmost demonstration of human calculation and mechanis-
tic control. After all, as Michael Hardt and Antonio Negri (2000) observe,

"Control of laboring activity can potentially be individualized and continuous in the virtual panopticon of network production (297)."[6]

Yet, this approach to management and control of the assembly line is critically accompanied by the flexible contingencies of post-Fordist, just-in-time labor. Worker absences, mechanical disruptions, missed deliveries, and rushed orders characterize the daily rhythms of the garments factories in Guangzhou. Indeed, the tension between contingency and control, as I emphasize, becomes a crucial aspect of post-Fordist lean manufacturing, one that has been intentionally designed to require the worker-manager to continuously regulate, calculate, and assess ongoing flows. Initial blueprints of this kanban approach have laid the imaginative groundwork for recreating and automating the Fordist assembly line.[7] By merging the principles of industrial manufacture into the realm of management, control over production processes emerges precisely via the changes and contingencies that arise unexpectedly throughout the manufacturing process.

The day-to-day work of managing the tensions between mobility and fixity as well as between contingency and control fall upon the migrant boss. These bosses must oversee the uneven rhythms of workers, objects, and money that float into and out of the *jiagongchang*. Without the security of corporate, governmental, or labor union organizations, migrants in the *jiagongchang* experience the intensification of the following two extreme approaches to mass production that operate synchronously, albeit in paradoxical ways: (1) the assertion of worker discipline by migrant bosses like the Wongs upon their temporary workers along the Fordist assembly line to complete or fulfill a production order, and (2) the structural mobility and responsiveness of just-in-time production. These two dimensions lie in direct contradiction to another, yet they also work together precisely through the movements of workers' labor and migration patterns. Specifically, the imperative to spatially reconfigure or "fix" production processes so as to continuously accumulate wealth in these workshops requires the extraction of labor power and raw materials via the contradictory rhythms of fixity and mobility (Marx 1885; Jessop 2004; Harvey 2001; Arrighi 2007). The everyday work of factory bosses, like the Wongs, shows the kinds of invisible labor, in conjunction with their work in garment assembly, that are required to resolve these contradictions. Straddling the worlds of factory labor and worker management, migrant bosses attempt to resolve the paradoxes that define these distinct realms, and they do so in the sticky encounters with both workers and other bosses along the supply chain.

Anthropologists have shed light on the social relationships and types of personhood that drive various forces of production and profit-making activities in an age of flexible production (Hsiung 1996; Yanagisako 2002; Elyachar 2005; Narotzky and Smith 2006). While these studies have underscored unequal relations of power in the everyday operation of industrial workshops, they have also tended to downplay how the spatial and temporal aspects of commodity mass production in home-based factories blur the categorical boundaries between worker and entrepreneur in an era of transnational subcontracting. Indeed, the spatiotemporal tensions that characterize the *jiagongchang* determine the dynamics of encounter between the workers and bosses as well as between factory owners and clients on the shop floor. Though the spatial fluidity of the home-based factory allows the speedy movement of people, commodities, and capital to float into and out of the factory space, the temporal demands of the production process require the need for migrant factory owners to discipline their hired workers in spite of the countless flows of people, money, and raw materials that characterize the factory floor. Bosses like the Wongs must confront these paradoxical dynamics while evading exploitation by their clients and controlling the rhythms of the assembly line.

Such tensions and contradictions are played out in the daily operations of the Wongs' *jiagongchang*. The Wongs' factory is located along a narrow alleyway lined with countless eateries and storefronts that lead to one of the back entrances of the towering Zhaocun fabric market. Sandwiched between a mobile phone store and a fabric warehouse, the fifty-square-foot factory sits semi-exposed to the outside world via a large, drawn metal gate. A red signpost hanging beside the front gate advertises the services that the factory offers, including pattern making, design, and mass production. The Wongs' two-level factory houses three parallel rows of twelve sewing machines: six are lined against the left wall and six are stationed along two center rows that face each other. Inside the combined kitchen and toilet space, a metal partition divides the cooking area from the bathroom. This partitioned room in the back corner serves as the only walled-off space in the factory.

Regulating the flows of people, aromas, and objects that drift through the factory gates that open to the urban village is difficult. On especially busy days, it is not unusual for a few pedestrians to stop dead in their tracks with hands wrapped behind their backs as they observe the lines of sewers, industriously working at their stations, taking note of the intricate garment production process. Young mothers in particular often approach the front worktable, eagerly caressing and admiring the colorful piles of finished clothing stacked around the front gate. In some instances, I found myself feeling rather uneasy when an eager onlooker unexpectedly snatched a piece of garment from the worktable to better admire the visual and tactile qualities of the finished piece. "Not to worry," Mrs. Wong assured me. She then further encouraged the admirer by asking, "Aren't the colors pretty? No, sorry. We don't sell these clothes piece by piece. We make them for our client." At that moment, I realized that she uses the products of her employee's labor as a means of promoting the factory's work in the hope of attracting additional walk-in clients.

In fact, the metal gates that stage the Wongs' factory space to the outside world have successfully attracted several longtime clients, reliable workers, and even foreign researchers like me. At the same time, the factory's exposure to passing thieves has resulted in stolen bikes and clothes. In addition, the factory's display to the outside world has also enabled strangers, including the neighborhood police and other officials, to take stock of the owners' financial success when business was good. Over the course of my field research, I witnessed inquisitive surveyors and money collectors dressed in various uniforms demanding payment of a variety of sanitation and fire safety fees. In one instance, a middle-aged female officer with whom the factory boss was not familiar approached the front worktable while surveying the piles of brightly colored girls' dresses filling the interior workspace. While the officer examined the clothes, she asked, "Wouldn't they make lovely gifts?" Suspiciously, Mrs. Wong boldly but calmly replied, "No, that idea has never crossed my mind. I've never heard of such a thing!" Her reply subsequently prompted the official to quietly leave the premises.

During the five years I spent with the Wongs, the industrial factory gates also served as a symbolic reminder of the Wongs' fluid way of life and their relatively unguarded orientation to the wider world as newly emerging migrant business owners in the garment district. As newly established business owners of a modest factory in Guangzhou, the Wongs lacked an existing network of personal contacts in the city, so they had to rely on walk-in clients and temporary workers they met on the streets of the urban village. As the Wongs slowly secured their business contacts, I saw them struggle with several unpredictably difficult workers who stormed off the factory floor in the middle of a production order. At the same time, they had to serve demanding clients and ward off money-grubbing officials. To be sure, the absence of physical partitions separating the exterior world from the interior factory defined the fluidity and precariousness of the working and living conditions among many producers of Guangzhou's fast fashion industry. On the one hand, the Wongs critically depended on clients and migrant workers who walked in from the street. On the other hand, they lacked a stable and reliable network of clients and workers, which left them vulnerable to theft, exhortation, and worker discontent.

The fluidity and openness that characterized the Wongs' workspace facilitated my own initial encounter with the couple. Since the evening when I met the Wongs for the first time, I had freely visited their factory three to four times a week. Whenever I dropped by, I felt welcomed into their intimate space. During my visits, I assisted them in packaging and in cutting loose threads off finished garments. Over the course of my 2.5 years of initial research, I had gained firsthand insights into the complexities of their work and family lives as migrants who struggled to become "bosses" of their own labor. I had spent numerous afternoons and evenings, eating and working alongside the Wongs and their hired laborers. My appearance as Chinese, combined with my privileged class position as an American researcher, led many migrant villagers and visitors to misrecognize me as a client of the Wongs, who frequently lent a hand or supervised a production order.

As the months passed, my presence became a regular fixture in the *jiagongchang*; the Wongs' factory felt like home to me, and I was no longer seen as a curious novelty. More importantly, my regular visits demonstrated a degree of investment and trust in my friendship with the migrant workers, which laid the foundation for my roles as a confidant and witness to the fragilities of their relationships and the complexities of their everyday experiences of factory work. My time spent in the factory enabled me to become acquainted with over three hundred piecework laborers and one hundred clients (from all parts of China and the world), who drifted into and out of the industrial workspace. I also observed five other *jiagongchang* in the area, though most of my time was spent in the Wongs' factory. Our conversations provided a mutual relief from the stress and monotony of cutting, sewing, and packaging.

Participant observation has allowed me to witness how, through their mutual encounters, actors along the fast fashion supply chain came to understand the contradictions of bosshood and the paradoxes of autonomy within the context of transnational subcontracting. Migrant laborers have learned to recognize and navigate the workings of inequality and power across wider relations of cross-cultural mass manufacture and exchange.

They have attempted to evade exploitation, as they confront the demands of the global market to extract labor and capital further down the commodity chain. The dynamics of inequality and power in a mutual encounter thus become critical lenses through which we can observe how market participants exploit, contest, and negotiate the disciplinary and exploitative effects of the supply chains.

Over the course of my research, I have learned that entrepreneurship and subcontracted labor are appealing to former industrial workers, because they enable migrants to call themselves the boss of their own labor. More importantly, it provides a platform upon which migrant bosses contract with bigger, more established bosses across the transnational supply chains, along with the economic opportunities and possibilities it promises to deliver. Some older migrants that I met in the urban village, for example, work mornings as janitors in the wholesale markets, and moonlight as scrap pickers in the afternoons and evenings. Other migrants who have opened small wholesale outlets in the area take up piecework in the *jiagongchang* for a few hours a day, or for days at a time, in order to generate some supplemental income to weather economic downturns. Many of these migrants frequently complain about how their bodies have been worn down from decades of hard work. Since their tired bodies can no longer withstand the backbreaking work of full-time wage work in the factories, temporary work at a *jiagongchang* provides an option of last resort.

Since wages are kept low and labor conditions remain unstable and uncertain in the *jiagongchang*, migrants view this line of work as a temporary stepping stone to more lucrative entrepreneurial endeavors. At the same time, the flexible rhythms of low-cost garment assembly typical of a *jiagongchang* critically rely on the uneven rhythms of workers' migratory pathways, allowing temporary laborers to float into and out of the shop floor and back again. When they are expelled from the ranks of bosshood, the migrant workers return to the factories where they earn a modest amount of savings and plot their next entrepreneurial ventures. The mushrooming of independent contractors operating these fragmented and small-scale sites of mass production has compelled migrants to move into and of wage work and self-employment and back again.

Ambiguous relations of power between factory workers and their bosses also emerge from these unstable conjunctures. In the highly fluid and precarious conditions of life and livelihood in the urban villages, migrants on the shop floor often find it difficult to discern who the "boss" is in a given situation. The Wongs' attempts to exercise control and discipline were often met by worker indifference, resistance, and outright protest. The ambiguities embedded within client/employer/employee relations offer limited spaces for negotiation and mobility. For migrants who emerged from the ranks of wage workers in the factories, asserting oneself as "boss" involves a spectrum of relationships and labor practices that leave them in conditions of ambivalence and frustration. Accumulation by exploitation, as they learn, is a relational and dynamic practice that involves the uncertain and inconsistent assertion of discipline and power.

Migrants' attempts to escape the oppressive conditions of factory labor, which they view as a dead end, combined with their risk-laden aspirations for entrepreneurial wealth and autonomy, lead them into ongoing situations of entrepreneurial deferment. The structural conditions of their migrant status, exacerbated by the disciplinary effects of transnational subcontracting, keep them from becoming physically and socially mobile. Last-minute deadlines, demanding clients, low profits, and market fluctuations bind the Wongs, who must work in the factory every day for over twelve hours a day. These structural dynamics produce forms of entrepreneurial subjecthood that remain fragmented and uneven.

In Guangzhou, the class-based roles of migrant boss and worker and of employer and employee become blurred as migrant laborers collectively declare their labor as "free," though their family and work lives remain uncertain and precarious. For migrants who have emerged in the *jiagongchang* from the ranks of wage workers, their experiences of stalled mobility involve a spectrum of relationships and labor practices that leave them in conditions of ambivalence and frustration. Over time, the demands and limitations of transnational subcontracting prevented the Wongs from accumulating the necessary wealth to achieve a level of financial security, thrusting them into an ambivalent condition of bosshood that was devoid of meaningful autonomy.

THE EVERYDAY RHYTHMS OF *JIAGONGCHANG*

Amid the ambivalent and precarious conditions of bosshood, migrant bosses and laborers must work together to coordinate the time-sensitive processes of fast fashion production while fulfilling the clients' requirements and responding quickly and flexibly to market fluctuations. Their work includes tagging garment labels, coordinating the necessary fabrics and accessories, attaching the tags to the finished garments, printing specific stock keeping unit (SKU) numbers, attaching embellishments or accessories, and packaging the finished goods. Most migrant bosses that I spoke with in the urban villages openly expressed their preference for collaborating with intermediary brokers who brought them international orders, since production turnovers are relatively slower, compared with domestic orders. Furthermore, forging connections with clients from abroad was frequently seen by migrant bosses as a source of cultural capital, since transnational connections lent a glimmer of possibility and relief from their conditions of socioeconomic exclusion in Guangzhou.

Clients typically arrange payments with the fabric or accessory wholesaler in advance of delivery. However, if for some reason clients fail to pay, then the *jiagongchang* owners, like the Wongs, have to bear the burden of paying for the raw materials out of their own pockets; this is a thorny situation that factory owners prefer to avoid. Alternatively, factory owners like the Wongs could return the materials delivered back to the sender, thereby delaying the entire production order. Or the owners, like the Wongs, could reprimand clients for their failures to pay or deliver the necessary fabrics or materials on time. In other instances, clients have purchased the wrong type of fabric for a particular style thereby also stalling the production process.

Usually, the Wongs' clients hastily coordinate all the necessary materials for production, and the Wongs assemble their work team based on the number of workers they need per order. The Wongs hire five to seven workers at one time and build their work teams based on existing contacts. Typically, after orders have been placed, the factory owners call upon their friends and family members for help. Since Mr. Wong's older brother operates a larger garment factory in the neighborhood, he often sends over workers from his factory when business there has tapered off. Another brother who works in the neighborhood as an ironer sometimes comes by with his wife to lend a hand. In the past, Mrs. Wong also invited her family friends from her home village in Guangxi to live and work with the couple for several months at a time. When new workers are needed, the Wongs will sometimes post advertisements on a small chalkboard that hangs by the front gate of their factory. At other times, Mrs. Wong will walk over by a pedestrian bridge in the neighborhood, where unemployed workers informally gather in the hope of securing temporary jobs.

Soon after the fabric has been delivered and the workers have been assembled, Mr. Wong and his son begin the arduous task of cutting the fabric (*lai bu*) on the second floor. Once the fabric arrives, Mr. Wong painstakingly lifts the long and heavy bolt of fabric and rests it upon his right shoulder. Because of the sheer weight of the fabric bolt, the entirety of his strained body sways in whatever direction the heavy object leans. He must grip the walls and the side handrails of the steep staircase with his left hand as he slowly ascends to the second floor. He then unrolls the fabric bolt on the large industrial table, while he and his son slice the ends with a mechanical saw that zips vertically from one end of the table to the other. As each piece is cut, Mr. Wong and his son stack the fabric pieces on top of one another on the table so that they form a mound that is several inches tall and about five feet wide.

After the fabric pieces have been cut and stacked, Mr. Wong then begins the highly skilled and meticulous process of arranging and cutting garment pieces according to specific cardboard patterns. This task of cutting the garment pieces requires the highest amount of skill and experience because arranging the pattern pieces by size and in such a way that utilizes the least amount of fabric by surface area is one of the most challenging tasks in garment manufacture. During this process, Mr. Wong must also consider the direction in which the fabric's threads fall (its warp and weft), as well as the ways in which fabric patterns are displayed after the garment pieces have been cut.

Once Mr. Wong cuts the separate garment pieces, they are then distributed to each worker according to the finished garment sizes for which they are responsible. Each sewer is usually assigned three or four batches of about 22 to 30 garments (ranging from 60 to 120 total garments per order), depending on the order. In general, five or six workers take about three to five days to complete an order of 1,000 garments. They are paid at a piece-rate of about 4–5 RMB a piece (approximately $0.50–$0.75 USD). Each worker completes just one or two steps in the wider garment assembly process, which follows a broader chain of mass manufacture. For example, workers who mass manufacture dresses that button up in the front must first assemble the two front flaps. The flaps are then brought back to the workers, who attach them to the back pieces before the top portion can be sewn together with the bottom skirt piece. Though some workers sew faster than others, all follow the same broader process of garment construction. Once their assigned batches of garments have been completed, they are paid in cash and are free to leave the factory.

Because the garment construction process follows particular chains (*lian*) of collective assembly, the delivery, preparation, and coordination of every single garment piece and accessory affect the entire garment production process. Often, once the workers complete one aspect of the garment manufacturing chain, they would cry out for Mr. or Mrs. Wong to retrieve the next portion of the garment identified by size and number. *"Laoban!"* (boss) or *"Laoban niang!"* (boss lady) they would cry out. "I need number 10, size 8." I would also frequently witness workers assisting each other in the retrieval of necessary garment pieces and in demonstrating certain methods of sewing and garment construction. When garment pieces or accessories failed to be prepared or delivered on time, workers would often express impatience, since the time during which they were left to wait could otherwise be spent earning wages in another factory nearby. During this time, they would leave the factory to run household errands or find short-term employment in another garment factory in the area.

Even when full-scale production in the factory proceeds according to schedule, the conditions of work are difficult to control. In a highly fluid environment where raw materials, commodities, clients, and migrant laborers float into and out of the factory throughout the day, Mr. and Mrs. Wong often find themselves simultaneously juggling the roles of boss and employee as well as the roles of wage worker and manager at unpredictable times. Frequently, Mr. Wong must join his employees off-site at a larger garment factory of a client in order to complete a production task or to redo a botched order. At the same time, Mrs. Wong spends most of her working day laboring alongside her employees on the factory floor in order to assist in completing the order. Most of the time, she assumes the role of a manager when walk-in clients enter the factory to discuss an order. As the so-called bosses of their time, labor, and means of production, Mr. and Mrs. Wong encounter limits to their personal autonomy as migrant entrepreneurs when they must determine their own class position while also managing class-based relations across the supply chain. This work is a necessary aspect of their efforts in coordinating the people, objects, and work rhythms both within and outside of their industrial workshop. Their everyday rhythms of labor demonstrate how the variable intensities of labor and managerial control across the supply chains for low-cost garments are key to keeping production costs low, sustaining low-volume output, and responding quickly to consumers' fickle demands.

Migrants' experiences of labor time thus critically illuminate how techniques of bodily control and subjective discipline have been rendered invisible within informal workshops but continue nonetheless to determine the unequal dynamics and forms of sociality that constitute transnational supply chains. Their engagements across different orders of industrial production entail changing between different roles and positions across the supply chain. To be sure, small-scale factory owners, as bosses of their labor and means of production, are no longer subject to constant surveillance and managerial control characteristic of Taylorism—however invisible the methods might be—yet the uneven temporal pulses and makeshift factory spaces that exemplify the post-Fordist just-in-time production of low-cost garments intensify their exploitative effects, while creating a surplus of available workers when the pace of market activity slackens (Postone 1993; Pun 2005).[8] After a production order is completed and the workers move out of the Wongs' *jiagongchang*, they continue to float in and out of the ranks of bosshood and wage labor. Migrant laborers experience a limited degree of mobility and the relative autonomy to pursue the life projects to which they aspire. Yet, the structural constraints of their rural and working-class identities in the urban villages leave them in conditions of displacement and precarity.

ENGENDERING PRECARITY

In light of the uncertain conditions involved in their line of work, migrants attempt to forge a sense of temporary protection from their conditions of precarity by bridging relations of care and sociality with their neighbors, coworkers, colleagues, and clients. Through these kin-based relations of care, small-scale migrant laborers and bosses try to mitigate the risks of bankruptcy and exploitation in their engagement with global supply chains by reconstructing the affective and spatiotemporal dimensions of family and work in the countryside, a realm of life and livelihood with which they are familiar. Within the *jiagongchang*, migrant workers perform the affective dimensions of a household, though these relations of social reproduction are often ephemeral and temporary, primarily serving the demands of industrial supply chains.[9]

In many cases, for example, migrant laborers demonstrate care for one another on the basis of kin-like relations. For instance, Mrs. Wong and her female employees often look after each other's children throughout the day while they labor at their respective sewing stations. Migrant bosses cook for themselves and for their employees in tight corners of the workshops that serve as kitchens and toilets. Jealousy and gossip frequently pervade through the alleyways of the urban villages, as migrant families compete over sought-after clients and as stories of domestic violence and abuse are shared among women. Those who return from larger garment factories nearby share stories about work conditions, market forecasts, and upcoming fashion trends. They also exchange crucial information about local crimes and accidents around the neighborhood, including cases of domestic violence, homicides, pedestrian accidents, and industrial fires. In one instance, Mrs. Wong and her employees assisted one woman who was emotionally struggling to leave a physically abusive husband. They offered her comfort and places to stay while she planned for her future.

Intergenerational migrant women, in particular, return more readily to the *jiagongchang* after their initial departure, seeking relief from debt or some form of protection from their precarious family lives. A forty-three-year-old woman, Mei Xue sought refuge at the Wong's factory after her husband beat her and threatened to kill her. The couple had a small business selling food sauces in her village, and the business unexpectedly went bankrupt. Her husband fell into depression and blamed her for their losses. Because of her undocumented status, she was reluctant to seek social services or to report the abuse to the police. After a few days of work in the factory, she disappeared, leaving us concerned about her welfare.

Similarly, a Chaozhou woman juggled her part-time work with her childcare responsibilities by bringing her three-year-old daughter to the Wongs' factory. She was looking for a temporary escape from her husband and father-in-law, whom she suspected was using drugs back in her home village. Reluctant to return home, she drifted from one factory in Guangzhou to another, bringing her young daughter with her wherever she went. Another woman who was in her late twenties, Jinglu, worked beside me for a few weeks at the packaging table. She needed to find some reprieve from her demanding parents, who incessantly pressured her to marry right away. Although she despised factory work, she felt that there was little else she could do. Eager to forge a life of her own, Jinglu strove to a find a way to break free from the constraints of marriage and factory work. After several weeks at the *jiagongchang*, Jinglu got into a bitter confrontation with Mrs. Wong about the quality of her packaging work. Jinglu left in a storm, and we never saw her again.

For many migrants who flow into and out of the factories, *jiagongchang* household workshops serve as provisional springboards for various types of class-based and geographic mobility. These cursory and unpredictable rhythms produce a feminized form of migratory sociality that draw upon the affective dimensions of family and "home," but they remain ambivalent, uncertain, and at times, even exploitative. Contrary to conventional ideas of household as spatial and affective realms of settlement, signaled by reproductive and accumulative practices, *jiagongchang* draw upon the affective dimensions of a household, along with the managerial discipline of an industrial factory, in order to serve as zones of transience and unsettlement. Migrant laborers nonetheless attempt to spatially anchor and temporarily link their labor capacities and other kin-based forms of social reproductive power to the transnational supply chains for fast fashion.

LEARNING TO "BOSS"

Despite the fluid rhythms of life and livelihood that define the *jiagongchang*, the Wongs must sell the products of their hired employees' labor to sustain their business. To accomplish this, the couple must keep their workers productive along the assembly line over a fixed period, while requiring them to fulfill all the detailed specifications of the production order. The workers, in turn, must endure the exploitative nature of their temporary work, including the long hours, monotonous labor, and low wages. The structural conditions dictated by this mode of flexible production ultimately make the Wongs' interests as factory owners necessarily contradict those of their workers, regardless of their shared experiences of work, their overlapping identities as migrant laborers, or their fictive kin relationships. In other words, the Wongs' and their workers' divergent roles within the production process are essentially in conflict with one another, ultimately leading to awkward exchanges, heated arguments, and sometimes even outright confrontations on the factory floor. These incommensurable conflicts of interests between the Wongs and their hired workers sometimes erupt, severing the fragile and tenuous bonds created over long periods of time through their shared experiences of factory work.

I came to realize the complexities of the boss-worker dynamic one afternoon. That day, Xiao Xue and her mother and unexpectedly dropped by the Wongs' workshop a day after the Chinese New Year holiday. At the time, Xiao Xue was a seventeen-year-old female migrant from Hunan who arrived in the Zhaocun garment district to take up wage labor. Her youthful exuberance had delighted Mrs. Wong. Since their initial meeting, they grew emotionally close to one another, and the women developed a fictive mother-daughter relationship. However, even though their intimate relations facilitated kindred acts of cooperation between the two, those well-intentioned feelings unintentionally worked to perpetuate the exploitative aspects of low-wage factory labor.

That afternoon, I climbed up to the second floor of the workshop to join the women in their joyful reunion. Xiao Xue and her mother greeted Mrs. Wong who was upstairs watching television. When she and Xiao Xue saw each other after a two-week absence, the two women acted like young girls catching up on juicy gossip that they had been eager to share. After a few rounds of joyous exchange, Mrs. Wong explained to Xiao Xue and her mother that her client from Malaysia intended to submit another order of children's clothing the next day. Since most of her workers had not yet returned from their native places for the New Year's, Mrs. Wong desperately needed Xiao Xue to start work right away. While Mrs. Wong explained her situation to Xiao Xue and her mother, the exuberance that was once written on the young girl's face immediately turned to dismay. With her eyes cast downward, she remained silent, almost refusing to acknowledge Mrs. Wong's request. Mrs. Wong then moved her body closer to Xiao Xue on her right-hand side, while her biological mother stood beside her on her left. Sandwiched between the two adults, Xiao Xue remained reticent. Mrs. Wong physically nudged her gently with her right arm, while her mother beckoned her quietly in her left ear with her soft words, "Come on. Do it just this one time . . ."

I was standing directly in front of the three women during this exchange. As I watched their discussion unfold before me, I could feel the anguish and disappointment that Xiao Xue felt in unexpectedly losing her last days of leisure and sleep. Her silence and sadness signaled her desire to remain a carefree teenager, a critical aspect of her life that she must once again forfeit as she resumed those long hours of monotonous and dreary factory work. I empathized with Xiao Xue's reluctance to forfeit her untroubled youth to the constraints of industrial labor. At the same time, however, her role as the (fictive) daughter reinforced her reluctant obligations to resume work despite her unwillingness, leaving her feeling that she had to fulfill Mrs. Wong's and her biological mother's wishes. Her mother's quiet urging signaled that her family relied upon Xiao Xue's wage-earning capacity as a critical source of income, a burden that seemed unfair to impose upon a young woman but that was, perhaps, necessary for her and her family's daily survival. At the same time, Mrs. Wong's subtle urging signaled her dependence on Xiao Xue's help in meeting a last-minute deadline. The older factory boss appealed to their fictional mother-daughter ties to convince

Xiao Xue to give up her vacation time. That day, Xiao Xue taught me the incredible sacrifices a young woman like her made for the sake of livelihood and filial piety, particularly within the context of low-wage labor. At the same time, I wondered the following: Were Mrs. Wong's affective appeals to Xiao Xue coercive or exploitative?

This vignette underscores how the Wongs' need to keep their temporary workers "fixed" or tied to the assembly line shaped the gendered dimensions of fictive mother-daughter love that conditioned the relations of inequality and exploitation (Harvey 2001). The labor of negotiating the boundaries of kin-based love and exploitation was necessary to facilitate the extraction of labor power across the supply chains for fast fashion. More precisely, this story demonstrates how familial love serves as a form of social labor that is critically mobilized by the demands of subcontracting low-wage, feminized workforce, particularly the need to sustain the speedy cycles of garment mass manufacture. This labor of love, as I suggest, sheds light on the practices of nurture and care that cannot be easily categorized as capitalistic or exploitative and, yet, that are paradoxically critical to capitalist discipline along with its exploitative effects. As this example shows, women such as Mrs. Wong and Xiao Xue must work through their desires for financial autonomy and the risks of exploitation that they face as factory laborers. Migrants' aspirations for better lives frequently expose them to the unequal and exploitative effects of market activities, leading to disappointments and emotional turmoil. Their stories demonstrate how performing gender and kinship ties serves as a force of capitalist accumulation but also as a means of encountering and negotiating the risks of exploitation and discontentment. These ambivalent and ongoing entanglements underscore the discrepant forms of desire and risk that shape migrants' experiences of labor as they intensify their participation in global commodity production and exchange.

On another occasion, about two months after the exchange between Xiao Xue and Mrs. Wong, I returned to the factory to find only many young migrant men and women at the sewing stations. The Chus, an elderly couple from Sichuan Province, who had developed a professional friendship with the Wongs, were unexpectedly absent from their usual workstations in the back corner. The new workers in the workshop that day appeared to be in their late teens at most. Some of them alternated between working at larger factories along the periphery of Guangzhou, and in smaller, household workshops like the Wongs' factory around the Zhaocun garment district. When I stepped inside the factory, I overheard

Mrs. Wong chatting with one of the younger female workers. Mrs. Wong asked about the working hours in the larger factories. According to the young worker, she was allowed only one rest day a month. At that moment, Mrs. Wong expressed her sympathy for the young worker, acknowledging the difficulties in enduring such a grueling work schedule.

That afternoon, the absence of the Chus concerned me. So I asked Mrs. Wong about their whereabouts and whether they would come back. Mrs. Wong hesitantly replied that they had returned to their home village and added with an odd, trembling voice. "Yes, eh, I don't know. They may or may not come back." Later that day, after I had inquired further about the Chus, she discreetly revealed to me that Mr. Chu had left under the most unpleasant circumstances. She explained that one afternoon, Mr. Chu left the factory to rest for lunch. During that time, as Mrs. Wong explained, their client rushed the Wongs to finish an urgent order. She also needed someone who was adept at sewing a particular synthetic fabric, which required a specialized skill. Subsequently, Mrs. Wong ordered a young man to sit at Mr. Chu's station temporarily to help finish the stitching on a sleeve.

When Mr. Chu returned from lunch, he discovered the young man at his station. Mr. Chu interpreted the young man's act of sitting at his station as a sign of disrespect toward him, a signal that Mr. Chu would simply be replaced. He subsequently reprimanded the Wongs for hiring too many inexperienced teenage workers, a management decision Mr. Chu vehemently opposed. Mr. Chu then blazed out in fury, taking his wife with him, never to return. As Mrs. Wong retold her story to me, she remarked, "You know how Mr. Chu is. He's got a hot temper." In her voice, I could not help but notice a tinge of sadness and regret, particularly because I had personally witnessed the special rapport the Wongs shared with Mr. Chu. In fact, everyone in the factory, including the Wongs, addressed him respectfully as Master Chu, or Chu Shifu, a title that accorded him honor and respect for his skills, experience, and hard work.

After I heard her story, I felt Mrs. Wong's grief for their loss of the friendship. I then recalled a moment I had witnessed months before when Mr. Wong bonded with Mr. Chu. This affective bond, I realized, compelled Mr. Chu to stay at the Wongs' factory and kept him from seeking better employment opportunities around the neighborhood. One time, I had witnessed Mr. Wong paying Mr. Chu his wages after a few days of labor. Mr. Wong at that time did not have necessary change to pay Mr. Chu the remaining 3–5 RMB ($0.50–$0.75 USD) owed to him. Out of their mutual respect and honor, Mr. Wong offered to hand him a 10 RMB ($1.50–$2.00 USD) note, but Mr. Chu insistently refused. During their exchange, I observed the mutual smiles and eye contact that acknowledged their close relationship. With a quick and unforeseen incident, it seemed that the foundations of their friendship had unexpectedly crumbled.

As the Wongs and the Chus labor across the assembly lines of garment mass manufacture, they experience the invisible effects of just-in-time industrial discipline through their encounters with clients (both Chinese and transnational) and with other migrant laborers across the supply chains. Uncertainties are part and parcel of transnational subcontracting. The ambiguous and fluid boundaries that define the migrant "boss" and the worker reveal the necessity of understanding the workings of power across global supply chains as emergent through face-to-face encounters. Rather than assuming the operations of power as an external force or as a bounded whole, the dynamics of encounter compel us to raise questions about how power is worked out and *recognized* and negotiated by those who are involved in an encounter or exchange. The relationship between the Wongs and the Chus thus illustrate Janet Roitman's (2005) arguments that the effects of power manifest precisely through its emergence, that is, through the play-by-play dynamics of encounter.

In this case, the dynamics of encounter ultimately lead to questions about who governs whom in an economic exchange and how the terms of labor, mobility, and class hierarchies are negotiated. These questions are particularly relevant in light of the fact that across the supply chains for fast fashion, mechanisms of power and discipline are increasingly rationalized, self-regulated, and made invisible by multinational corporate and state agents through audit practices, which include quality standards, price controls, and production deadlines.[10] These measures trickle downward among intermediary agents, or self-declared "bosses," along the supply chain, the majority of whom remain decentralized and far away from the physical sites of production.

Furthermore, migrant wage workers like the Chus contest various disciplinary measures through various strategies of contingency, including labor disputes, missed deadlines, and contestations over quality. When disagreements over the workmanship of garments surface between the boss and employee, wage workers verbally disagree or simply leave the shop floor. Meanwhile, migrant bosses find themselves renegotiating their role as "boss" vis-à-vis their temporary employees. The ambiguity in what separates the factory bosses from their part-time employees often leaves the parties uncertain about where to locate and assert authority within a given situation. When disputes between the Wongs and their workers over the quality of the clothes erupt, they must renegotiate the boss-worker hierarchy amid the painstaking work of collectively keeping up with the relentless production process.

After Mrs. Wong's revelation, I tried to imagine the unfolding of events. I could not help but imagine the insult Mr. Chu must have felt when he discovered that he had apparently been replaced. Since Mr. Chu embodied the figure of honor and pride in factory labor, he must have been quite perplexed by how a young man could unexpectedly replace him at his workstation. Mr. Chu's fury highlighted for me the unevenness of class identifications and conceptions of work across the generational spectrum of workers who must confront each other when they work elbow to elbow on the factory floor (Rofel 1999). Mr. Chu's storming out of the factory gestured an absolute rejection of the changes that characterize the emergent form of flexible production that the Wongs and their workers must embrace. Mr. Chu's sudden absence conveyed the message that he would not accept those uncomfortable changes, nor would he participate in them. His rejection also affirmed that neither he nor any other worker could be simply replaced.

Later, I wondered whether Mr. Chu's breakaway from the Wongs' factory floor meant as great a loss for Mr. Chu as it was for the Wongs. When Mrs. Wong recalled the incident, she regretfully commented that Mr. Chu could easily find another position at another factory in the neighborhood. After all, other owners and workers in the neighborhood knew Mr. Chu, signaling that he had established an honorable reputation for himself in the surrounding neighborhood. In fact, Mrs. Wong stated, "You know, he can find a job anywhere among the factories here." Her comment thus registered a sense of loss. At the same time, however, Mr. Chu's interpretation of the incident as personally offensive must have meant that the young man's presence signaled a threat to him—that somehow that Mr. Chu believed his labor and life history could be easily erased.

Mr. Chu's unexpected departure demonstrates the Wongs' dependency upon their temporary workers, despite the couple assuming the role of bosses within the highly exploitative context of transnational subcontracting. The tenuous and intergenerational relationships that were forged amid the constant movement of workers onto and off the factory floor attest to the tension between dependency and exploitation, which the Wongs negotiated vis-à-vis their workers as they struggled to keep up with the demands of just-in-time mass manufacture. In this highly mobile and fluid environment, the Wongs had to learn to control and extract the labor power of their workers through various disciplinary mechanisms, as we have seen in the case of Xiao Xue. In the *jiagongchang*, however, these mechanisms, as the Wongs' encounter with Mr. Chu demonstrates, are quite limited. As such, the Wongs might declare themselves the "bosses" of their labor, but in practice, as they gradually realized, they were not the actual bosses of their temporary workers in the ways that they had expected to be. Such unstable dynamics of power highlight the fragilities and uncertainties of bosshood that characterize encounters across transnational supply chains.

THE ART OF "READING" AND EVADING EXPLOITATION

The ambivalent encounters between the boss and worker in the *jiagongchang* also extend to client-manufacturer relations. The Wongs also had to learn to sort out these complex dynamics through their strategies of reading their clients. During the first year of my visits to the Wongs, I expected the boss-client dynamic to be rather straightforward. Clients, both domestic and transnational, who occupy more powerful positions further up the commodity chain, represented themselves or subcontracted from others. They sought to pay the lowest prices in exchange for the labor and expertise of the Wongs and their workers. I expected the clients to be unyielding in their demands and uncompassionate to the conditions upon which these migrant laborers struggled to stay afloat financially. Much to my surprise, I had noticed that Mrs. Wong, who handled most of the couple's client relations, refused production orders offered by some domestic and transnational subcontractors. Despite the necessity of building their client base, Mrs. Wong would turn away from potential collaborations by citing a lack of time, labor force, or the appropriate machines to handle a particular fabric or design.

When I asked Mrs. Wong to explain why she refused particular production orders, she reasoned that the designs were too time-consuming, or that the foreign markets that they served did not promise enough profits to justify the Wongs' time and efforts. The frilly designs of lace dresses for Japanese clients, for example, were too complicated and time-consuming, while the women's cotton T-shirts for African consumers paid too little to justify their labor time. Gradually, I began to realize that Mrs. Wong had learned to "read" or decode the demeanor of clients and the materiality of garments along a calculus of labor time and potential exploitation. For

Mrs. Wong, the art of reading entailed not only decoding her clients' interests in undercutting her labor. It involved also anticipating potential long-term collaborations that would lead to other possibilities later, including transnational connections, introduction to other clients, and meaningful friendships.

In other words, the Wongs looked for some level of guarantee that they would receive a nonmonetary return on their time and effort. For the Wongs, these considerations would make the risks of exploitation worthwhile. In one instance, Mrs. Wong flatly refused a Chinese female contractor who inquired about a production job. She was dressed in a black sequined top and high heels. Mrs. Wong appeared exasperated and rejected her outright on the basis that she was not the type of person who would work hard for her money, since the kind of work subcontractors do was *xin ku*, or entailed struggle. "Look at how she's dressed! Do you think she's the type who works hard? We would have to be at her beck and call!" In this highly fluid and uncertain market environment, the art of reading clients, I realized, was essential for the Wongs in situating their clients' roles and demands within a broader context of precarity and exploitation.

As intermediary agents, subcontractors know that they must serve other bosses further up the chain. Even clients of the Wongs have explained to me that because of the demands placed upon them by their bosses, they find themselves relying on the good graces of their hired manufacturers to prioritize their production orders over those of their competitors. Clients must also trust that the factory bosses they hire do not undercut them by producing garments of low quality. Techniques for situating and decoding the larger chain of command and exploitation are thus shared by factory bosses and subcontracting clients alike.

The broader organization of transnational subcontracting across global supply chains necessitates migrants' developing strategies to evade the exploitative effects of labor governance. Corporate oversight across supply chains operates precisely through its invisibility as well as through its ability to offload unexpected costs and social responsibility onto third-party contractors at its discretion. Transnational subcontracting practices, which include offshore production away from the sites of consumption, yield dispersed sites of governance and power, whereby multinational corporations and their intermediary agents govern the production process without any direct face-to-face contact with the manufacturers on whom they rely (Appel 2019). Relying on digital technologies, multinational companies remain physically absent from the production sites with which they contract, yet their presence is palpable through the transcontinental movements of commodities and capital, which they capture through data collected in real time (Chua 2018). These powerful players assert their influence over the daily operations of the assembly line by hiring independent contractors to mediate communications with manufacturers and by establishing certain quality-control measures and price-fixes on the finished goods.

While multinational corporate retailers can extract monetary profits from transnational subcontracting arrangements and pass the risks downward along the supply chain, small-scale subcontracted agents take on riskier, more uncertain investments of time, money, and labor by relying on contingent factors that materialize only through scalar encounters across the chain. Subcontractors, for example, frequently disagree about the labor conditions, debt, deadlines, market forecasts, future trends, and quality, all while keeping in mind the conditions of their exploitation by *their* own bosses further up the supply chain. By coming together in negotiation or in collaborative partnerships, factory bosses like the Wongs and their clients across the supply chain position themselves vis-à-vis one another to situate and come to know, albeit partially and temporarily, the conditions of their mutual precarity based on their subcontracted labor. Their experiences of cross-scalar encounters in and across the *jiagongchang* become revelatory moments in which the dynamic modes of power and labor discipline that sustain the demands of flexible, just-in-time mass manufacture materialize and are made apparent to all participants. The class-based and scalar dynamics of encounter also provide subcontractors opportunities to leverage their economic interests and to evade, or at least, negotiate the terms of their own exploitation. This strategy, as I would learn, entailed several unexpected contingencies and improvisations that materialized through the unfolding of a heated exchange.

One day I observed an interesting encounter between Mrs. Wong and Mr. Liu, a younger male client from South Korea. On the afternoon Mr. Liu approached the Wongs' factory, he was accompanied by another young South Korean man who was of similar age and stature as his colleague. I recalled having seen Mr. Liu one week earlier, when he came by the Wongs' to coordinate a production order for about 1,000 men's button-up plaid shirts. On the afternoon in question, I simply assumed that the man accompanying Mr. Liu was Mr. Liu's client, since I had witnessed Mr. Liu engage in some translation work from Chinese to Korean for him. As Mrs. Wong and her four female workers sat at their respective sewing stations that day, Mr. Liu and his male colleague entered the factory floor by ducking their heads below the steel gates and quietly stepping into the industrial workshop. In contrast to the surroundings of the working-class neighborhood, the two young men looked clean, chic, and especially well-groomed. Mr. Liu was wearing a crisp white T-shirt with a rounded collar and shorts, while his friend wore a pair of beige khakis and a long-sleeved, button-up sports shirt in a warm crème color. As Mr. Liu politely greeted Mrs. Wong from across the factory floor, the two men lingered by the front gates, trying to open and inspect the contents of two large bundles of clothing that lay beside the left-hand corner of the factory entrance.

To my bewilderment, Mrs. Wong seemed to have ignored Mr. Liu's greeting, even though it was obvious to everyone on the shop floor that the two Korean men had come by to see her. For several minutes, as the two men lingered by the front gates and chatted between themselves, Mrs. Wong left them waiting by simply failing to acknowledge their presence. Feeling a bit uncomfortable about the situation, I nudged Mrs. Wong to greet them by informing her of their arrival. Feigning surprise, Mrs. Wong turned her head in the direction of the two men and reluctantly greeted them in return. As Mr. Liu tried to untie the bundle and pull the contents out of the large sack, he asked Mrs. Wong if she could confirm whether the garments were part of his order of men's plaid shirts. Mrs. Wong then attempted to dodge his question by ignoring it altogether. Instead, Mrs. Wong feigned utter ignorance. She explained that only Mr. Wong knew whether the garments were theirs and instructed them to sit upstairs in their living quarters and to wait until Mr. Wong returned. In an exasperated tone of voice, Mrs. Wong then turned to the direction of her Chinese workers and mumbled in Cantonese, "These young-uns haven't paid their deposit in full. They can't just take the goods and leave! They will just have to deal with my husband." I then asked her whether Mr. Liu was a new client. She responded, "No, we've worked with him for a few years now, and we've never really had any problems with him. But just recently, he has picked up a new client from Korea, and we don't know anything about this new boss. We just don't know what kind of person this new boss is. He is simply too risky."

At that moment, I realized that Mrs. Wong's instruction to have them wait was a deliberate strategy to keep them from leaving with the goods before they paid the deposit in full. Her strategy enabled her to assert a degree of control over the situation and to protect herself from the clients' possible attempt to cheat the couple of their money without directly confronting the two men. Unaware of her tactics, the two men obligingly climbed up the steel stairs to the second-floor room and patiently waited for Mr. Wong's return. Thirty minutes passed while the two men remained upstairs engaging in conversation, while Mrs. Wong and her workers diligently worked at their respective sewing stations. Over time, however, the men's voices slowly grew louder, and I could hear some rustling from above. Shortly afterward, Mr. Liu descended the stairs and impatiently inquired about Mr. Wong's whereabouts.

Growing irritated, Mr. Liu turned to Mrs. Wong and spoke to her in Putonghua. He asked, "How much longer will we have to wait? I've tried calling Mr. Wong over the past thirty minutes and he won't pick up the phone. It's already 5:30 p.m., and I still have a full schedule ahead of me. I can't wait much longer . . ." Mrs. Wong then tried to quell Mr. Liu's growing exasperation and attempted to maintain control over the situation by keeping Mr. Liu at bay. In reply, she assured them that Mr. Wong would return to the factory soon. Until then, they would simply have to wait. At that moment, it was clear from Mr. Liu's brewing exasperation that Mrs. Wong's delay tactic was slowly becoming ineffective. After a few minutes of chatter, the men then turned to the bundle and tried to open it in order to inspect its contents. Because of the heavy and durable material of the bag, Mr. Liu failed to open it with his bare hands and asked Mrs. Wong to pass him a pair of scissors.

As Mrs. Wong's delay tactic gradually collapsed before our eyes, her exchange with Mr. Liu slowly became more and more contentious. Within a few minutes, Mrs. Wong gave in and revealed the stacks of men's plaid shirts, individually folded and packaged in clear plastic bags. Annoyed by the pressure exerted by the two men, Mrs. Wong then complained out loud, "You know, we haven't received the full payment from you." Mr. Liu then sighed and frowned. The exchange between them suddenly grew more heated. In an annoyed and exasperated tone of voice, he replied, "Look, don't worry. We won't steal away with the goods without paying you. We simply want to take a look at the goods to check whether the details and the quality were correct."

At that moment, I suddenly noticed from their body language how Mrs. Wong and Mr. Liu took on specific gendered and intergenerational roles while they bickered about the details of the transaction. Mrs. Wong seemed to have abandoned her timid and passive demeanor and took on a somewhat patronizing tone of a female elder talking down to a younger and more naive newcomer to the garment industry. In reply, she stated in a stern yet calm tone of voice, "Ok, ok. I know that you will eventually pay." (Mrs. Wong likely made this statement in an attempt to temper Mr. Liu's growing exasperation toward her.) "But I'm just informing you that we don't usually deliver the goods to our client before receiving our payment. We're in the middle of a very large production order for another client. We put in extra effort to subcontract your order to another factory to ensure that it would be delivered to you on time. We put in a lot of time and effort to arrange this for you." Mr. Liu impatiently replied with an exasperated sigh similar to that of a son talking back to his mother, "Of course, I know! I know! I promise you. I won't leave with the goods and not pay you. I just want to inspect the garments to make sure that everything is done right!"

Shortly after Mrs. Wong cut open the bundle, she and the two men remained standing around in a semicircle by the left-hand corner of the front gates as the clients discussed the details of the plaid shirts in their native Korean language. Minutes later, Mr. Wong finally returned. Just as Mrs. Wong informed her husband that the clients were preparing to pick up the bag of assembled clothing, he immediately turned toward the two men and asked whether they had transferred the money to his bank account, thereby confirming Mrs. Wong's suspicion of Mr. Liu's intention to leave the factory premises with the goods before rightfully paying the Wongs. Mr. Liu explained to Mr. Wong that he had submitted the money online the day before. After a few minutes of discussion among the men, Mrs. Wong quickly retreated to her sewing station, and Mr. Wong went upstairs to check the status of his bank account on his computer.

Within minutes, Mr. Liu called upon Mr. Wong to return downstairs. Panicked, Mr. Liu noticed that the fabric of the plaid shirts was not the material that he had initially requested. Mr. Liu explained, "Look at this fabric. I cannot sell this low-quality material in Korea. Unlike the Chinese, Korean buyers care about quality." Calmly, Mr. Wong then descended the stairs and joined his two Korean clients by the front gate. Mr. Wong gestured to the bag on one hand and then nudged the tip of his cigarette with the other. With a slight air of indifference, Mr. Wong explained that he simply relayed the specificities of Mr. Liu's requests to the factory boss who handled the production order, implying that the responsibility for the botched order fell upon Mr. Liu and not himself. As Mr. Liu and his friend conversed in Korean, I slowly and quietly approached Mr. Wong and asked him to clarify the situation for me. He remarked in Cantonese, "Ah, now it's become a really complicated situation (ma fan) for them right now. We used up so much time and effort to arrange with a subcontractor to produce this order, but now they've realized that the fabric of all the garments was wrong." At that moment, I wondered to myself who was responsible for the mistake. I then caught a glance of the two Korean men and realized that at that moment, determining who was responsible for the mistake no longer mattered. Mr. Liu had to answer to *his* boss and client and had to frantically brainstorm ways to redo the order by tomorrow's production deadline.

As Mr. Liu and Mrs. Wong's initial encounter demonstrates, quality standards and the just-in-time delivery of commodities dictate the conditions upon which workers organize their labor, even if there is no single system upon which they operate. To be sure, price and quality have often become highly contested discursive realms upon which migrant wage workers, factory bosses, and transnational clients dispute the terms of labor and exchange. By controlling the prices and quality of the finished products, corporate agents like Mr. Liu attempt to manage the minute operations of the Wongs' manufacturing process, thereby coloring the everyday encounters between employers and employees on the shop floor. Sometimes, depending on the situation, these management tactics border on outright exploitation. Third-party contractors like Mr. Liu attempt to shrug off the risks and costs of low-cost manufacture—including worker protests, unionization, industrial accidents, and environmental damage—to participants further down the supply chain. Based on their experience, the Wongs evidently were familiar with these tactics by corporate agents, so they learned to "read" clients and evade further exploitation. Luckily for them in this case, the couple successfully delayed responding to Mr. Liu's demands. Their strategy has paid off once both parties realized that Mr. Liu needed to backtrack from his performance of authority vis-à-vis Mrs. Wong in order to answer to *his* boss further up the supply chain.

PERFORMING BOSSHOOD ACROSS UNEVEN ENCOUNTERS

In an attempt to save himself from the wrath of his boss, Mr. Liu tried to negotiate with Mr. Wong. First, Mr. Liu complained that the factory owner to whom Mr. Wong subcontracted the job failed to meet his requirements by misunderstanding the details of the production order or by negligently overlooking certain quality standards. Mr. Liu then asked Mr. Wong whether he could send back the bundle of clothes and have the factory owner redo the entire order by tomorrow. However, like a professional or an old hand in the garment manufacturing industry, Mr. Wong failed to budge. Mr. Wong simply stated that the mistake was not theirs but was Mr. Liu's.

As I returned to my seat beside Mrs. Wong who was working diligently at her sewing station, I observed the two Korean men pace back and forth along the street directly in front of the factory. Mr. Liu grew visibly nervous and exasperated. His frown turned to a blank stare as he thought of alternative solutions to this sticky situation. At one point, I saw Mr. Liu's colleague plop his head into his hands as Mr. Liu called his boss to discuss the problem with him. After Mr. Liu ended his call, he turned to us looking nervous and exhausted. Aware of Mr. Liu's dilemma, Mrs. Wong called out to Mr. Liu and asked him about the status of the situation. In reply, he stated, "Whew! He (Mr. Liu's boss) is really angry right now. I don't know what to say." Over time, as rounds of negotiation went on between Mr. Liu and the Wongs, I noticed a subtle transformation in Mr. Liu's demeanor, which went from that of a young boss making demands upon the Wongs to that of a young fledging client seeking to appeal to the sympathies of the Wongs and their workers.

Upon waiting for his boss's arrival, Mr. Liu's disposition toward the Wongs almost completely transformed. His defensive and stern attitude slowly dissipated, revealing a somewhat vulnerable and meek young man. Nervously, Mr. Liu explained to the Wongs, as well as to the workers on the shop floor, that he was dreading the impending confrontation with his boss. His display of nervousness and vulnerability served as a bridge that affectively connected the Wongs with him. In a way, his performance evoked the Wongs' empathy by displaying their mutual positions as precarious employees of stern and unforgiving bosses (of course, including Mr. Liu before he discovered the botched order).

In fact, Mr. Liu began to coach all of us inside the factory on how to conduct ourselves in front of his Korean boss. He turned to one of the Wongs' workers as if he were a colleague in the Wongs' factory and said, "Don't say anything about him in Putonghua. Even though he is Korean, he has lived and worked in Guangzhou for many years. His Putonghua is fluent. He will understand anything you say." He then continued, "He is very, very serious. He has also been in this industry for many years and can read through people immediately. Just pretend you don't know anything about this order . . ." Mrs. Wong then giggled at Mr. Liu's somewhat humorous and exaggerated display of fear and nervousness toward his boss, signaling an understanding of the man's intent to garner an audience that was sympathetic to his uneasy relationship with his own boss. Acknowledging Mr. Liu's appeal, Mrs. Wong then whispered to me, "Ah yes, there are many Koreans in the garment industry who have lived in Guangzhou for a long,

long time. Many speak Putonghua very well and can sometimes be ruthless bosses."

When Mr. Liu's boss finally arrived, all of us inside on the factory floor remained silent with our heads down in an uncomfortable anticipation of the boss's wrath. Indeed, Mr. Liu's boss, a tall and handsome man in his early thirties, stood in front of factory gates, silently inspecting the bags of finished garments, which were now deemed unsalable. While the boss remained reticent with his eyebrows furrowed, Mrs. Wong caught a glance at him from across the factory floor and remarked, "Oh yeah. You can tell he is angry. He must be a tough boss, ha-ha. . . ." Meanwhile, Mr. Liu stood beside his employer, looking up at him with scared and bewildered eyes. Every once in a while, he tried to steal glances at Mrs. Wong and her workers, in full knowledge that all of us on the factory floor were waiting for the boss to publicly reprimand Mr. Liu for his mistake.

Luckily for all of us who witnessed the exchange, the Korean boss remained calm in spite of his annoyance and frustration. The three Korean men, including Mr. Liu, his colleague, and his boss, discussed possible solutions to the problem at hand, while everyone else inside the factory continued their work at their stations. After about half an hour of discussion, the head boss made a phone call to one of the factory owners nearby to ask whether he could place a last-minute production order. Apparently, they planned to take the garments to another factory to redo a part of the production order. While the men were talking, I observed Mr. Liu's display of guilt and passivity in front of his boss. He simply listened to his boss's orders without any complaints or resistance, a disposition that starkly contrasted to his behavior toward the Wongs earlier in the afternoon. As the men prepared to leave, they arranged a pedicab driver to deliver the bundles of garments to another factory nearby. Before his departure, Mr. Liu caught Mrs. Wong's eye from far across the shop floor, signaling a sense of mutual compassion toward one another despite their confrontation. In response, Mrs. Wong chuckled, subtly acknowledging Mr. Liu's precarious position as an employee/agent and thereby smoothing out any residual tensions between them. Mrs. Wong's quick change of attitude toward Mr. Liu surprised me, particularly since Mrs. Wong initially held a strong sense of suspicion and distrust toward Mr. Liu. At the same time, Mr. Liu's subtle but palpable change of behavior and disposition toward the Wongs indicated the ambiguity and fluidity of the position as "boss" among independent contractors.

The unexpected unfolding of events during Mrs. Wong's exchange with Mr. Liu demonstrated to me how each incremental node along the supply chains for fast fashion brought together discrepant and overlapping sets of demands and expectations related to product quality, production deadlines, and monetary transfer, all of which were determined and influenced by other aspects of the production chain. As intermediaries along the transcontinental supply chain, Mr. Liu and Mrs. Wong bore the quality demands and production costs that their respective bosses and employee/subcontractors expected in order make a profit. In this case, the production time that higher-quality goods required and the low costs that transnational clients such as Mr. Liu and his boss demanded from the Wongs and other local manufacturers lay in direct opposition to the interests of factory bosses and their wage workers. Consequently, transnational jobbers and local manufacturers attempt to reconcile this opposition during the process of negotiating the terms of labor and profit exchange.

As this ethnographic example shows, determining the "boss" of the employer-employee relationship becomes an improvisational game of performance and play, which draws upon roles of gender, ethnicity, and intergenerational authority. These roles, as I emphasize, are mutually strategic, since both parties attempt to dictate the terms of transaction in anticipation of the other party's actions and motives. For example, Mrs. Wong used delay as a tactic to avoid confronting Mr. Liu about her suspicions of him, and she later took on the position of an older woman trying to manage the temperament and impatience of a younger man. At the same time, performances of particular ethnic roles are also implicitly present. Mr. Liu, aware of his social capital as a South Korean boss in China's garment industry, drew upon his knowledge of product quality in his attempts to (unsuccessfully) convince Mr. Wong to redo the entire order.[11]

Before Mr. Liu's boss arrived at the Wongs' factory door, Mrs. Wong could only speculate on the likelihood that Mr. Liu would submit his payment in full. Mr. Liu had the leveraging power to negotiate the terms of exchange as if he were the "boss" of the transaction. Only until both parties realized that the terms of their profits and exchange were *both* determined by Mr. Liu's boss did Mr. Liu's demeanor toward Mrs. Wong change and both contractors worked as collaborators. Only at the point of encounter were the operations of power across the supply chain made visible and intelligible to Mrs. Wong and her client, highlighting the mutual precarity of their roles as subcontractors.

Like Guangzhou's urban villages, *jiagongchang* act as temporary spaces of transition for migrants who move between rural and urban spaces as well as between entrepreneurship and industrial wage work, since these urban villages have been slated for demolition by the municipal government in the near future. Migrant residents here are fully aware that the pressures of urbanization and capital flight will eventually impact the urban villages and the *jiagongchang*, leaving behind permanent zones of social abandonment. By attempting to disarticulate themselves from the exploitative obligations of industrial wage work, migrants find themselves negotiating the fine line between the disciplinary constraints of factory labor and the emancipatory promises of entrepreneurship despite the exclusions and uncertainties they face due to the *hukou* policy of population control. Intergenerational migrants, both young and old, often complain about the isolating and exploitative conditions characteristic of large-scale factory labor and find temporary and piece-rate labor in the *jiagongchang*. In the meantime, they wait to look for other employment and entrepreneurial possibilities.

Their attempts to accumulate capital through their labor mobility in the urban villages, however, are only temporary since they are fully aware that the land upon which the urban villages are built will eventually be sold (*hui gui*) to the municipal government and to real estate corporations before it will be fully incorporated into the urban core. As a middle-aged, female worker from Fujian once stated, "[Our work in the factory] is a matter of self-responsibility [or depending on oneself]" (*kao ziji*). One must make money for oneself in order to ensure a good living." She complained about the difficulties of earning a living at her advanced age. She described her body as worn out by years of labor and said that she could no longer work as efficiently or as strenuously as the younger workers. Over time, her body could only endure the slower-paced labor such as cutting thread, even though these tasks paid significantly less than sewing and other more physically demanding jobs. During dinner, she revealed to the workers in the factory that she had stolen work time (*tou gong zuo*) from her regular job at the fabric store so that she could earn a little extra money on the side. She added that in the past hour of snipping loose threads, she had earned only 3 RMB because some clothing styles were so difficult to work with.

Another middle-aged mother from Guangxi reflected on her labor as a garment worker by stating, "I've been doing this for a long, long time. . . ." I then asked her if she would often make her own clothes, but she fell silent as the machine buzzed with fervor. Afterward, I added that I hoped to learn how to sew my own clothes someday. In surprise, she immediately rejected the idea by saying that a student like me does not (and should not) learn how to make clothes. "Why would you want to do this? It would be a waste of time for you. I've been doing this for over twenty years! Sometimes I get so tired at the end of the day and just want to give up doing this. But I think to myself and wonder what else I could possibly do. Then I realize there's nothing else. So I just give up and keep up with this [work]."

The unfavorable experiences of factory employment within Guangzhou's fast fashion sector have led some wage workers to express their growing ambivalence toward factory labor. Paradoxically, their aspirations for entrepreneurship and financial freedom leave them even more dependent and vulnerable to the exploitative conditions of factory labor. The pressures of meeting tight production deadlines and of facilitating the rapid turnover of fashion commodities have tested the limits and the well-being and bodily capacities of factory workers. Although the informal organization of garment production characteristic of the Wongs' factory-workshop grants wage workers a certain degree of mobility, they nevertheless face long working hours, low wages, and monotonous working conditions. Consequently, they view their temporary labor as a stepping stone to entrepreneurial ventures or to permanent retirement from wage work but only until they return to the factory floors.

Once, during a weeklong idle phase between orders, I suggested to Mrs. Wong that she take the time to catch up on sleep and rest. She then immediately responded, "You don't know what it's like in our line of work. We can't take breaks because we don't know where our money will come from." She and her workers face the challenge of balancing demanding work schedules, during which garment production consumed every waking hour, with their concerns for earning enough money to cover their living costs and family expenses during idle periods. When I asked the couple about their plans for their future, they simply said, "We don't know. Next year, we may be here. Maybe not. We just don't know where the market will take us." Uncertainty for the future has become a permanent condition of livelihood and labor for the Wongs and other migrant bosses.

Within these spatiotemporal opportunities and disjunctures, migrants must negotiate their long-term aspirations with the short-term risks of self-employment and small-scale entrepreneurship. As intermediary contractors across the supply chain for fast fashion in Guangzhou, migrant entrepreneurs assert themselves as "boss." Few, however, know who the actual boss is in advance of a mutual encounter or negotiation, particularly among those interactions based on short-term contracts and working relationships. Unlike a conventional factory setting where the wage relation determines the roles and expectations of a capitalist or a worker, relations of production and labor across the supply chains are more fluid, dynamic, and ambiguous, since piecework and non-waged relations predominate. At first glance, non-waged employment based on temporary or project-based work seems to offer individual subcontractors more autonomy in controlling the conditions of their labor and in determining the terms of their exchange. Over time, however, they gradually realize that they must all take on more risks of exploitation and displacement in return for the *promise* of wealth and economic opportunity. Yet, their investments in capital, time, and emotional energy into their own enterprises leave them reluctant to cut their losses and to forfeit their long-term aspirations for themselves and their loved ones. Consequently, they become entangled in the webs of stalled mobility.

More specifically, migrant bosses find themselves caught between the necessity of having to accumulate profit and capital over time, and the inability to do so in light of rapidly changing fashion trends, market competition, and policing by more powerful bosses. Capitalist accumulation, as David Harvey (2001) and others inform us, requires a certain degree of "fixity" or stability in both dimensions of time and space in order for capital to grow. By contrast, in the world of transnational subcontracting, spatial fixity and temporal stability are no longer the primary strategies of accumulation, particularly for the financially vulnerable migrant populations. Rather, the ongoing circulation of people, commodities, and money through migration, commodity speculation, and unregulated redistribution of wealth have become mechanisms through which migrant labor is disciplined and through which Guangzhou's migrant populations anchor their entrepreneurial dreams and desires across the supply chains for fast fashion.

3 Surveillance and Regulation in the *Shenfen* (Identification) Economy

One afternoon, Sylvianne, a twenty-six-year-old female trader from Senegal, and I were enjoying a pizza and salad in a local restaurant in the heart of Xiaobei. Outside, the damp and odorous alleyways of the Xiaobei and Sanyuanli urban villages were alive with economic activity. Residents frequenting the hair salons, mobile phone shops, restaurants, grocers, tailors, and kindergarten playgrounds animated the contours of transregional exchanges and village life in these commercial and residential hubs. What started out as a calm and relaxing lunch between friends suddenly turned into an anxiety-provoking spectacle when local police officers unexpectedly entered the restaurant. The uniformed officers immediately ordered the managers to lock the front door, preventing anyone from exiting while they carefully inspected the passports and visas of the foreign patrons. Everyone in the restaurant froze silently in their places, fearful of making a sound. The officers approached the African men who were sitting behind us before they spoke to Sylvianne and me.

When one of the uniformed men turned in our direction, I asked politely in Cantonese whether Sylvianne and I needed to show our papers. Assuming that I was a Chinese local, the officer let us off the hook. After about ten minutes of making the rounds, the officers walked out of the restaurant in search of other Africans in the neighborhood. Sylvianne breathed a sigh of relief, since she had accidentally left her documents at home. Possible arrest and fines would have prevented her from running her business smoothly, exacerbating the stress and anxieties that already accompanied the pressures of making financial ends meet. After the incident, Sylvianne admitted that encounters such as this often led her to doubt whether her family's businesses in Guangzhou could weather the financial uncertainties and bureaucratic hurdles she often confronted. To be sure, the urban villages of Xiaobei and Sanyuanli fostered an atmosphere of criminality based on racist and misguided views about African migrants.

This ethnographic scene illustrates how West African migrant bosses like Sylvianne, who move about the marketplaces, factory spaces, and street corners of Guangzhou, become caught up in the larger inequalities of place-based regulation and control. Such regulatory activities are tied to unbridled real estate speculation and industrialization in the urban villages of what I call Guangzhou's burgeoning "shenfen (identification) economy." The shenfen economy is an extralegal economy run by nonstate actors who follow and surveil migrant bosses' activities across the supply chains for fast fashion. These strategies of scrutiny, inspection, and ultimately extortion exert procedural intimidation on migrant populations as well as on other vulnerable groups via their daily rhythms and everyday market activities.

While Guangzhi Huang (2020) insightfully argues that racial discrimination against African populations in Guangzhou stems from the municipal government's tendency to equate African migrants with Chinese rural migrants and label them as rural and chaotic (luan), I contend that the strategies of regulation of migrant populations by the police and private security officers are varied and uneven. In fact, they may be generative; that is, they promote the profits that transnational and domestic migrant bosses make. The surveillance and regulatory tactics, as I demonstrate, do not aim to suppress or limit migrants' entrepreneurial and profit-driven activities. Rather, they rest firmly upon the rhythmic activities of the market (not the state) so as to extract and siphon portions of migrants' profits for themselves.

My use of the term shadow, in describing the shenfen economy, is specific and deliberate since the tactics of regulation and control exercised by private security officers and village landlords upon the migrant population closely follow the bosses' trail of cash and profits, linking their rent-seeking pursuits with the migrants' profit-driven activities. Thus, in contrast to modes of regulation and surveillance practiced by officers via state-backed policing—which aims to deter, suppress, and control the mobility

3.1 An advertisement for African textiles, 2018. Photo by Nellie Chu.

of migrants, along with the flows of cash and goods they exchange—the *shenfen* economy mobilizes mechanisms of shadowing and coercion by nonstate actors with the aim of siphoning off a small portion of migrants' profits through rent and fee collection, regardless of whether these actions are sanctioned by the state or not.

These forms of regulation and surveillance, for example, comprise a range of visual, affective, and material practices. Propaganda posters, public service announcements, and other community ads serve as forms of visual deterrence, informing residents of the strict enforcement by the police of the sale of foreign currency, drugs, and counterfeit goods. Meanwhile, police inspections by officers who regularly patrol the streets of Xiaobei remind residents and tourists that they are subject to identification check and visa inspection (Castillo 2016; Lan 2015, 2016b; Wilczak 2018). Since 2018, a small police station and checkpoint have been built along a busy intersection in Xiaobei in an attempt to control the traffic of migrants, goods, and money that pass through the streets (Wilczak 2018; G. Huang 2020). The infrastructure and visual tools of the police operate as modes of deterrence at most times of the day, yet they can quickly transform into tools of direct containment and violence when the situation arises.

The *shenfen* economy, which consists of an invisible group of nonstate actors, including peasant landlords (colloquially referred to as the *tu er dai*) and the private security officers they hire, utilizes document checks and other administrative procedures to target and criminalize migrants as a means of regulating the flows of people, goods, and money into and out of the urban villages. The *tu er dai* is a group of former peasants who have turned into landlords nearly overnight, and who now govern the villages almost completely—and oddly, they do so through their absence. The term is a play on words from the popular term, *tu er dai* (the second generation of the wealthy class), or the generation of extremely wealthy urbanites in China (N. Chu 2022). The word *tu*, which means "earth," refers to this group's peasant background. According to the *hukou* household registration system, holders of the land use-rights are still considered rural citizens, even though some have become wealthy peasants who rent apartment spaces to rural migrants in search of jobs and affordable housing.

Nearly all the *tu er dai*—who once were members of former Maoist collectives whose livelihoods once depended on crops grown on this land on which the urban villages have since arisen—have moved away from the urban villages and into the fully urbanized districts of the city (N. Chu 2022). Shortly after the introduction of market reforms in 1978, these village landlords revitalized pre-Maoist corporate lineages to which their shared land was tied. Many of southern China's agricultural collectives during the Maoist period were organized by lineage surnames. Membership to these collectives allows them to claim use-rights to this land. These peasant landlords have been quickly elevated to the rentier class thanks to their collective possession of use-rights to village land.

In this chapter, I illustrate how the manufacture and exchange of fast fashion among migrant bosses in Guangzhou's urban villages intersect with the rent-seeking interests of the peasant landlords. The crossing of these divergent profit-seeking activities fosters the emergence of the *shenfen* economy. Ethnographic vignettes in this chapter shed light on the mechanisms through which the *shenfen* economy operates as well as on the personal and societal impacts the officers' regulatory activities have on the rural Chinese and West African migrant populations, even if these "regulatory" activities are not officially sanctioned by the state. Such regulatory mechanisms include arbitrary fee collection from small-scale bosses, the racialization of West African migrants, affective control over rural Chinese and West African migrants, and regulation/valuation via the *suzhi* (human quality) discourse. In the sections that follow, I detail the ways in which the tactics of regulation and surveillance among nonstate actors in the *shenfen* economy unfold alongside the fast fashion supply chains through migrants' encounters with private security and other uniformed officials in the urban villages.

These tactics of regulation and surveillance involve the construction of discursive categories of race, criminality, and counterfeiting as they are mobilized through the everyday rhythms of market labor and exchange in Guangzhou. Discourses such as these are critical to the functioning of both the supply chains of fast fashion and the overlapping *shenfen* economy. Through them, the fast fashion supply chains mobilize the assembly lines of low-cost migrant labor, while the *shenfen* economy attempts to extract rent and other fee payments by regulating the movements of money, migrants, and commodities into and out of the urban villages. In turn, peasant landlords claim portions of the rent payments and fees for themselves, some of which are then reinvested in apartments and other infrastructural projects that further facilitate the fast fashion industry in the urban villages.

THE *SHENFEN* ECONOMY

In Guangzhou's urban villages, the *shenfen* economy operates along the edges of formal and informal governance. Since the use-rights to the land upon which the urban villages are built belong to members of the village collectives, regulation of traffic and safety in the urban villages falls within the domain of the *tu er dai* peasant landlords. In turn, the peasant landlords hire private security officers to oversee these activities. Meanwhile, the municipal police reserve the right to detain migrants anywhere and at any time. For this reason, the official municipal police frequently overlap awkwardly with the private security forces, resulting in a situation where few migrants know to which branch of the police, and corresponding authority, the officers they confront belong.[1] This lack of public transparency enhances the regulatory authority of the officers as they perform their street-level "security." In practice, the officers' regulatory and rent-seeking activities put rural Chinese and African migrants directly in the eye of danger, unrest, and undue exclusion. In other words, migrant bosses' market engagements lead them to become the primary targets of economic regulation and rampant extraction by officers of the *shenfen* economy. In this way, brutality, as Charmaine Chua (2020) argues, is not an exception but a core component of normalized, state-sanctioned violence, even when it involves nonstate actors and market-based activities.[2]

As a case in point, in Zhaocun urban village, where Mrs. Wong lived and worked, rural Chinese migrants were similarly targets of violence, derision, and criminalization. Later on the day on which Sylvianne and I had lunch, after we parted ways, I took the bus to the Wongs' *jiagongchang* household workshop. As I descended from the bus and approached the pedestrian bridge that was situated by the front entrance of the urban village, I saw several men careening down the bridge, running with their arms flying desperately. The men were migrant street vendors (*zou gui*) who were attempting to escape from the patrolling *chengguan* officers (uniformed officers hired by the municipal government exclusively to detain street vendors, hawkers, and pedicab drivers). The officers had apparently made a surprise visit to the bridge that day with the primary aim of capturing these vendors. About five or six street vendors had fled the scene, leaving a bundle of plastic iPhone covers and cases wrapped in a purple cotton mattress blanket.

As I approached the scene of the chase, I saw a handful of transparent iPhone screen covers scattered on the ground. A young man desperately crouched on the wet concrete picking up every piece of plastic. In front of the crouching man stood about five or six *chengguan* officers dressed in green, heavily padded jackets and matching pants with black lace-up military boots. They stood around in a semi-circle with feet shoulder-width apart, directing another officer holding a video camera to document the scene of events. With voices of authority, the officers discussed in Cantonese the best position for the cameraman to stand in so that he could capture the most accurate shot. I overheard one officer say to another, "Here, here. Take a shot from here." A burly, bearded officer picked up the purple bundle and hugged it like a bear with both hands, while slowly sauntering with a group of officers back to their van that was parked in front of the neighborhood gates by the village entrance. Two officers diverted from the large group that was returning to the parked van. One of them turned around and walked underneath the bridge in search of more street vendors.

While I observed the scene, I noticed how spectators had gathered at a distance. They were gripped by discomfort and fear, shocked by the violence that could potentially ensue when the *chengguan* carried out their campaign to forcibly drive out the vendors. Some observers tried to disrupt the tense atmosphere by pretending to go about their day, undeterred from their ordinary activities. Others speculated that the *chengguan* officers resold these goods back to the very same migrants from whom they had just confiscated them. The vendors who were able to escape remained on the other side of the bridge, standing by the sidelines with an uncomfortable smile, probably relieved that they had been able to escape the officers this time. I briefly followed the two officers who walked underneath the bridge. It was not long before the guards turned around empty-handed and slowly walked back to the van to rejoin the other officers.

Brutality in Guangzhou's *shenfen* economy is intimately tied to market exchange across the fast fashion supply chains via the tactics of shadowing and surveillance. I thus focus on the shadowing of migrants' market activities in Guangzhou's urban villages to ask the following questions: How do the everyday operations of fast fashion supply chains determine the kinds of policing and economic regulation that emerge in the urban villages? How do migrant bosses confront these embodied forms of street-level policing and economic regulation? How do these regulatory constraints determine migrants' gendered and racialized experiences of bosshood?

Rather than establishing clear and consistent definitions of legality and illegality in the urban villages, the municipal government and its arms of law enforcement establish their legitimacy through the wholesale criminalization of rural and African migrants, a practice based on the assumption that these populations are backward, uneducated, and uncivil (*bu wenming*). For urban residents who claim rightful inclusion in the cities but who remain far removed from these migrant communities, scenes of rural migrants, hidden or sequestered within the dark and shabby apartment buildings of Guangzhou's urban villages, conjure the belief that these undocumented populations feed into the world of criminality and low-wage labor. State-sponsored media often tell stories of murder, hit-and-run accidents, and drug use. As Guangzhi Huang (2019, 2020) describes in his research on policing in Guangzhou's urban villages, the Yuexi District government released a 2015 video celebrating the "clean-up" campaign of Xiaobei, Sanyuanli, and the surrounding Dengfeng urban villages. This video described "illegal peddling and chaotic informal market" activities as social problems that plagued the community prior to the state campaigns (Huang 2020: 155). These popular images and narratives magnify and reinforce people's negative perceptions of urban villages and of the migrant populations who live there. These popular discourses justify the exploitative and extortive practices of regulating migrant bosshood by state and nonstate actors.

Such exclusionary tactics challenge the conception of the state, including its mechanisms of regulation and surveillance across the transnational supply chains, as a coherent and top-down entity that is all-encompassing and unchanging in its practices, serving to constrain market transaction and exchange (Mitchell 1991). Instead, the mechanisms and force of the regulatory *shenfen* economy are constructed from the ground up—namely through intimate, face-to-face encounters that cross the boundaries of legality and illegality—as well as through fear and extortion. Indeed, migrants' experiences of surveillance and extortion in the *shenfen* economy show how discourses of criminalization do the work of the state in regulating and extracting profits from bosses' everyday market exchanges across the fast fashion supply chains. While some ethnographic studies have discussed at length the violent and extortive practices of police agents in China (Dutton 1998; Solinger 1999; L. Zhang 2002; Alexander and Chan 2004; Han 2010; G. Huang 2019), these works tend to assume that the logics of the market and the state are separate. By contrast, I shed light on the racialized extractive and regulatory practices that take place aligned with the vicissitudes of fast fashion production and market exchange, which produce regulatory effects that in turn shape the everyday rhythms of migratory life and entrepreneurial enterprise in Guangzhou's urban villages.

Within the *shenfen* economy, nonstate officers encounter migrant bosses who labor across the fast fashion supply chains. Officers intimately shadow migrants' market activities, extracting rents and fees from them. In the course of the officers' surveillance activities, they draw upon discourses of discrimination and criminalization in order to demonstrate to Chinese urban citizens that local authorities promote economic trade and investment through the protection of private property (Mitchell 1991). These activities operate squarely upon the market rhythms via the logics of evaluating quality, legitimacy, and authenticity. In this way, exclusionary valuations based on hierarchies of quality and legality are critical in making supply chains of fast fashion work.

REGULATION IN THE *SHENFEN* ECONOMY

Private, nonstate officers in the *shenfen* economy draw their regulatory authority from the municipal police force in the name of public security, even though they operate separately from them. Amid the rhythms of economic activity in the urban villages, armies of officers dressed in assorted police and military uniforms regularly patrol the streets of Zhaocun and Xiaobei. These security officers across Guangzhou and other major cities in China are the primary agents of migration control by the state, making them one of the most powerful arms of regulation and enforcement (Han 2010).[3] By *security officers* (both public and private), I am referring to a range of state and nonstate agents who straddle the public and private realms of market exchange, along with the regulatory activities they exercise. They assume the authority (whether state-sanctioned or not) to regulate the everyday mobility and work lives of domestic and transnational migrants. Unlike the city police whose authority stems directly from the municipal government, private security officers are hired by third parties, who in turn work for landlords, real estate developers, and business owners; yet these officers draw their authority from the public police force. As an administrative organ, private security officers in the *shenfen economy*, retain the power to detain people and to check anyone's ID cards and paperwork at any time (Han 2010).[4] As such, the *shenfen* economy demonstrates the regulatory powers of the Guangzhou city police (Han 2010).[5] By doing so, these security officers perform a continuum of violence work across fast fashion supply chains that intersect private and public realms (Seigel 2018). Their extortive and exploitative practices feed into a secondary economy of cash-based extraction based on the collections of various fees and fines.[6]

Amid the ambiguity of authority in governance and property ownership, the *shenfen* economy operates alongside Guangzhou's official police force, paradoxically through the lack of consistency, if not through the outright absence, of police enforcement. Although the presence of private officers in the *shenfen* economy remains an everyday fixture in the urban villages, labor codes, electric and fire safety, waste management, and counterfeiting practices remain largely unenforced. Instead, security officers construct their authority by performing the *threat* of enforcement, oftentimes through intimidation, but *without the actual act* of enforcement. In other words, the uniformed security officers in the *shenfen* economy construct their power through the withholding of their authority, while turning a blind eye to many of the economic activities that take place across the fast fashion supply chains. The extraction of rent and fees along the supply chains serve as sources of profit accumulation for the security officers and the landlords who hire them.

Along the perimeter of the urban villages, for instance, the *chengguan* officers, private security guards, and other uniformed officers pursue migrants and constrain their activities by patrolling the traffic of goods, vehicles, people, and money that animate the fast fashion supply chains here. The patrolling of traffic into and out of Zhaocun, for example, has intensified since 2016, when police officers stepped up their efforts to crack down on street vending and other semilegal activities in the urban village. They have set up a checkpoint station where, at various times of the day, they restrict certain motorbikes and vehicles from entering the village. Though their presence creates a spectacle of authority and intimidation, migrants and visitors (including me) in the urban villages are frequently confused by the source of their power and legitimacy. Some are privately contracted by village landlords, while others report to the street, district, or municipal governments.

The administrative forms of regulation and governance characteristic of the *shenfen* economy articulate with the day-to-day functioning of fast fashion supply chains in the urban villages, where identification documents become mechanisms of gatekeeping and fee extraction. The fragmented, cellular, and semiformal organization of the fast fashion supply chains enable, if not actively foster, a shadow economy of semilegal rent-seeking and fee-collecting activities that exploit the vulnerable conditions of migrant workers while further intimidating them into complicity. While migrants (documented and undocumented) float into and out of the urban villages earning piecework wages, the *jiagongchangs* remain situated in the densely and haphazardly constructed apartment buildings that are owned by Cantonese peasant landlords. Rents in the urban villages are relatively inexpensive, drawing migrants into these working-class neighborhoods when jobs are available, while forcing them to leave when employment becomes scarce or when factories close. The small-scale and informal characteristics of just-in-time mass manufacture facilitate the fluid and temporary conditions of labor and production across the supply chains.

This organization of low-cost manufacturing articulates with the everyday business of fee collection in Guangzhou. Since the beginning of market reforms in the late 1970s, the responsibility of enforcing criminal laws and public safety devolved to local state agencies and bureaus. To this end, the central state established a system of monetary incentives for district- and street-level police force to demonstrate its authority over migrant populations. In this system, the police officers must meet daily quotas, which are calculated by various statistical formulas for the minimum number of arrests made and fines levied in a day. Promotions of individual officers by rank are given based on regular performance evaluations. Moreover, budgets for an entire police force, per station and per department—and which are usually insufficient—are determined based on performance and evaluation by the municipal government (G. Huang

2019). The decentralized system of promotion and monetary compensation statistically calculated by the number of arrests made and raids conducted by the police fosters an economy of illicit fee extraction wholly sanctioned by the public and by the state. This is particularly evident in the urban villages, where the jurisdictional boundaries between what is enforceable and unenforceable by the municipal government is spatially ambiguous and varies according to the negotiations with specific village collectives.

As the socioeconomic divides in infrastructure and economic development continue to drive a wedge between urban cores and urban villages, the cash-based policing of migratory, low-waged labor remains tolerated, if not glorified, by urban residents and by the municipal government. Since residents outside the urban villages assume that the police and private security officers keep neighborhoods safe and secure for the benefit of migrant communities, few publicly acknowledge or intervene in the predatory tactics of the uniformed men. But private officers and even state-hired police officers are rumored to have pocketed handsome sums of money through bribes, fees, and other forms of extortion. In one instance, I was indulging in a bowl of noodle soup when a group of restaurant employees watched a traffic officer catch a man who was biking in the opposite direction along a narrow lane. The officer took him to a dark corner in a parking lot and stealthily accepted what looked from a distance to be a roll of cash. The employees responded in an uproar, crying out how abusive and corrupt the police were. One employee even speculated that the man was only in costume and was not a legitimate police officer.

AFFECTIVE CONTROL

Migrants' encounters with the officers are not only administrative and procedural but also intimate and laden with fear and intimidation. The bodily presence of uniformed officers on the streets accentuates the culture of predation and extraction that pervades the urban villages by facilitating a secondary economy of fee collection and rent-seeking practices that operates alongside the fast fashion supply chains. These figures of authority represent unyielding, heavy-handed punishment and suppression of crime (G. Huang 2019). Across the fast fashion supply chains, state effects manifest via affective dimensions of fear and intimidation as consequences of the officers' indiscriminate and unpredictable enforcement of power and authority. For example, newly arrived migrants often feel fearful, frustrated, and confused by the culture of surveillance and predation that they encounter. This culture of fear and intimidation that animates the everyday rhythms of migrant bosshood becomes particularly apparent when inspections and clean-up campaigns entail face-to-face encounters. Confrontations with the police become particularly heated when police violence emerges across a spectrum of physical, epistemic, psychic, and economic injury (Seigel 2018). These effects are meant to lend coherence to the public image of the Chinese state (Mitchell 1999).

In most cases, the aggressive profiling of rural migrants becomes normalized as a routine aspect of regulation and surveillance such that the boundaries of violence and the everyday become ambiguous and difficult to decipher. In more heated and potentially violent situations that require negotiation with the officers, some African migrants turn for assistance to their Chinese-speaking friends or to members of their respective national and religious associations in Xiaobei. Chinese and African migrants who are apprehended by the police and other uniformed officers try to defuse explosive situations by relying on the mercy of the officers to let them go. In these situations, officers reserve the authority to indiscriminately decide whom to let go, when, and under what conditions. Migrants may intimidate, argue back, cry, or beg. Such cases highlight the highly affective and precarious conditions under which these migrants must work and live.

One such encounter occurred in the Wongs' factory when two female officers who appeared to be serving the neighborhood or street committee arrived with pens and writing boards in their hands. They were dressed in blue uniforms with arm badges and matching hats, indicating their membership to a particular authority. From the demeanor of Mrs. Wong and these two female officers, I could tell that the three of them had had previous encounters and that there was residual tension among them. When they approached Mrs. Wong at the front table, one of the women immediately pulled out her writing board and started to scribble something on couple receipts. Meanwhile, they announced their arrival by demanding water fees for the year. Mrs. Wong immediately pulled out some cash from her pants pocket and began slowly tugging at a 100 RMB bill, loosening it from her hand. "Two hundred," the officer demanded. "This time, 100 RMB is not enough. If you need money, take it from your workers." Mrs. Wong then reluctantly gave the officers another 100 RMB.

Once the officers saw that Mrs. Wong complied with their demands, they started to glow about the Wongs' cooking, particularly the sticky rice (*zongzi*) from their hometown. When the officers recognized Mrs. Wong's unfriendly attitude toward them, they eventually backed off and directed their gaze toward the dresses that were lying on the front worktable. "Very pretty," one of the women said to me. Mrs. Wong then immediately explained to them that the goods did not belong to me, and that I was just a student studying at a nearby university. "Oh, I see," the officer slyly answered. She then clarified my relationship with Mrs. Wong by stating, "You're a friend of Mrs. Wong and you're only here to help out." As the officer stepped back, ready to depart, her verbal clarification reminded us that she was keeping an eye on who was coming into and out of the factory and the wider neighborhood.

Surprisingly, Mrs. Wong kept her composure, which stood in stark contrast from her displays of fear and nervousness when other officers had visited the workshop. Perhaps the reason was that these two officers were women, which would underscore the subtle ways in which power materialized through gendered face-to-face encounters. The police eventually left without inspecting the workers' documents. Mrs. Wong then returned to her station and resumed her work at the sewing machine. A temporary wage worker, Ms. Ma, then criticized Mrs. Wong for being too honest and for revealing too much information to the authorities. She stated, "You should have told them that only you lived there and left it at that." Mrs. Wong kept her gaze downward at her sewing and smiled in embarrassment. She quietly mumbled, "Oh, it's no big deal." Interestingly, Mr. Wong remained silent throughout the entire encounter, leaving Mrs. Wong to manage the situation. Shortly after the authorities left the factory, all of us resumed our work as though nothing had happened.

I inquired about the subtle contrast in Mrs. Wong's demeanor later in the afternoon when we paused to have dinner. I naively asked Mrs. Wong why she and the officers appeared to have a tense relationship, even though Mrs. Wong kept her composure in her interactions with them. I recalled times when she would engage in a playful banter with other female officers by sharing neighborhood gossip or exchanging delightful snacks from their respective hometowns. Mrs. Wong explained that it was nearly impossible to tell which officers in the neighborhood worked for whom. Sometimes, the directives from one officer, such as the placement of a garbage can or the display of a business license, directly contradicted another officer's orders. "You have to read the person," she explained. "Some are empathetic, and others are not." Mrs. Wong then elaborated that some confrontations required her to talk back and to resist, while at other times, confrontations demanded that the Wongs submit quietly to their orders.

Even though her explanation seemed reasonable to me at that time—since she had many encounters with officers in the urban villages in the past—I was convinced that Mrs. Wong's tactic of reading officers offered no guarantee of justice or protection if a potentially violent or extortive situation arose. As I witnessed in other parts of the urban village, officers could shut down a migrant business and cut off critical sources of livelihood at any time. Although the Wongs and their migrant employees generally did not allow the atmosphere of fear or intimidation to encroach upon the everyday rhythms of their family and work lives in the urban village, migrants' continual exposure to potential harassment, extortion, and violence by the police and other security officers highlighted the risks and structural vulnerabilities they must take up to forge a livelihood in the urban villages.

CATCH AND RELEASE: RACIALIZATION AND CRIMINALIZATION OF AFRICANS AS "COUNTERFEITERS"

"See, these Chinese! I don't understand them. They see you and they think that you are working as a spy for me. That's the kind of thing that goes on around here. I just don't understand it!" cried Sylvianne. She, Nancy, and I were lounging in her clothing boutique when a young Chinese man from across the hall of the mall peeped in through the dusty glass doors to watch us. Nancy was a thirty-five-year-old trader from the Congo. She and her husband were in Guangzhou to purchase fashion and other small commodities to resell in their home country. As soon as Sylvianne turned her head away from the door, the young Chinese man vanished from sight. I soon realized that he was curious about me, an unfamiliar Chinese visitor who appeared to be on good terms with Sylvianne. As soon as we turned our heads in his direction again, we caught the mysterious man stealing glances at us. He dodged our line of sight once more and returned to his shop. With an exasperated sigh, Sylvianne explained that her experiences with entrepreneurship in China led her to become knowledgeable about various acts of surveillance and competition among the participants in Guangzhou's business circles. Such experiences, she admitted, deepened the migrant community's sense of alienation as foreigners attempting to eke out a livelihood in China.

At the time of our meeting, Sylvianne had been residing in Guangzhou for five years. In 2011, she arrived in Guangzhou, following in the footsteps of her father and cousins. Her father, the patriarch of a large transnational family whose kin networks extended from Senegal to China and Spain, operated a trading and logistics company in Xiaobei's Zhongnan building; his company facilitated the export of Chinese-made commodities to France, Spain, Nigeria, the Congo, and Senegal. These commodities included foodstuffs, motorcycles, automobiles, elevators, household appliances, and clothing. The father-daughter duo, along with several of Sylvianne's male cousins, had shared living and office quarters in Guangzhou so that they could collectively oversee the daily operations of the family business.

Despite their entrepreneurial successes in Xiaobei and Sanyuanli, racism remains an everyday fact of life for migrant traders like Sylvianne and her family members (Cheng 2011; Castillo 2016, 2018, 2020; Huynh 2015; Lan 2015, 2016b; Mathews et al. 2015; Wilczak 2018). Widespread ambivalence toward Black populations in China as well as outright anti-Black discrimination draw variously from histories of disparaging rural populations from the dynastic period to the present day, as well as from encounters with Western colonialism, diplomatic and student exchanges during the Maoist period, and China's rise as a player in the global capitalist economy (Lan 2016b; G. Huang 2020).[7] Anthropologists and social scientists who conducted extensive fieldwork in Xiaobei before the COVID-19 pandemic interviewed African migrants in Xiaobei who had been barred from getting onto taxi cabs or entering restaurants based on their skin color (Lan 2016b; Castillo 2016, 2020). Other African migrants in Xiaobei also complained that Chinese residents would avoid sitting next to them on public buses (Castillo 2020b). During my research, I encountered Chinese landlords who refused to rent their apartments to African migrants. Africans, more than any other foreign group in China, are likely to be singled out for passport and identification inspection (Lan 2016b). For them, racial tensions are experienced and felt through the day-to-day exchanges that take place across the fast fashion supply chains in Guangzhou. Africans become targets of evaluation based on spectrums of legitimacy and criminality, which are cast across the discursive hierarchies of commodity price and quality.[8]

As market intermediaries, migrant entrepreneurs who labor across the supply chains for fast fashion in Guangzhou, including African migrants in this case, are often looked upon with ambivalence and suspicion. The *shenfen* economy marks African migrant bosses as targets for social exclusion and unbridled extraction. The racial criminalization of migrants lends the state the appearance of being a coherent, legitimate, and stable entity that offers protection to urbanized citizens from the fluctuations of the market as well as from the dangers of unruly migrant delinquents (Mitchell 1991).

The racialization of African migrant bosses serves to justify the extractive and exploitative tactics upon which the state and peasant landlords rely to regulate the flows of money, migrants, and commodities into and out of the urban villages. As Shanshan Lan (2016a, 300) describes—citing Michael Omni and Howard Winant (1994)—racialization involves the projection of "racial meaning to a previously racially unclassified relationship, social practice, or group." In the case of Africans in Xiaobei, the ranking, evaluation, and regulation of these migrants demonstrate the ways in which categories of race, particularly within the context of supply chain capitalism, follow hierarchies of quality, value, and profitability. In turn, these racialized and market-based dynamics lend legitimacy and coherence to the Chinese state. They foster an economy of unbridled fee collection and an atmosphere of prevailing fear and uncertainty for both Africans and Chinese groups.

As such, powerful agents of the state derive their authority precisely through these seemingly oppositional dynamics. The figure of the migrant boss (*laoban*) converges uneasily with the aspirations of small-scale migrant entrepreneurs to produce a chain of exploitation and extraction. More specifically, the figure of the migrant boss serves to project the aura of the state (as well as the exercise of its authority) as a stabilizing and protective force against the incoherence and unpredictability of the supply chains. Place-based ambiguities and disputes over property relations among peasant landlords and the municipal government result in a web of extortive relations between the police and migrant bosses. The propping up of real estate value by the *tu er dai* landlords through the wholesale criminalization of the "counterfeit" and those who trade with them intensifies the racialized and gendered policing of private homes, residential living rooms, wholesale markets, stalls, and other infrastructures of fast fashion.

While Shanshan Lan (2016b) cogently argues that racial ideologies as well as the racialization of African migrants in Guangzhou are diverse and uneven based on overlapping histories of Western colonialism, Sino-African relations, and China's intensified participation in the global capitalist economy, I argue that the evaluation and the cultural meanings of Blackness as race must be seen as intersections of the broader structural dynamics of capitalist collaboration and competition, commodity fetishism, market evaluation, and migrant bosshood that materialize on the ground via everyday transactions and exchanges across the supply chains.[9]

For instance, in Guangzhou, many Chinese residents (both local and migrant populations) project an aura of criminality and danger onto the

African and Middle Eastern migrants, who are commonly depicted as drug dealers, users, and illegal money lenders (Haugen 2012; Lan 2016b; Castillo 2020b; G. Huang 2020).[10] Chinese residents consequently deride the wealth that African migrants make by delegitimizing their entrepreneurial activities and by excluding them from property rentals and ownership. The Chinese describe commodities sold in Xiaobei and Sanyuanli as fakes with the lowest prices and the lowest quality, appropriate only for underdeveloped African markets. Profits made in Xiaobei and Sanyuanli are mistakenly assumed to be minimal, even though local Guangzhou residents (both Chinese and Africans) have witnessed the enormous wealth that has been generated there. Other residents refuse to rent their apartments and commercial spaces to African migrants. By delegitimizing the economic activities of African migrants, landlords and the officers they hire maintain their local authority and pursue their own profit-seeking, regulatory interests vis-à-vis the central state. This racialized ranking of people and commodities creates a culture of illegitimacy and illegality among African migrant populations based solely on discursive constructions of market value, demonstrating "the legal production of African illegality" (Lan 2015, 290).

Mass campaigns that racialize and criminalize African migrants intensify the race-based tensions that brew under the surface of everyday life in China. As G. Huang (2020) argues, Blackness operates as a form of leverage exercised by the Guangzhou municipal government in exerting social control and regulation over its transnational migrant population, often conflating Blackness with rurality. In this way, African and Chinese rural migrants become subject to intensified surveillance and scrutiny. Since 2008, the local Public Security Bureau in Xiaobei has organized mass campaigns known as *san fei*, or "triple illegal," explicitly targeting African migrants attempting to enter, stay, and work in China without appropriate documents (Lan 2015; Wilczak 2018; G. Huang 2019). This campaign was part of the Guangdong Act passed by the provincial government of Guangdong to expand the authority of the local police in regulating the mobility and activities of foreign migrants in an attempt to curb their population expansion and economic influence (Lan 2015; Wilczak 2018). The campaign entails street-level and door-to-door inspections as well as stop-and-frisk measures by the district police to fine or arrest African migrants who do not possess proper documents and identification (Lan 2015; Wilczak 2018). Uniformed Chinese officials routinely walk along the streets of Xiaobei and Sanyuanli to surveil the neighborhood. Officers enter restaurants, private homes, and street corners unannounced and demand to be shown documentation of migrants' statuses and business licenses. If migrants are found without valid identification and paperwork, which is a frequent occurrence, officers levy hefty fines, close their businesses, arrest, and detain them. These state-endorsed, top-down movements promote predatory forms of surveillance and policing that color the everyday lives of Africans in Xiaobei and Sanyuanli.

While much is known about the brutal policing and unyielding crackdown on African migrants in Guangzhou, we know less about how relative inconsistency of law enforcement by the district or street-level police intensifies African migrants' conditions of ambivalence and vulnerability. The day-to-day forms of economic regulation and law enforcement outside of mass campaigns by the municipal state have been less frequently documented. The power of the police, as Seigel (2018) asserts, lies not in its overt presence but rather in its latency and potentiality. Violence may not necessarily materialize in every police encounter, yet urban citizens often unquestionably lend the police legitimacy and authority even in its absence and inconsistency. Indeed, the quasi-legal activities that enable migrant bosshood to flourish emerge in the gaps laid by police who turn a blind eye to them (Weller 2012). In other words, the authority of the police stems not only from enforcement of the law but also from its reservation of authority—even if it decides *not* to wield its power.

At the time of my research, officers who patrolled the streets at the neighborhood or district level frequently turned a blind eye to illegal or semilegal activities, such as sex work, street vending, or under-the-table money-lending, which left an ambiguous boundary between the licit and the illicit (Lan 2015). For example, after an afternoon of closure, restaurants and vendors are usually allowed to resume business again until the next inspection is announced. For those familiar with these tactics of catch and release, African migrants and Chinese store owners speculate that village landlords and government officials on the street or district level must receive handsome fees or favorable bribes, though few migrants know this with absolute certainty.[11]

Normally between the hours of 2 p.m. and 5 p.m., for example, West African street hawkers fill the streets that line the perimeter of a large wholesale market for export clothing, hoping to sell copied fashions, including Nike sneakers, Gucci belts, Louis Vuitton bags, and Dolce & Gabbana wallets. These hawkers carefully lay out their fashions along the streets or on the front hoods of parked cars for passersby to visually browse through the inventory before they are lured into buying the goods. Whenever officers arrive unexpectedly, the hawkers run, sometimes forfeiting their goods, and sometimes setting up shop at another street corner. Informal sellers frequently sacrifice one day's worth of business in order pay off fines, bribes, and other forms of punishment from the police. After the police officers depart, however, the hawkers immediately return and resume their street businesses for the remaining hours of the day. With full knowledge of these underground market activities, the police merely turn a blind eye to them; yet they have the capacity to forcibly suppress them at any time.

Exchanges of fast fashion among West African migrants in Xiaobei and Sanyuanli's *shenfen* economy take place within the discursive gaps between the law, its enforcement, and the culture of criminality that surround it. Since urban villages themselves are spaces of administrative and legal ambiguity, local authorities are not necessarily interested in suppressing the growth of economic trade and exchange. After all, gray market activities bring in cash to village landlords and other local authorities. Rather, local police forces have a vested interest in *regulating* the flow of migrants, goods, and money across the blurred boundaries between the legal and the illegal; thus, local law enforcement attempts to control transnational migrants' access to markets and capital. The inspection of IDs, potential counterfeits, and licenses lends legitimacy to the uniformed officers who decide whether to enforce the law at any given moment. Local authorities thereby direct the volume of commodities and money flowing through the system, often intervening via taxation and bribery, but not outright stopping these flows.

By permitting the economic exchanges of West African and Chinese migrant bosses to flourish in the urban villages, on the one hand, while regulating the conditions and terms on which they operate, on the other, landlords and the police implicitly endorse a shadow economy of small-scale entrepreneurship among migrants in the urban villages. They do so to oversee the migrants' movements and extract capital from them. Such forms of erratic and indirect regulation across the municipal, district, and street levels of governance render certain forms of licit economic practices illegal so that the state can maintain its exercise of authority, the display of which emerges at the point of cross-cultural encounter (Roitman 2005). Maintaining conditions of illegality establishes and authenticates the exercise of power by the state over migrants' economic relations and forms of wealth.

Moreover, local Chinese residents falsely assume that the fashion goods that Africans buy in Xiaobei and Sanyuanli and resell in export markets are illegitimate or outright illegal. Wholesale markets that cater to African traders are commonly assumed, by industry participants, to sell the "real fakes," or cheap, low-quality clothing, bags, shoes, and other accessories that are constructed using poor production techniques (*shou gong*) and made with shoddy material.[12] In these wholesale markets, Chinese sellers take customers to back-alley boutiques and stalls hidden behind curtains or tucked away in cellars or other dark corners of the building. Other sellers will publicly display bags and other leather goods in open air stalls but will keep tags and logos unattached so that they can pass as so-called original products. Urban residents frequently associate these clandestine practices and low-quality counterfeits with crime and low-quality people (Wilczak 2018). Based on these assumptions, urban residents justify the criminalization and policing of West African migrants. In this way, the racialization and criminalization of African traders do the work that local enforcement agencies alone cannot do; that is, law enforcement agencies reserve the discretionary right to exercise wholesale authority over these populations without having to expend the necessary legal authority, finances, and manpower to do so.

The race-based criminalization of African migrants thus authenticates the power of local authorities to constrain, turn a blind eye to, or even to collaborate in illegal or extralegal activities at their discretion. This is achieved through the delegitimization of migrants' accumulative practices via discourses of counterfeit goods. In the West African communities in Guangzhou, state effect—that is, the construction of the state as a coherent entity—operates precisely through the everyday encounters and exchanges that take place in the fast fashion markets (Mitchell 1999). The everyday rhythms of fast fashion enable local police forces to maintain discretionary powers to enforce the boundaries of legality and illegality at their discretion. Along these lines, migrant bosshood, fast fashion, and the regulation of migrant business activities are made possible precisely by the blurring of boundaries between legality and illegality as they manifest through day-to-day encounters.

REGULATION VIA QUALITY/*SUZHI* DISCOURSE

Regulation and surveillance in the *shenfen* economy are also enacted through the discursive hierarchies of race and human quality (*suzhi*), which operate as powerful regulatory devices along the fast fashion supply chains. The *shenfen* economy and fast fashion supply chains thus converge via discourses of quality; that is, commodity quality and human quality converge to further criminalize domestic and transnational migrants, while making their status as the so-called floating population (*liudong renkou*) even more vulnerable to extraction and exploitation. By reflecting on the ways in which migrant bosses, including Sylvianne and Mrs. Wong, criticize the exclusions they face as small-scale migrant entrepreneurs, my analysis captures migrants' senses of ambivalence toward bosshood as they confront challenges to their attempts to accumulate capital.

Like Guangzhou's *san fei* (triple illegal) campaign that targets African migrants, rural Chinese migrants are also singled out as *san fei* or *san wu* (the three withouts), those without ID, without a temporary residence permit, and without employment (Han 2010; G. Huang 2020).[13] The *hukou* household registration system institutionalizes rural migrants' displacement by permanently marking their presence in the cities as illegal and temporary (Solinger 1999; L. Zhang 2002; Florence 2006; Yan 2008; Han 2010). Discourses of danger and uncivility (*bu wenming*) target members of the floating population, leaving them vulnerable to various forms of discrimination, policing, and street violence.[14] A walk through an urban village, for example, often entails an encounter with the *chengguan*, who sometimes unexpectedly take over entire streets in order to carry out various confiscations, arrests, and clean-up campaigns. Their presence creates an atmosphere of fear and intimidation, tactics that officers use to regulate and to extort fees from migrants. State effects in this urban village operate through the creation of fear, uncertainty, and potential violence (Mitchell 1999).

In one instance I witnessed, a group of policemen dressed in dark blue uniforms unexpectedly entered the workshop. Unlike the Wongs' previous encounter with the police, the three officers seemed particularly well-mannered, kind, and respectful. The three men appeared to be in their twenties. One of the men passed the gates and entered the factory interior, visually inspecting the surrounding space while asking Mrs. Wong for her identification papers. Mrs. Wong politely obliged, directing Mr. Wong to bring down the paperwork from upstairs. Mr. Wong did so and handed his wife a large brown envelope. Mrs. Wong took out a plastic card with a black-and-white photo of her face (her ID card). She then took out several pages of documents of black and white paper, which might have been the business license.

After leafing through the documents and inspecting the ID card, the young officer asked Mrs. Wong where the couple lived. She replied matter-of-factly that she and her husband lived in the second-floor attic and pointed to the makeshift room in the top corner of the factory. The officer pointed to the unstable cardboard walls surrounding the attic, and commented about the dangers of the steel ladder, the attic walls, and the wiring that hung disorderly along the cement walls. With a slight tone of sternness, he stated, "Well, I'm warning you now. Someone is going to come and point out how unsafe this place is. It normally wouldn't be a problem, but since more than one person lives here, someone will come by and inspect this place." His comment seemed to have implied that another officer would certainly come soon, expose these unsafe conditions, and present them fines.

In response, Mrs. Wong cordially accepted the officer's warnings without any resistance. The young man then proceeded to ask Mrs. Wong about the workers' identification papers, verifying whether they had the proper documentation. Out of concern for the workers, Mrs. Wong assured the officer that they indeed had them, so it would be unnecessary for the workers to pull them out. As I turned my attention from the policemen to the workers on the other side of the factory floor, I noticed that the workers had kept on working in silence, without even glancing at the policemen standing at the front entrance. The possibility that any one of these migrants could have been fined, arrested, or detained by the police compelled the workers to keep their heads down in fear. Their silence conveyed trepidation and uncertainty. I could sense that they wanted to avoid unnecessary confrontation, implicitly acknowledging the power of the police who reserved the right to punish these migrants at their discretion. Luckily, the police left without any further inspection. Yet for the Chinese rural migrants, intimidation, fear, and the possibility of fines and punishment remained latent under the surface of migrant entrepreneurial practices in the urban villages.

Such acts of policing reinforce the prevailing prejudices against African and rural Chinese migrants and are based on discourses of human quality or *suzhi* that are used to justify the ongoing criminalization of these migrants in the urban villages (L. Zhang 2002; Siu 2007; Han 2010; Haugen 2012; Lan 2016b; Wilczak 2018; G. Huang 2020). Like the race-based exclusions that the criminalization of West African migrants seeks to achieve, *suzhi* operates as a discursive mode of moral evaluation and social control by aligning with the principles of commodification and free market capitalism (G. Huang 2020). Though generally undefinable, ideas about human quality exist as a social fact, engendering prescriptive norms and value judgments of *zuo ren*, or being human (Anagnost 2004; Kipnis 2006; Yan 2008). The discourse of *suzhi* mobilizes the language of modernization and economic development by casting the urbanized, middle-class consumer as a figure of capitalist aspiration and desire in contrast to the relatively backward migrant laborer (Anagnost 2004; Kipnis 2006; Yan 2008). In effect, the discourse of *suzhi* privileges cities as the locus of modernity, while signifying the countryside as a wasteland of backwardness (Yan 2008). *Suzhi* discourses thus govern the migration of rural people into Chinese cities by eliciting their desires to become urban citizens.[15]

The ranking and social disciplining of migrant populations based on judgments of *suzhi* becomes visible in the urban villages, where regulatory governance and the politics of capturing migrants' hard-earned profits operate by preying upon migrants' accumulative practices as well as on their physical mobility. *Jiagongchang* become sites of surveillance, and acts of policing unfold along the rhythms of fast fashion exchange. When the garment manufacturing season starts in full swing during late July and early August, the district teems with market activity. In the Wongs' workshop, officers hired by the village landlords come by at different times of day to check migrants' identification papers and to collect sanitation, utility, and other so-called management fees. When clothes begin to pile up along the factory floor and when workers appear particularly busy, Mr. and Mrs. Wong become particularly vulnerable to officers' unexpected demands for payment. By contrast, fewer officers come by during the fashion low season, including the summer months, as well as over Chinese New Year, when most migrants leave Guangzhou and return to their native places. Rather than controlling and subsequently curtailing the district's commercial activities, rent-seeking practices by village leaders aim to funnel or channel migrant entrepreneurs' profits into the coffers of the landlords' corporate lineages.

"MONEY CHANGES PEOPLE!": RESISTANCE AND COUNTER-DISCOURSES IN THE WORLD OF FAST FASHION

The fear and frustration that percolate beneath the African-Chinese supply chains cast a shadow of doubt among the growing numbers of young African women who migrate to China and aspire to become businesswomen in their own right. Many are forced to reassess the social costs and dangers of transnational migration and entrepreneurship.

Nancy's role as a female migrant entrepreneur from the Congo, for example, often left her feeling lonely. Her family business kept her busy, for the most part, and she rarely found the time to socialize. When she did, there were few African women with whom she could relate, since most residents in her neighborhood were men. In fact, Nancy seldom ventured alone beyond her home and her place of business, since experiencing African men's sexualizing gaze when walking through the public areas of Xiaobei often left her feeling vulnerable and unsafe. Aside from men's intrusive stares, Nancy also mentioned occasions when she encountered acts of racism from local Guangzhou residents. Occasionally there were cases of young male African traders in Xiaobei, who were violently beaten to death by the police and robbed by local thieves; this caused feelings of insecurity, anger, and danger among transnational migrants in the area. Consequently, many young African women like Nancy attempted to establish their family and work lives in Guangzhou, while struggling to overcome deep-seated feelings of isolation and vulnerability.

In addition to the gender and racial inequalities migrants encountered in Guangzhou, they also faced everyday pressures of making ends meet and competition with other aspiring young men and women migrants who also sought to realize their dreams of establishing their businesses in Guangzhou. While defining the ethical parameters of entrepreneurship, they worked through the meaning of entrepreneurship as they encountered various acts of jealousy, competition, and exploitation. These experiences enabled migrant entrepreneurs to make sense of and exert control over uncertainties that unfolded as they learned to become foreign entrepreneurs in Guangzhou.

Nancy, for instance, recounted stories of undercutting and cheating among local retail store and factory owners whom she had encountered through her business dealings in Guangzhou. She recalled a time when a family of Chinese store owners next door were arguing viciously over a client. Apparently, a cousin of the store owner operated a competing store in the mall and would assist in the running of her cousin's business from time to time. One day, while her cousin was away from the store, the woman had successfully convinced a foreign client to place a large order of clothing and shoes at her own store rather than at her cousin's shop. Once the cousin became privy to the woman's backhanded dealings, a dramatic argument ensued, leaving their stall neighbors to witness the altercation in discomfort and horror.

Sylvianne held similar feelings of ambivalence toward her life in Guangzhou. She was extremely proud of how successfully she had managed her father's businesses in China. They were engaged in talks with the Senegalese government about shipping dozens of elevators from China to Africa for the government's construction projects. During a recent trip to Europe, she purchased and shipped a Mercedes Benz sedan back to her hometown. Despite her financial successes, she felt that her life remained at a crossroads. Her father had arranged for her to marry an older man who already had two other wives. Even though she had feelings for her fiancée, she loved running her business even more. In Guangzhou, she played the role of a young matriarch to her extended family by providing her cousins with food and shelter while they learned the ropes of the family's transnational business. If she returned to Senegal, she would have to give up much of her personal autonomy and enter the life of her husband's family, along with his wives and children. In leaving China, she would no longer be the business-minded world traveler she had struggled to become. And yet, because of the police harassment she faced on the streets, malls, and even in her home, she increasingly felt that she had no choice but to leave the country. The intensified hostility that she felt from the police and from her market competitors left her feeling that there was no future for her as a transnational entrepreneurial woman.

While such paradoxes and ambivalences of small-scale self-employment and entrepreneurship within unregulated economies across the Global South may be thought of as "relative autonomy" or as "competing desires" (Narotzky and Smith 2006; Millar 2018), Sylvianne's lived experiences of racialized policing and discrimination demonstrate the gendered and class-based limitations that pose structural constraints to transnational and domestic migrants in their efforts to accumulate wealth and other sources of financial security. These constraints are part and parcel of the gatekeeping measures of the *shenfen* economy, within which fast fashion supply chains are critically embedded. More specifically, migrant bosses in Guangzhou face competition for market dominance from state agents and local landlords as well as from other migrant bosses.

Sylvianne recounted a time when a childhood friend had arrived in Guangzhou from Senegal to establish her own women's fashion line. This friend enlisted Sylvianne's help in establishing vital business contacts with local Chinese manufacturers whose products she needed. Sylvianne dutifully introduced her Senegalese friend to a local manufacturer with whom she thought she had good, trusted relations. This local manufacturer produced primarily jeans, which served the needs of Sylvianne's friend perfectly. Upon seeing Sylvianne and her friend one day, the factory owner quoted them a certain price. This price was calculated based on the mutual understanding that Sylvianne, as the intermediary agent, would receive a commission for her introductory services. However, when Sylvianne left the factory, the owner apparently had chased her friend down without Sylvianne's knowledge and offered her a much lower price with the aim of undercutting Sylvianne's intermediary role. Apparently, the factory owner promised to uphold the discounted price if Sylvianne's friend would directly patronize the factory-owner's manufacturing services on a regular basis. Sylvianne had somehow gotten wind of these backhanded deals and had reluctantly ended not only her business partnership with the factory owner but also her friendship with her former childhood acquaintance. While retelling her story, Sylvianne cried out, "I don't know why, but money changes people!"

DISRUPTIVE ENCOUNTERS

For Mr. and Mrs. Wong, the pressures of dealing with the police and other authorities directly impeded their plans to expand their workshop and to accumulate wealth. The couple had planned to extend their informal garment workshop in Guangzhou's garment district by opening a satellite factory inside their newly built five-story house in their hometown of Guigang, in Guangxi Province. Their house was the only property they owned, and it served as an emblem of pride, a testament to the migrant couple's hard work. At that time, their aspiration seemed to have made practical sense. The Wongs could capitalize on the newly built railway system between Guigang and Guangzhou, and Mrs. Wong could finally uphold her gendered obligations as a mother and stay home with her two teenage sons. Since labor costs were lower in Guangxi than those in Guangzhou, the Wongs would maintain their small-scale workshop in Guangzhou, where Mr. Wong would receive production orders from domestic and transnational clients who passed through the garment district. Then, mass manufacture would take place within their home-based factory in Guangxi, where Mrs. Wong would manage and oversee the entire production processes. After the garments were manufactured, the finished products would be delivered overnight via the newly built high-speed train that connected the interior regions of Guangxi to Guangzhou in a matter of three to four hours. The finished garments would be then packaged by Mr. Wong and his employees at their assembly site in Guangzhou before they were sent to their clients. These cross-border linkages of labor, capital, and commodities would be spatially and temporally coordinated by the Wongs to serve the "just-in-time" delivery and export of fast fashion.

The scheduled cycles of cross-border production and delivery worked seamlessly for the first year and a half after the Wongs began their operations in Guangxi. However, in the weeks leading up to my visit with Mrs. Wong in the summer of 2017, several public utility officials asked the Wongs to pay a certain amount in fees for laying electricity cables in their house in Guangxi. She informed me that the utility officials had visited their home and demanded a few hundred to a few thousand RMB here and there. "It's so corrupt over there," Mrs. Wong stated. "In Guangzhou, once they get the electricity line (lai dian xian), they just asked for a few hundred yuan, and that would be it. That's not how they do it over there [Guigang]." At one point, the Wongs maintained they had paid officials up to 20,000 RMB over the course of the two years they had been in operation in Guangxi. "Initially, they asked for only a few hundred yuan to complete job. As soon as they figured out that we were building a house, more and more people came by and demanded various forms of payment from us. Now, I must deal with (gao hao) the bills." As Mrs. Wong explained her dilemma to me, I realized the particularities of how a commercial land or industrial space was governed and managed. She then explained further, "At first, we thought that the intermediary agent who helped us submit our payment was trustworthy, but then the problems [the demands for payment] kept coming back to us." Mrs. Wong thus drew broad comparisons between doing business in Guangzhou and in her native place in Guangxi. Networks of patron-client relationships (presumably between landowners, lessees, and other interested people or third parties) were organized along a place-based division of profits and rents that were collected through the scaling of electricity lines and other forms of infrastructure in and across a particular location.

While the Wongs assumed that hiring workers in Guangxi would save labor costs, they did not anticipate the extra costs of bribes and other fees. To be sure, the movement of labor and infrastructure involved negotiations and compromises that, at times, might hamper the seemingly smooth and seamless movement of people, commodities, and production facilities. Having operation facilities both in Guangdong and Guangxi might have offered them flexibility (since Mr. and Mrs. Wong could move in between these sites), but leaving machines and employees idle imposed an unforeseen cost for the couple. In light of these additional financial demands, Mrs. Wong explained that she could not provide work and pay for her current seven or eight employees in Guangxi. Mrs. Wong simply informed them that she needed to return to Guangzhou without a precise date of return and rehire.

To this day, the factory remains idle and the Wongs' dreams of expansion and accumulation in Guangxi have not come to fruition. Without effective protection in the form of legal assistance, personal connections, and wealth, the Wongs remain vulnerable to the regulatory effects of the *shenfen* economy, as personified by local officials and extra-legal authorities who demand a cut of their potential profits. State agents and extralegal authorities disrupted the Wongs' attempts to accumulate wealth by preying upon their entrepreneurial activities while safeguarding the financial and propertied interests of larger bosses in Guigang.

THE STATE EFFECTS OF FAST FASHION

In the context of fast fashion in Guangzhou, the police force is frequently perceived as an autonomous entity that stands apart from the unrestrained fluctuations of market activity and its attendant flows of migrant laborers, transnational traders, and capital. Migrant bosses, for example, often blame the ups and downs of the global markets for fast fashion for their unsold inventory and subsequent financial losses, while the state is seen as the locus of cohesion and stability. The so-called informal economy serves to reinforce state legitimacy by serving as a source of unsanctioned market exchange via the exclusion and criminalization of the people, commodities, and money that sustain it. As shown throughout this chapter, migrants, counterfeits, and bosses who straddle awkwardly the labor and capital divide are frequently targeted so as to maintain the state-market distinction.

The reinforcement of the state as an independent and cohesive entity as well as an enforcer of protection and legality is done precisely through the representation of unsanctioned informal market activities as unruly, uncivilized, and criminal.[16] These representations of the informal economy enable state agencies and other local authorities to stand apart from the financial and social risks of market participation, while simultaneously serving as predatory regulators by preying upon migrant bosses' economic activities without being accountable to them. In effect, the state attempts to confine and enclose the migratory population by operating according to the logics of mobility and exchange. Much like the rhythms of the market, governance by the state follows the market logics of rationality and cost-effectiveness, where it asserts its carceral authority precisely through its absence. This is evident in the officers' timely arrival in the Wongs' factory when production orders fill up as well as in their presence along the alleyways in Sanyuanli when West African vendors sell their fashion objects informally on the streets. The state, after all, implements institutional mechanisms to protect private property and capital accumulation in the interests of the landholding classes at the expense of migrant groups, while it accumulates its own wealth and power.[17]

Across Guangzhou's fast fashion supply chains, policing, as an exemplary feature of the carceral state, links up with the profit-driven interests of local landholders in the real estate market to leverage their contested claims to profits and jurisdictional authority over mixed-use public and private land. The municipal government's exercise of authority over property relations and market activities emerges precisely along the jurisdictional folds of urban and peri-urban land, where direct governance by the state remains ambiguous and contested. At the same time, its authority critically depends on migrants' shouldering of financial risks and exposure to personal vulnerability, as demonstrated by the regulatory and sexualized gazes that haunted the everyday activities of Sylvianne and Mrs. Wong. Regulatory practices follow the everyday rhythms of migrants' labor and trade, revealing the ways in which the state and nonstate authorities attempt to strike a delicate balance between the sanctioning of market activity (thus profiting from such activity) and the subsequent clamping down of it. The culture of racialized criminalization and the economy of extraction create what Jean and John Comaroff (2006) describe in their study of the burgeoning informal sectors in South Africa as a feature of the postcolonial and neoliberal order: "parallel modes of production and profiteering, sometimes even of governance and taxation, thereby establishing a simulacra of social order" (5).

The intersection between the secondary economy of policing and migrants' engagements with the transnational supply chains of fast fashion thus underscores the constitutive relationship between the ongoing policing of migrants by the state and village landlords via the fast fashion markets. Carceral capitalism, after all, is a race-based and embodied form of accumulation driven by the logics of urban renewal and nationalist development (Rodriguez 2019; Chua 2020). It also operates through the temporal, spatial, and affective dimensions of the fast fashion bosshood. Fast fashion bosshood allows for a spectrum of claim- and profit-making schemes that animate ongoing land disputes, unresolved property relations, and profit-driven law enforcement agencies. It brings the worlds of Sylvianne and Mrs. Wong into the dynamics of ongoing negotiations with the police and other officers, cultivating a spectrum of discourses and practices through which they leverage their claims.

Within the context of state-backed promotions, monetary compensation, and illicit extortion, the criminalization of rural Chinese and African migrants guarantees a handsome return to those who stand to profit from it: namely, village landlords and law enforcement bureaus. As the costs of living in the urban centers continue to rise, strategies of predation and extraction exercised upon the migrant classes intensify, often resulting in violent encounters and even large-scale protests. In 2009, for example, protests within the African community erupted on the streets of Xiaobei and Sanyuanli when a Nigerian man jumped out of a window to his death, trying to escape from the police. Furthermore, in 2012, over one hundred African traders organized public protests after a twenty-six-year-old Nigerian man died in police custody without further investigation (Beech 2012; Branigan 2012; Castillo 2016; Lan 2016b, 2017). In solidarity with the Black Lives Matter movements across the world, African traders went to the streets of Xiaobei again in 2020, when scores of African migrants found themselves homeless after being expelled from hotels, restaurants, and even their own apartments.

In Zhaocun, protests among Chinese rural migrants broke out in 2018, when private police officers stepped up their tactics of confiscating and fining pedicab drivers (who are indispensable to the flows of commodities and people in this garment manufacturing sector), only to resell the bikes back to the original owners. These alarming events illustrate the capacity of rural Chinese and African migrants to mobilize resistance to these heavy-handed policing practices. In its efforts to control the public representation of migrants in Guangzhou, however, the state-controlled media uses these watershed moments to further criminalize these so-called unruly groups as threats to public order, exacerbating the racialized and discriminatory tensions between migrants and local urban citizens.

Migrant bosses' experiences of racialization and criminalization thus demonstrate how the aura of the state materializes across their profit-driven practices of precarious accumulation. To be sure, migrants are exposed to extreme degrees of racial profiling, discrimination, and criminalization due to their status as domestic and transnational migrants. As such, their precarious forms of accumulation cannot be framed along a single, linear trajectory of market expansion, particularly not via rural-to-urban development. It also cannot be described by a single template of market liberalization or upgrading, as migrants attempt to transform their social positions from worker to entrepreneur. Rather, precarious accumulation materializes in uneven, unpredictable, and erratic ways. For these migrant bosses, the accumulation of wealth and financial security remain "patchy" (Tsing 2015), that is, open-ended, provisional, and uncertain. Such patchy forms of accumulation are part and parcel to sustaining the place-based real estate markets, the local police forces and the global supply chains of fast fashion within which they critically intersect. While migrants labor tirelessly to scale their modest manufacturing and labor capabilities to the global supply chains of fast fashion, they search for market niches through which they may find what they perceive as quick and easy money. Yet, as they perform the indispensable work of incorporating post-Maoist transformations of land, migration, and surplus labor into Guangzhou's urban fabric, precarious accumulation exposes migrant bosses to the extortive conditions of their self-enterprise and low-cost labor.

4 Speculative Real Estate and Flexible Appropriation

In March 2014, shortly after the Chinese New Year, a mob of frantic buyers, shopkeepers, and itinerant workers swarmed the area outside the Xi Fang Hang international fashion wholesale market in central Guangzhou. Panicked hordes of shoppers and workers attempted in a mad stampede to flee the building when a violent brawl broke out inside the market, leaving several men stumbling about with streaks of blood dripping from their foreheads. Fearful that a riot had broken out among the crowds, police officers quickly descended upon the scene in their attempts to restore civility and order. Although no one was critically injured and the day-to-day business of garment wholesaling was almost immediately restored, tensions among small-scale business owners, building managers, and real estate speculators escalated in the aftermath of the violent eruption.

Fights like these regularly broke out in the Xi Fang Hang market, and while people speculated about their causes, it was ultimately impossible to determine which rumors were true. A state-sponsored newspaper speculated that the confrontation in March 2014 might have been an act of terrorism, linking the event with public stabbings in the railway stations of Kunming and Guangzhou. For those who regularly visited the market, however, this sensationalized report merely masked the deepening divisions in access to wealth and real estate that characterized this commercial space. Many observers that I spoke to speculated that this confrontation arose among competing bosses who rented out or subleased commercial spaces to migrant wholesalers who operated businesses in the market.[1]

Apparently, a building manager of the Xi Fang Hang market had accused a wholesaler of using a pattern in one of her garments that closely resembled a design trademarked by an internationally recognized luxury brand. The wholesaler disputed this charge, claiming that her garment was an original design. Another wholesaler in the marketplace remarked, "Of course, [the dispute] had to do with money—kickbacks, really. We as wholesalers don't know the types of collusive relationships and business interests that are tied to their monthly collections of rent." This statement referred to kickbacks paid by lessees of the building to landlords and managers for turning a blind eye to the selling of copied fashions. The comment implied there was a web of social relationships that structured the ways in which stalls and commercial spaces within the building were allotted and subleased. For those who regularly visited the market—where disputes over design copying and counterfeiting flared up on a regular basis—this altercation unmasked the deepening divisions in access to wealth and real estate that characterized this commercial space.

As one of the most well-known and long-standing wholesale markets for women's low-cost clothing and accessories in China, Xi Fang Hang stands at a critical intersection of countless fast fashion commodity chains that serve markets across the Middle East, East Asia, South Asia, Africa, and Europe, and Latin America. For most domestic and international visitors, Xi Fang Hang refers to the towering, multistoried building and surrounding shops that operate as one of Guangzhou's wholesale hubs for low-cost fashion garments and accessories. As the site of the Opium War and the historic port of departure along the Maritime Silk Road, Xi Fang Hang symbolizes Guangzhou's legacy of colonial trade while serving as a logistic anchor for the transnational flows of entrepreneurial aspirations, commodities, and capital in the present day.[2]

Yet, despite its reputation for fashion and cosmopolitanism, Xi Fang Hang is notorious among industry insiders for the secondary economy of extortion and extraction that animates the global supply chains for fast fashion. Inside the market, thousands of small-scale migrant entrepreneurs, most of whom are Chinese and South Koreans, find themselves bankrupted by or indebted to so-called big bosses (*da laoban*). These big bosses are landlords, long-standing wholesalers, and building managers, most of whom are of local Cantonese origin. These powerful and wealthy bosses monopolize the property markets in Guangzhou and forecast worldwide market trends while also setting domestic industry standards for the prices and quality of cotton, metal (for zippers and buttons), and other raw materials. More importantly, these bosses coercively manage and collect rent in the building. Amid the chaos of blaring music, eye-catching styles, and pushy stall owners, landlords and building managers carefully schedule and map fee collection and rent-seeking practices throughout the market, governing the ways in which fast fashion commodities are produced and exchanged. Indeed, the differences in access to rental income, transnational consumer markets, and knowledge of future market trends between the wealthier, more established local bosses and the struggling, small-scale migrant entrepreneurs sustain the daily rhythms of this fast fashion market.

While the issues of counterfeiting and kickbacks seemed, at first glance, to be two different and unrelated aspects of the March 2014 fight, I found out, upon closer inspection, that they were in fact inextricably linked. In the weeks following the incident, I visited the market eager to find out what transpired in the aftermath of the bloody brawl. Cantonese-speaking women and men in police uniforms patrolled the numerous stalls and hallways that lined the interior spaces of the market. Some inspectors sat on folding chairs assembled in a tight circle by the front entrance of the lobby, showing a commanding and stern presence. Other uniformed inspectors roamed the floors, designating where shoppers should queue for the elevators, how shopkeepers should arrange their interior lights, and even when young migrant sellers should eat their lunch. Meanwhile, building managers shooed away older female vendors who informally sold homemade snacks to shoppers and sellers in the market. While African migrants in Xiaobei encounter racial profiling and surveillance by the local police, migrant wholesalers in the Xi Fang Hang market face the risks of debt and extortion that stem from property management practices in the market. To negotiate and evade these forms of regulation, migrant wholesalers engage in design-copying and flexible appropriation practices.

This chapter follows the movement of fast fashion commodities from their sites of mass manufacture to the buying and selling of them in the wholesale markets in Guangzhou. It also describes the work of small-scale migrant wholesalers who facilitate these commodity flows. Migrant wholesalers are typically the clients of the migrant factory owners in the *jiagongchang* described in chapter 2. As wholesalers, they occupy a more economically privileged position than factory bosses like the Wongs, yet their status as migrants keeps them excluded from property ownership in Guangzhou, leaving them vulnerable to the speculative fluctuations of the global fast fashion and real estate markets.

The ethnographic analysis in this chapter charts the rhythms of fast fashion exchange among these migrant wholesalers, revealing how the boom-and-bust cycles within Guangzhou's wholesale markets emerge from the intersection of global fast fashion exchange and rampant local real estate speculation. These cycles of fast fashion boom and bust are accompanied by the regulation of wholesaling practices by Cantonese building managers and local wealthy bosses. Competing participants in the city's fast fashion sector—landlords, managers, wealthy wholesalers, migrant bosses, and consumers—converge to speculate on the profits that they can make through the ubiquitous practice of buying low and selling high.

Indeed, frenzied market speculation in fast fashion and real estate development is what makes Guangzhou's wholesale markets for low-cost, just-in-time fashion different from the factories, *jiangongchang*, and other manufacturing nodes along the commodity chain. Even though migrant factory owners in the *jiagongchang* pay attention to the speculative activities of their clients—since these activities determine the conditions of their labor—most of the rampant speculation, along with the windfall of profits and accompanying losses, takes place in the halls of the wholesale markets. Small-scale migrant bosses in these wholesale markets must confront the risky and predatory dynamics of real estate speculation while struggling to catch up to the speedy turnover of fast fashions. The extractive economy of collusion and rent-seeking emerges like a shadow alongside the creative and entrepreneurial practices of fast fashion bosses who seek to escape it. This dual and ongoing dynamic inadvertently intensifies the aura of high stakes and high rewards that fast fashion promises.

The management of private property serves as a conduit for monetary extraction in this predatory "fee" economy. Amid the inflationary and speculative rhythms that animate the wholesale market, how do fast fashion bosses capitalize on the instabilities of the real estate and fast fashion markets? How do the various policing and regulation practices that unfold within the market enable or constrain the bosses' attempts to hedge market risks? In what ways do these attempts further expose market participation to conditions of precarity? How do they resolve the tensions between their constant exposure to potential debt and losses with their desires for entrepreneurial wealth?

Here, rent-seeking activities and fee extraction drive the flexible forms of creative appropriation that undergird Guangzhou's fast fashion markets. To successfully navigate this highly competitive market, fast fashion bosses attempt to hedge the economic risks associated with market competition, economic downturns, and rent/fee hikes—both in the global markets for fast fashion as well as in the local economies of real estate speculation—by engaging in various practices of design-copying and other forms of what I call *flexible appropriation*. Flexible appropriation is an aspect of precarious accumulation, which mobilizes techniques of arbitrage by exploiting differentials in commodity price and quality between divergent markets. Strategies of flexible appropriation include retagging garments, reassembling garment pieces, and "flipping" finished goods (*chao huo*) from one market to another so that wholesalers and other fast fashion bosses can increase their prices and profit margins while evading the timely rhythms of rent collection and fee extraction exercised by landlords and the police.

To be sure, fast fashion as a global industry is predicated on the appropriation or "copying" of couture runway looks to meet consumer demands for low-cost and designer-inspired fashions. Indeed, scholars argue that fashion as an industry and as a creative practice is defined by maintaining the fine line between sameness and difference (W. Benjamin 1969; Taussig 1983; Coombe 1998; Lipovetsky 2002). But what is particular and noteworthy about the migrant wholesaler bosses in the Xi Fang Hang market is that their appropriation practices are not inherent to the everyday functioning of fast fashion. They are strategies that hedge financial risks posed not only by fluctuations in the global fashion markets but also by the rent-seeking and extractive practices characteristic of the local real estate market. Migrant wholesalers engage in fashion forecasts to speculate on the new trends that might bring in a windfall of profits. Some create original designs, while many others borrow, change, or directly copy runway designs and mass-produce them for wholesale at low cost. Many wholesalers, as I further explain below, simultaneously engage in practices of flexible appropriation.

Meanwhile, migrant wholesalers must strategically time the selling of their inventories to dodge the landlords, uniformed officers, and bigger bosses who try to skim off and extract portions of the migrants' profits. If the timing of their speculative wholesaling is off (which unfortunately is often the case), migrant bosses are left to sell overstock or unsold clothing on the street, taking on the risk of further policing and regulation on the streets. Collectively, the speculative strategies by the migrant wholesalers are attempts to engage in, and ultimately to anchor their livelihoods upon, the rhythms and practices of runaway capitalism in these wholesale markets as they attempt to minimize the exploitative effects of the extortion that impedes their accumulative practices.

While many anthropological accounts have extensively examined various forms of design and artistic appropriation, fewer studies have analyzed the diversity of creative practices such as retagging and flipping (or the physical movement of commodities), what I describe as flexible appropriation, which are often conflated with "copying" or "counterfeiting." Scholarly works on design-copying have primarily focused on the links between citationality, authenticity, and fashion. Moreover, these studies have tended to focus on branding and intellectual property rights in the social construction of logos and their counterfeits (Coombe 1998; Vann 2008; Y.-C. Lin 2011; Nakassis 2013; K. Thomas 2009, 2016). Indeed, historically distinct understandings of creativity, originality, and their relationships to copies and fakes characterize various worlds of commodity mass production (Vann 2008; K. Thomas 2016; Y.-C. Lin 2011). In other contexts, as other scholars have highlighted, the ongoing tension or friction between practices of creativity and copying operates as a generative force that yields the ongoing production of "newness" within creative industries such as art, digital media, and fashion (L. Pang 2012; Tsing 2005; Moon 2014).[3]

Specifically, in fashion, the creation of styles must be constantly replaced by the incoming flow of new trends (Mason 2008; English 2013; Moon 2016).[4] Within the logic of intellectual property law, branded commodities such as fashion must constantly be displaced by their reproductions, which are marked by both aesthetic likeness and difference, in order for the cultural categories of authenticity and counterfeit to remain ideologically stable (L. Pang 2012). Likewise, practices of fashion and self-styling underscore the ways in which students and other practitioners within Beijing's burgeoning art schools display their aesthetic fluidity and creativity by dressing and performing stylistic differences while conforming to the rigid structural dynamics of aesthetic and political containment, as manifested in teacher-student relationships, state propaganda, and the global art markets (Chumley 2016). While cultural theorists Laikwan Pang and Lily Chumley point to the widening social inequalities masked by these oppositions, some legal studies experts praise such paradoxes by highlighting the creative and productive energies generated by the ongoing turnover of fashion trends (Raustiala and Sprigman 2006). They argue that design-copying paradoxically benefits the creative capacities of fashion designers and helps to reinforce intellectual property laws governing design practices. Though these analyses insightfully point to the relational

dynamics and contradictions inherent in the notions of the copy, originality, and authenticity, I suggest that these works overlook the wider social
impacts of design-copying upon participants other than consumers, designers, and art practitioners within the wider political economy of transnational supply chains.

Flexible appropriation sheds light on the broader class-based relations
of inequality and precariousness within the context of runaway capitalism in ways that exceed the concepts of individualized creativity and the
linear drive toward innovation among art and design practitioners.[5] In
Guangzhou, commodity chains, including those of fast fashion, articulate
with practices of real estate speculation and place-based entanglements
of bosshood and territorial power among local landlords and migrant entrepreneurs. As fast fashion commodities float into and out of the Xi Fang
Hang market, wholesalers turn to flexible appropriation to hedge their financial stakes against local real estate speculators and commercial management companies who unfairly exploit the demands among competing
wholesalers (both domestic and transnational) to lease commercial spaces
within this building. Local landlords and their managers also extort additional payments and fees by demanding exorbitant rent, drafting unfair
leasing contracts, and colluding with third-party agents to enter secretive
subleasing arrangements. These leasing practices place undue financial
burdens upon migrant wholesalers who must also keep up with the speculative turnover of fast fashion styles and trends. They do so by subverting
the necessity of continuously introducing new trends through novel practices of design appropriation.[6] Flexible appropriation comprises the ways
in which the practices of flipping, retagging, and reassembling garments
are embedded within a broader political economy of migratory regulation
and extraction.

My ethnographic analysis of flexible appropriation in the Xi Fang Hang
market focuses on the speculative dimensions of fast fashion exchange and
the volatile rhythms of property management. I illustrate the novel practices
of creation and appropriation that migrant bosses employ as they strive to
achieve their aspirations for entrepreneurship. Flexible appropriation in
Guangzhou's Xi Fang Hang wholesale market brings together the material
sector of fashion mass manufacturing with the immaterial world of finance
capital—conventionally seen as two separate domains—to underscore the
various forms of speculation in the global fashion and the local real estate
markets as well as the ways in which migrant bosses confront regulation
and extraction. The everyday speculative exchanges of fast fashion critically

link up with the day-to-day speculative rhythms of the real estate market in such a way that the value of real estate becomes inextricably tied to indices of price, quality, and style of a fast fashion commodity.[7]

By engaging in flexible appropriation, fast fashion bosses inadvertently reproduce the socioeconomic hierarchy of debt and extraction they struggle to overcome. They find themselves increasingly vulnerable to debt, extortion, and even violent confrontation. The practices of flexible appropriation enable these migrant bosses to hedge economic risks and manage the inflationary pressures of increasing rent and extortionary demands of management. These practices, however, also lead to disputes among local building managers and competing bosses over copying and ownership, which in turn open opportunities for uniformed officers, managers, and other interested parties to extort money under the guise of copyright protection and brand regulation. The pervasiveness of design-copying among competing bosses in Guangzhou also further accelerates the turnover of fashion commodities in the industry and intensifies the wider pressures of market competition and dwindling profits. As such, despite these creative and entrepreneurial schemes, their speculative practices collectively destabilize the market while exacerbating the unequal access to profits that animate this market.

THE RHYTHMS OF SPECULATIVE LABOR AMONG MIGRANT WHOLESALERS

I begin my ethnographic analysis by describing the labor of migrant wholesalers and how their work differs from that of migrant bosses who run factories and *jiagongchang* at the less profitable nodes of the fast fashion supply chain. The labor of the migrant wholesalers in the Xi Fang Hang market brings together the speculative rhythms of the global fast fashion industry with the risky dynamics of the local real estate economy in Guangzhou. Migrants' speculative engagements with the global fast fashion supply chains demonstrate the enormous financial risks they take on as they continuously chase after the windfall of profits that small-scale entrepreneurship and self-employment promise.

Despite the extreme wealth that wholesalers in the Xi Fang Hang market are rumored to accumulate, small-scale migrant wholesalers often encounter tremendous competition as well as unforgiving amounts of debt as they struggle to chase the latest trends while avoiding the predatory practices of more powerful bosses, uniformed officers, and landlords. Small-scale migrant wholesalers emphasize the speed at which clothes must be translated from the pictorial image to the actual finished garments. The entire process, starting from placing an order with the local manufacturer to choosing the appropriate fabrics and accessories, to mass manufacturing, to final assembly in packages involves only about a two- to three-day turnaround.

During the peak fashion seasons in the fall and the spring, wholesalers, agents/brokers, and manufacturers anticipate future trends for the coming year; they hope to identify profit-making opportunities that will enable them to weather extreme market fluctuations. They begin by flipping through popular fashion magazines geared toward young, female, and mostly urban shoppers. They comb through noted fashion publications including *Vogue China*, *Marie Claire*, *ViVi*, and *Oggi* magazines in order the survey the latest colors, fabrics, patterns, and styles. Fashion forecasting websites and fashion magazines from China and abroad have become the engines of market information that enable various participants along the commodity chains to quickly identify future trends and compete to become the first to capitalize on the latest fads. Online forums enable netizens to exchange questions and advice on garment design and manufacturing. Participants also share their reviews and stories of their experiences with manufacturers throughout the Pearl River Delta region, thus facilitating an open-source platform for the distribution of valuable market information. Informal bookstores offer shelves of pictorial catalogs showcasing ideas for future trends. Many shopkeepers set up tables stacked with fashion magazines along sidewalks in the garment district in Guangzhou. Private companies, which offer online subscription access to the latest couture fashion shows around the world, have also sprung up along the walkways leading to the wholesale markets around the garment district. Thanks to the technological advancements in photography, the internet, and design applications that enable consumers to dictate the terms and the scheduling of the production processes, market participants must constantly anticipate possible losses in profits and entire business ventures in face of extreme market fluctuations.

Aided by modern technologies including the internet, mobile phones, iPhones, and iPads, migrant wholesalers bring selected images with them as they scour the fabric market in Guangzhou's garment district to search for the newest and most popular fabrics, accessories, and raw materials.

They then bring these materials to the garment factories and *jiagongchang* located behind the fabric market. Since migrant owners in the *jiagongchang* do not provide any fabrics or raw materials for the customers, the costs of raw materials are passed from the manufacturers to the migrant wholesalers, who must provide the fabrics and other raw materials themselves. After the mass manufacture of garments is complete, the finished products are then whisked away to the wholesale markets around town for distribution and sale.

Bringing samples to local manufacturers for mass production requires wholesalers to manage costs and make careful assessments of time. While some time is primarily spent scouring through magazines, internet sites, and other market stalls for new clothing styles, buying or picking up fabrics and other raw materials consumes most of their time. Wholesalers must often wait for two to three hours at the fabric market while the materials are retrieved from storage. Time and energy are also expended inspecting the merchandise carefully before wholesalers sell the products on the open market. Oftentimes, inventories must be returned to the manufacturer because the quality of workmanship is poor.

Migrant wholesalers' hectic work schedules attest to the difficulties in sustaining a fledging business in the Xi Fang Hang wholesale market. Usually, these shop owners begin their workdays by arriving at their stall before 6 o'clock in the morning, when market doors open to accommodate clients who must travel long distances to get there. With help from their employees, they manage their stalls until 2 o'clock in the afternoon before they close for the day. Afterward, they head to the garment district in Guangzhou to prepare for the next day's batch of new clothing. There, they circle around the massive fabric markets in search of fabrics, accessories, and other raw materials. They then bring the items via pedicabs to the hundreds of home-based factory workshops nearby. Some may visit more than one factory since these wholesalers oftentimes must juggle more than one style of clothing.

Depending on the production specificities of a particular garment, some of these small-scale wholesalers must cooperate with more than one manufacturer. These manufacturer-client relationships often require time and effort to nurture since wholesalers critically rely on the goodwill of the manufacturers to not steal or sell off their designs and work product to any competitors. Timing particular production orders also requires good faith on the part of the local manufacturers, since deadlines are often rushed and last-minute. In such cases, the manufacturer must mobilize their team of low-wage factory employees to work overtime to meet certain production deadlines for little pay in return. In the evenings, wholesalers search for new designs and prepare for the next business day.

To cover the costs of rent and garment production, most wholesalers moonlight as intermediary brokers or *jobbers* for corporate fashion brands by introducing their clients to local manufacturers in Guangzhou or by handling production orders in their own factories. Migrant wholesalers manage orders for their transnational clients based on the clients' specifications for designs, fabrics, and measurements. Although the incomes earned through their work as jobbers are modest at best, the monies serve as a reliable source of capital that sustains migrant wholesalers' independent labels. Consequently, migrant wholesalers often find themselves juggling the intricate timing of capital inflows and outflows as they wait for their clients' payments, while placing their own production orders and paying off their debts and rents to factory owners, building managers, and other wholesalers. At the same time, migrant wholesalers must come up with new fashion styles in order to generate new sources of income while they push to sell off their current inventory as soon as possible.

Because of the tight and unforgiving cycles of payment and debt, the constant creation and delivery of new styles pose new risks of monetary losses. For migrant wholesalers, the work of choosing garment samples almost always entails a certain degree of risk, because there is no guarantee that a certain style will sell. They must balance between minimizing financial risks by choosing the same or similar styles that are popular and are guaranteed to sell, while marking themselves as unique or slightly different enough to avoid an oversaturation of similar looks and styles. A migrant wholesaler in the Xi Fang Hang market once explained to me that she tends to choose simpler styles for her clients. For her, styles that are too trendy or too flashy are too risky, so they are "not worth making." Leftover inventory that fails to sell in time during the appropriate fashion season is stored in warehouses before it is cleared at discounted prices. Unsold goods that impede the continuous flow of commodities and capital thus cut into the potential investment opportunities of wholesalers. Indeed, one bad investment decision at any time may set off a ripple effect of debt for other market participants along the supply chain. Meanwhile, debts can quickly accumulate, potentially leading small-scale migrant wholesalers down a spiral of debt, delinquency, and bankruptcy.

As migrant wholesalers chase after the newest trends that circulate in the global fashion markets, they must confront unequal to access to capitalist accumulation that is reflected in the spatial organization of the Xi Fang Hang market. The spatial organization of the Xi Fang Hang market critically marks the socioeconomic divisions in fast fashion bosshood that are key to its operation. Each market level indicates the global markets it serves and, consequently, the costs of running a stall there as well as the profits that the fashion objects can generate for the wholesalers based on commodity prices.

On days that I walk through the market, I am often met by throngs of faceless crowds that pack the narrow corridors that line the shop floors. The cramming of stalls and clothing along the first three levels of the market obstructs shoppers' paths. Mounds of loose duct tape, plastic wrapping, and cellophane bags are scattered across the narrow corridors. Thousands of tiny stalls, most of which are only five feet by seven feet and separated by simple steel frames, are jammed beside each other forming narrow rows along massive market floors. Collages of photographs cut out from fashion magazines don the interiors of the cramped stalls. These photos illustrate the innumerable ways in which consumers can appropriate the newest trends by purchasing garments designed to imitate these looks.

A muscular man in his late forties pushes aggressively through the crowds while keeping his eyes cast down to the floor. The enormous plastic bundle resting upon his shoulder keeps him from holding his neck upright. Young migrant women in their early twenties, dressed in the latest outfits, stand eagerly beside their makeshift stalls, brazenly calling out to passersby and beckoning them to explore their array of the most fashionable women's clothing. "New styles! New styles! Come take a look . . ." Dressed in the latest styles and decked out in full makeup , these women have come from the countryside and lower-tiered cities of China to witness and to participate in one of the most lucrative and fast-paced fashion industries in the world today.

Tightly cramped, informal stalls occupy the first four levels of the building. These stalls sell clothing and accessories to intermediary buyers primarily from lower-tiered cities in China and from export hubs throughout Southeast Asia, including Taiwan, Malaysia, Singapore, Vietnam, and Indonesia. Most clothing styles featured in Xi Fang Hang are categorized as "Asian," suggesting the strategic location of the market in linking Guangzhou to Asia and other regions throughout the Global South. Most migrant entrepreneurs on the lower market levels pull photographs from fashion magazines published in Japan and Korea as inspiration for the styles that they appropriate and display. The styles on display here are generally casual junior wear featuring brightly colored prints, flowery dresses, eye-catching accessories, and message T-shirts. Their stalls attract the most shoppers, as evidenced by the crowds of onlookers who flood the hallways. Shoppers visit the market to buy garments at low volumes (at most 10–20 pieces per order). The lower market floors offer the trendiest fashions at the lowest price points, which generally range from 20 RMB to 100 RMB per piece.

The upper floors of the building consist of more formalized boutiques that look as if they are set up in offices rather than in the makeshift stalls on the lower floors. The clothing and accessories that are sold here, which often feature subdued colors, boxy and angular styles, and solids (rather than prints), are usually more expensive and frequently appeal to shoppers who prefer more formal, professional looks. Consequently, fewer shoppers roam the halls of the upper levels. Bosses who occupy these upper floors, most of whom are longtime Chinese and South Korean wholesalers, sell their products to their clients from other first-tier cities in China as well as to clients from South Korea and Japan. These clients, who are often long-term patrons, frequently order over the phone or via the internet. Tenants on the upper floors are also wealthier and more established players in the industry, as compared to the small-scale migrant entrepreneurs who set up their stalls on the lower levels. For this reason, these upper-floor tenants tend to sell their goods at higher volumes (from several hundred to several thousand pieces per order) and at higher costs.

These spatial inequalities have only intensified since the 2008 financial crisis. Since that time, Xi Fang Hang market has seen fewer customers, including fewer *shui fei jie*, or walk-in, clients. Those remaining customers include foreign clients, who before the 2007–8 financial crises had placed orders in massive quantities at a time. Those who continue to shop at Xi Fang Hang now, however, spend less. Sophie, a Guangzhou-based migrant wholesaler in the Xi Fang Hang market, recalls encountering clients who before 2008 bought clothes more freely regardless of price. Now, she adds, clients unfailingly try to negotiate for a better deal at any price. She also recalls friends who lost their investments in the stock markets in China. They include former clients of hers, who eventually canceled their orders for her garments. If clients cancel orders before they receive the actual shipment, they will typically bail out of the order after paying only 50 percent. Sophie's financial losses eventually led her to close her once-thriving business. To this

4.1 A fashion showroom in Guangzhou's Xi Fang Hang market, 2018. Photo by Nellie Chu.

day, Sophie still owes the other 50 percent of a canceled order to a local manufacturer. She candidly admits that she still owes money to other factory owners from her unsuccessful sales.

Other stall owners and market sellers also described to me changes in the spatial organization of the market, drawing direct connections between Xi Fang Hang's exorbitant rents and the behind-the-scenes brokering of deals among the more established bosses, building managers, and real estate speculators. For instance, some industry insiders remarked how the size of stall spaces has diminished over the years, even though rents continue to increase. Such inflationary measures, as stall keepers describe them, are not merely consequences of the 2008 financial crisis, the sharp rise of cotton prices since 2010, or other major economic downturns. Some acquaintances in the Xi Fang Hang market attribute the building's rising rents and other barriers to market access to the monopolization of a small group of local landlords who dictate the leasing contracts of multiple wholesale markets across the city.

Helen, a young migrant wholesaler from Dongbei whose showroom occupies the ninth floor, once speculated to me that organizing stalls into small units in Xi Fang Hang enables additional building managers who are tasked with supervising certain floors to collect a steady stream of commission from rent (through management fees), which are paid by their tenants. This strategic respacing of the market floors constitutes the managers' attempt to secure a bigger share of tenants' monthly profits while minimizing their own financial risks. Because of these changes, the second and third floors are increasingly crammed with people and garments as more competitors jostle to gain a competitive edge amid the market frenzy.

Some market sellers shared rumors about the building managers' attempts to hedge their bets on the burgeoning domestic market for fast fashion, underscoring the speculative activities among wealthy bosses and struggling migrant bosses alike. The sellers noted to me that certain spatial transformations within the market reflect the industry's gradual orientation to China's domestic market in lieu of its former emphasis on exports, signaling the ways in which the hierarchization of fashion and space in Xi Fang Hang reflects the changing geopolitical contours of the world economy. They speculated, too, that this reorientation is reflected not only in the stylistic transformation of the garments but also in the interior decoration of the showrooms. They observed this emerging "Chinese flavor," which they describe as the clothing styles that are on display in the stalls and boutiques, such as bolder prints, brighter colors, and flirtier styles.

Some observers note the Sinicization of Korean characters in the naming of boutiques on the upper floors. One designer couple from South Korea, with whom I strolled through the market corridors, once pointed out to me that one store used a name reflecting Korean-like script that is not actually the Korean language at all but simply an attempt by Chinese entrepreneurs to capture an impression of Koreanness.

The growing dominance of Chinese business owners within the Xi Fang Hang market has been accompanied by the shrinking presence of South Korean entrepreneurs within the building. This emerging trend is spatially evidenced by the clustering of a few stalls that are owned and operated by South Korean migrants. This cluster, named the "Korean Style Zone," is located in a small corner space on the second floor. This colorful and brightly lit corner is occupied by several South Korean entrepreneurs who are predominantly male and in their late thirties and early forties. Many can be found sitting in the back corners of their stalls, chatting with their clients, or conducting various forms of accounting, while their younger, mostly female employees sell clothing to shoppers who pass by.

PREDATORY ACCUMULATION

The spatial, temporal, and bureaucratic organization of the management structures within the Xi Fang Hang building reflect the extractive and policing activities that are part and parcel of the everyday order of conducting business there. Each of the nine floors of the market is supervised by a manager (usually a person who is fluent in the local dialect of Cantonese) who is responsible for leasing market stalls and boutiques to renters. Every supervisor leads a team of four to five assistants, who help carry out tasks assigned by their boss. Much like the uniformed officers who patrol the urban villages, floor-level supervisors act as gatekeepers who supervise the flow of goods and customers circulating into and out of the market floors. In the afternoons, uniformed officers make daily rounds along the hallways to confirm that certain security measures, fire safety codes, and intellectual property laws are enforced and followed by visitors, tenants, and employees. Meanwhile, their assistants check for legitimate *hukou* identification and valid business licenses on a weekly basis among the bosses and their employees to confirm that no one working inside the building is an undocumented migrant. Individuals caught without proper IDs and licenses face arrest and immediate business closure.

In addition to these formal management practices, rumors circulate wildly among stall owners about collusion, extortion, and other secretive schemes of the landlords. Apparently, landlords arrange collusive subleasing arrangements with third-party agents, many of whom are family or personal friends, to protect their property and legal interests in case tenants collectively sue or protest the landlords. In one instance, a South Korean wholesaler on the ninth floor of the building explained to me that the installation of electrical fixtures involved negotiating with two to three parties, all of whom were related to the landlord and received a financial cut in the wholesaler's five-year lease. In this scheme, each party serves to protect the others, so that when conflicts with tenants arise, they are mediated by different intermediary parties. Ultimately, the landlords remain invisible and protected from disputes with unsatisfied tenants.

In fact, a construction company owned by a wealthy Guangzhou-based Cantonese real estate developer occupies a large office space on the ninth floor of Xi Fang Hang, indicating the regularity of speculative remodeling that is required by the building management. The strategic location of this construction office within the building has led market sellers and visitors to complain that some business managers share a portion of their income from rent with other so-called insiders through various forms of kickbacks. For instance, Helen explained that any building repair must be handled by the building management for a fee. She states, "If they change a light or even hammer a nail on the wall, managers charge you 300 RMB for the job." Additionally, a factory owner who handles the production of many garments sold at Xi Fang Hang once told me, "Many of my clients describe how difficult it is to do business there, because the rent is too expensive. Do you think that just by remodeling they'll really upgrade [the market]? They [the management] will just fix a light fixture here or nail something there and they'll charge you double the rent for it!" Other shoppers described how undercover shoppers would regularly scope the markets to observe which stalls attracted the most clients. When management saw that a stall owner's business was succeeding, then the management fees for that space would increase accordingly.

Thus, the influence and authority that building managers maintain foster intricate webs of profitable and cushy patron-client relationships among supervisors, clients, and other powerful bosses. Oftentimes, building administrators expect monetary kickbacks when they assist in facilitating business mergers (usually through introductions among personal friends and existing tenants within the building), terminate long-term leases of tenants before their contracts expire, and overlook certain exceptions to legal codes or business procedures such as allowing certain counterfeit items to be sold on market premises or permitting some bosses (but not others) to operate without proper licenses and identification papers.

Managers usually allow a number of informal and secretive businesses to operate on the upper levels of the Xi Fang Hang wholesale market in exchange for compensation fees or kickbacks. These ventures are typically run by long-standing insiders of Guangzhou's garment industry, most of whom are Cantonese locals who act as intermediary brokers between building managers and newly arrived tenants who are interested in expanding their businesses. They covertly mediate disputes among competing bosses over allegations of design-copying and counterfeiting, arrange available stall spaces and boutiques for potential clients, take bribes to avoid counterfeiting charges, facilitate business alliances, and gather market forecasting details. Outside observers suspect that the Xi Fang Hang building management is increasingly being monopolized by a small group of established entrepreneurs who have had very successful businesses there since the early inception of this wholesale market in the 1990s. Rumors surrounding the ongoing spatial transformations underscore the growing sense of inequality and inaccessibility among struggling migrant entrepreneurs who are located on the lower floors of the building vis-à-vis their more established competitors.

RUNAWAY CAPITAL

The Xi Fang Hang building managers' regulatory activities work according to the yearly cycles of fast fashion, which generate lucrative opportunities for monetary extractions from their renters. Managers' own incomes critically depend on the cycles of fast fashion. Rather than enforcing a strict tightening, or lockdown, of economic activity, managers stand by to passively regulate the ongoing flow of cash, people, and commodities and attempt to extract a portion of their tenants' profit by levying rents and fees. Building managers exploit the temporal gaps in the turnover of the fashion season by regulating the inflows and outflows of tenants and market spaces. The timing of fashion seasons, along with their cyclical flows of commodities and capital into and out of the market floors, generate opportunities for building managers to inflate rent and management fees.

During the months of July, August, and September, and leading up to Guangzhou's famous trade show, the Canton Fair, most international clients filter through Guangzhou in search of the newest fall trends. This September trade show marks the beginning of the fall season, and it coincides with Fashion Week in New York, Paris, and London. Many new stalls and boutiques pop up in the wholesale markets, while factories that handle garments for direct export to Europe and North America receive production orders in July in preparation for the following spring's collection. The most intensive and frequent management work is conducted at this time in order to regulate the heavy traffic of visitors and goods that pass through the market floors.

The weeks following the annual Chinese New Year are characterized by an influx of new renters and business operations in the building. During this time, each renter on the market's floors are expected to provide a *hongbao*, or lucky money, placed in a red envelope (or 50 to 200 RMB) that is given to every building manager. These gifts act as symbolic gestures to sustain relationships of reciprocity (*guanxi*) between tenants and building managers in case special favors, including exceptions to intellectual property laws, must be curried in the future. March and April mark the beginning of the spring season, when regulation and fee collections by building management are also frequent, while the period from June through August, a term known locally as *dam gui* (off-season), is characterized as the slowest business period in the year. At this time, building managers clear out the spaces once occupied by former tenants while they solicit and interview potential new clients. Unlike the months of February and early September, during which most of the merchandise is cleared out at discounted rates (a process referred to as *qing huo*), the months of June through August typically serve as periods of rest or unemployment for many migrants. During this time, business in the markets slows down dramatically, and many garment factories temporarily close, forcing migrants to return to their home villages.

During the summer off-season, the Xi Fang Hang market temporarily closes so that all tenants can renovate their interior spaces. Throughout these summer months, building managers attempt to solicit tenants by guiding them through the vacant spaces and discussing the market's rental terms. The turnover of tenants and rental spaces allows managers to raise the costs of leasing there. Building managers have a personal interest in maintaining the ongoing turnover of new lessees, since it is easier to extort cash fees and other payments from newcomers than from established tenants. More established, long-term occupants tend to cultivate close ties to more powerful building administrators, so they are more difficult to bribe.

Migrant entrepreneurs within Guangzhou's fast fashion sector often emphasize the fierce competition for fast money that pervades the lower floors of this wholesale market. Indeed, the dynamics of global fast fashion is synchronized with the speculative dynamics of real estate speculation in Xi Fang Hang. The rapid turnover of commodities and capital from the market's premises is astounding. Hallways are usually packed with delivery men bringing goods in, and shoppers tugging massive bundles of clothing behind them as they leave the market. New styles flood the market stalls nearly every week. Stalls frequently go out of business and are filled by new owners nearly every year. Meanwhile, many market sellers can be seen holding and counting thick stacks of 100 RMB bills in their hands as they frantically fill out receipts and calculate totals of purchases made by their customers. In one instance, I witnessed a young female market seller wearing a short skirt and a pair of high heels physically attack an older male customer with a full soda can for attempting to steal 70 RMB from her denim pocket. The lure of quick money adds to the intensity of an already chaotic environment. Xi Fang Hang market is thus known among industry participants who are based in Guangzhou for its large number of conflicts that frequently escalate into violent outbursts.[8]

Despite the enormous risks entailed in running a stall at Xi Fang Hang, budding entrepreneurs, particularly migrants from outside Guangzhou, nonetheless attempt to stake a claim in this market by pooling their family's resources in the hope of striking it rich while enjoying the independence that comes with being their own bosses. Most novice Chinese bosses are young women in their late twenties or early thirties, who have migrated from the countryside to experiment in entrepreneurship. For them, the promise of bosshood in Guangzhou offers them a sense of freedom and cosmopolitanism, on the one hand, while providing them with the ability to fulfill their sense of filial piety by financially supporting their family members back home, on the other. Small-scale migrant entrepreneurs often pool their modest family savings to start a stall, only to lose it within a span of three to four years.

Ling, a savvy twenty-six-year-old woman, recently closed down her five-foot-by-seven-foot stall after running her business, a wholesale business for women's beach dresses, for only two years. She had started the business based on savings she had collected from her family in nearby Foshan. The failing of her business, however, did not deter her from wanting

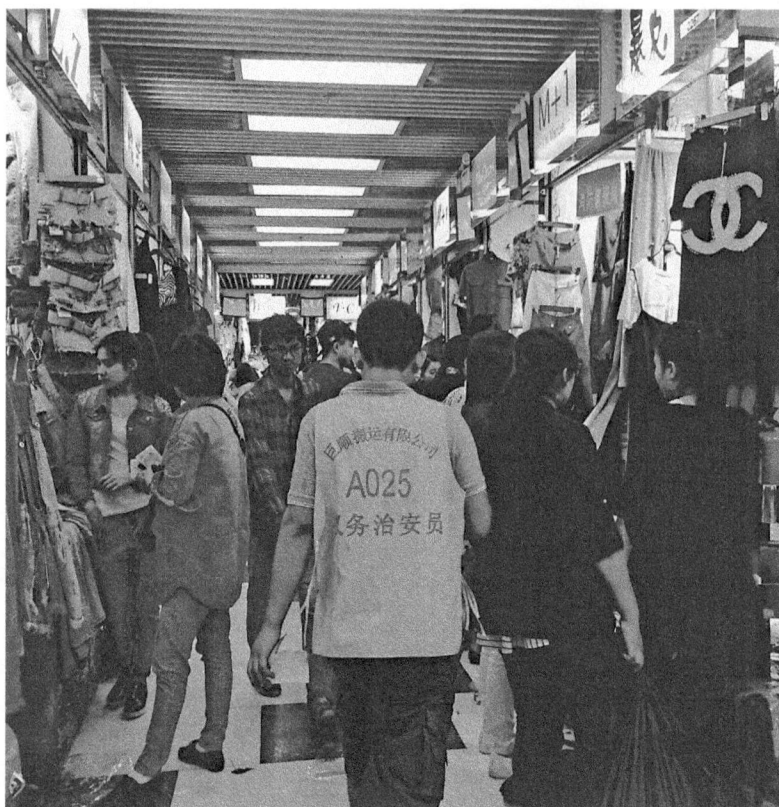

4.2 A typical hallway in a busy fashion wholesale market in Guangzhou, 2018. Photo by Nellie Chu.

to return to the market again. She was now taking the time to plot her next business scheme. Her experience of becoming a boss left her even more determined to own property in Guangzhou one day. Ultimately, she dreamed of resuming her business in this market so that she could one day strike her luck and make vast profits despite having already failed once. With her eyes beaming, she exclaimed, "Just before the 2008 market crash, some bosses (*laoban*) were making as much as 10,000 RMB a day! If you can make it there, you can make volumes of money. The returns are huge . . ."

As the myths of high-stakes risks and high rewards circulate among shopkeepers, keeping their entrepreneurial dreams alive, bosses on the market floors must keep up with the high price tag that comes with renting stalls there. In fact, stall owners that I spoke with often complained about how difficult it was to maintain their businesses there because of the market's exorbitant rent. A compact, five-foot-by-seven-foot stall on the first two levels of the market costs over 100,000 RMB per month ($15,500 USD), five times the average monthly income of a Guangzhou resident. Spacious offices on the fourth through ninth floors cost as much as 400,000 RMB ($62,000 USD) per month. Contracts are renewed every three to five years, and rents continue to rise despite the steep downturn in business activity since the global economic slowdown that began in 2008. Consequently, the turnover rate of new businesses entering this market and failed businesses exiting remains high. The average stall lasts only ten to twelve months. A longtime wholesaler of garment accessories in the building has once remarked, "They [the building managers] don't care whether you can afford it [the rent increases] or not; they'll just raise the rent for the next lessor who is willing to pay. They can find another tenant at any time. If you can't pay, then you'll have to leave!"

At the same time, the flows of money, commodities, and entrepreneurial dreams produce tremendous wealth for the owners and managers of the building. Proximate to manufacturing sites including the Zhaocun garment district, Xi Fang Hang facilitates practices that exemplify *speed to market*, that is, the ability to deliver consistent flows of new styles within short periods of time. Among the market's ambitious entrepreneurs, this practice proves to be critical to business success. Because of the intense competition and the pressure to make quick money, stall owners emphasize the speed at which clothes can be translated from the pictorial image to the actual finished garments; but these processes cannot be divorced from the spatial dimensions through which the evaluation of quality and fashion are organized. Along with the pressures of featuring thousands of new styles nearly every week, each owner must pay exorbitant rents and management fees. These financial and creative demands lead the stall owners who occupy the nearly one thousand stalls on the first three floors of Xi Fang Hang market into a cascade of debt and design-copying.

FLIPPING, OR *CHAO HUO*

In anticipation of the regulatory activities that take place at the beginning of each fashion season, before landlords and managers rotate throughout the building, wholesalers buy garments and accessories from lower-end markets, retag them under their own labels, and then resell them at higher prices in the Xi Fang Hang marketplace. At the same time, they sell their own appropriated designs to transnational and secondary wholesalers who will retag and resell these fast fashions on to other markets outside of Guangzhou. This chain of appropriation is colloquially referred to as "flipping," or reselling, fast fashions (*chao huo*). Broadly speaking, the notion of flipping garments, or *chao huo*, entails the traveling of objects through a hierarchy of market spaces based on commodity prices, quality, and labor values. *Chao huo* moves objects across different market spaces that, in turn, are critically linked to the speculative activities of the real estate industry.[9]

Most wholesalers and other migrant bosses from the Xi Fang Hang market exploit the gaps in rent prices and regulatory oversight within the hierarchy of wholesale markets and supply chains in Guangzhou. They source their goods from the inexpensive Sha He market across town. Sha He is a large wholesale market in the central district of the city; it sells low-end garments with simple cuts and designs. Sha He's garment pieces (called *choi pin*) often have straightforward lines and lower quality cuts that facilitate easy and quick assembly by unskilled and low-paid sewers. The shoppers who frequent the Sha He markets are often assumed to be poorer migrants from the countryside outside Guangzhou, who lack the cosmopolitan, sophisticated qualities (*suzhi*) to belong to the exclusive world of fashion. Xi Fang Hang sellers and other garment manufacturers oftentimes remark that Sha He clothes, generally priced from 30 to 100 RMB, will probably last through two washings at the most. Like the Zhaocun garment district, the Sha He markets are perceived as chaotic (*luan*) and dangerous. Some locals have warned me of potential thieves who apparently linger around the area, though I have never encountered or witnessed any criminal acts there.

Buyers at the Sha He market would purchase the inventory in bulk, retag the clothing, and resell them as their own in the more lucrative Xi Fang Hang market where the items generated greater profits. Few wholesalers, however, acknowledge the fact that much of their clothing originated from the low-end Sha He market, since Sha He is often excluded from the realm of fashion. After the garments and accessories are sold on from the Xi Fang Hang market, they are passed through to the more fashionable and cosmopolitan corridors of the Huimei market and on to markets abroad. Huimei, which I discussed in chapter 1, is a market that, at the time of my research, features the trendiest and most expensive clothing among all garment wholesale markets in Guangzhou. Industry insiders commonly describe Huimei as the "Korean" market, indicating its cosmopolitan and cutting-edge characteristics. Huimei's links to the outside world enables this market to demand even more exorbitant rents and higher prices for their garments. These pathways of traveling people and objects demonstrate how these capital flows and price speculation are anchored upon the rhythms of property regulation and real estate speculation within these markets.

Although flexible appropriation enables fast fashion bosses to hedge market risks amid rapidly changing trends, design-copying leaves them vulnerable to regulation and policing based on copyright laws. As we saw in chapter 3, uniformed officers in the urban villages demand higher fees from migrant bosses who receive a regular cash flow from walk-in clients, landlords, and building managers of the wholesale markets. In Xi Fang Hang, officers collect higher fees from tenants whose businesses appear to be successful. Contrary to the practices of authentication and branding by internationally recognized labels, bosses increase the prices of their fast fashion garments and accessories by circulating commodities *away* from their sources.[10] Whereas high fashion, whether it is couture or ready-to-wear, lays its claims to value and authenticity through branding and symbolic proximity to its source, fast fashion constructs its value through its circulation across divergent contexts of symbolic references and signification.[11]

Across the back walls of many market stalls in the Xi Fang Hang market, for instance, many nonbranded leather bags, belts, and other accessories are carefully placed on full display. These bags and accessories do not have any visible brands or logos attached, yet their material shapes and forms are almost identical to those that are sold in licensed retail outlets in Milan, Paris, New York, and Shanghai. In order to dodge tax and copyright regulations, stall owners have devised a practice of displaying only the bare skeletal body of the bags. After the customers purchase these bags, the owners then attach the logos onto the product so that it finally resembles the original, trademarked version. In this sense, the low-priced bag mirrors the hoodie as a "sign, a screen, expectation, and force" (Mimi Nguyen 2015). A copy-designed bag, much like a hoodie, operates simultaneously, to different degrees, as that which defines the sign as an index, an icon, and a symbol (Peirce 1955). A copy-designed bag resembles the material features of the original sample (the index), draws upon the qualities of designer fashion (the icon), while gesturing toward abstract, more generalized features of luxury, class, and taste (the symbol). The boundaries that separate the various roles of the signs are thus unclear. These ambiguities of brand signification become even more evident when the fashion object moves through various indices of valuation and marketability of fast fashions, as I will demonstrate below. Authorship among migrant bosses in Guangzhou's world of fast fashion remains hidden and obscured amid this indexical ambiguity in order to conceal the source of wealth, dodge regulation, and secure a steady accumulation of runaway profits.

In short, the flows of money and commodities, however ephemeral and mobile they might be, are tied to the spaces and places upon which the wholesale markets themselves are situated. Sellers often complain about the rising rents at the city's wholesale markets, particularly at Xi Fang Hang, Huimei, and the Zhaocun fabric market, as well as at other venues surrounding the railway station. Competition in the wholesale garment industry is made more difficult because of the inflated rents in the commercial real estate industry. The rising rents at Xi Fang Hang, Huimei, and other wholesale markets result in a rapid turnover of commercial tenants because the costs of operating a stall make survival in the industry nearly impossible. For example, Ling closed her stall only after two years because of the exorbitant rent at Xi Fang Hang. Even her former boss from Hong Kong who ran a market stall at the highly profitable Baima garment wholesale market, close to the Guangzhou railway station, eventually moved to Beijing to escape the highly competitive garment industry in Guangzhou. By the end of August 2014, Sophie and Ling were forced to join the masses of tenants who failed to renew their leases and who gave up their business and commercial stalls to competitors.

FLIPPING RISK

While migrant bosses attempt to increase their profits through flipping, they must also gauge the inventory of their competitors so that a certain style or trend does not oversaturate a market by overcopying. Whenever bosses anticipate that a certain garment style is oversaturated by competitors' copying practices, they move their inventory to alternative markets so as to territorialize or carve out new market spaces. They must constantly resolve the contradiction of tirelessly catching up with the quick changes in fashion trends while ensuring that they avoid overproduction of existing inventory. Calculations of risk are thus managed through the movement of commodities across the various marketplaces that constitute the fast fashion supply chain. Migrant bosses accomplish this difficult task, while discreetly keeping tabs on the inventory of their competitors. Bosses must first keep a daily stock of commodities that are currently in trend (or "in fashion") and those that are quickly expiring, or those that have been left behind from the trending cycle ("out of fashion"). Fast fashion's ceaseless production of new styles within shorter periods of time requires wholesalers to maintain the rapid inflows of new trends and money as well as outflows of old inventory in order to make room for new goods. By the time the popular fashion magazines are out on newsstands, the pictures have already been distributed around China via the internet and copied for reproduction one week earlier. The key to minimizing the bosses' risk is, therefore, to quickly convert their commodities back to money so that their capital can be quickly reinvested in order to design and produce new clothing.

The ongoing circulation of fast fashions into and out of various markets enables bosses to exploit the categorical fluidity that copy-design objects signify. In light of the rapidly changing trends that real estate speculation generates, bosses are forced to constantly circulate their inventory so as to acquire enough provisional capital to cover the next season's production costs. As a means of managing the relentless sequences of rapidly moving commodities, money, and clients, they invent mechanisms to mark time and commodity prices by appropriating local categories through which they describe the quick successions of roving objects, money, and customers.

Approximately one week after inventory arrives from the garment factories and generally before building managers begin their seasonal rotations around the stalls, sellers designate their stock as *ya huo* (to pawn) in order to describe unsold clothing that is static or inert. At this stage, commodities retain the physical forms of the original samples, similar to the ways in which branded logos serve as iconic symbols of luxury fashion, yet because the fashion trend has passed, these objects no longer demand the highest exchange value. The character *ya* (押) generally means to mortgage or to pawn objects, implying that retention of this extra inventory is already seen as a form of debt, or immobile capital. In other words, the term *ya huo* refers to garments that are immobile, unable to be converted into liquid capital. They sit in the stall waiting to be sold over time (usually for the duration of a few weeks), while the capital that would have been spent to produce other garments remains unusable and blocked from supporting other investments. The longer that the inventory sits inert, the lower the profits the wholesalers can gain from the sale of their goods.

Within the course of two weeks, this inert product is eventually bought by clients or discounted as unsold inventory. By this time, building managers have begun their rotations around the stalls and boutiques in the marketplace. Bosses rely on consistent conversions of material garments into liquid capital, flows of commodities into cash that will balance their business ventures. Many migrant bosses temporarily work for bigger, more established bosses as third-party agents by overseeing larger production orders for them. This form of employment provides fledgling entrepreneurs with alternative sources of liquid capital with which to support their independent clothing lines, as they gradually establish a foothold in the competitive industry. However, a Guangzhou-based wholesaler once explained to me the limits of her self-enterprise. She explained that she could not rely solely on her overseas clients for capital to sustain her independent business, stating, "They [the overseas clients] can leave at any time [depending on the fluctuations of the market]." Despite these uncertainties, she planned to slowly build up her own brand in Guangzhou, so that she could eventually develop a solid, stable, and independent source of capital and profit.

Market sellers designate the term *mei huo* or "tail goods" to describe the few remaining styles or garment pieces toward the end of the fashion cycle. Those with unsold goods often sell their *mei huo* illegally on the streets during the late evening hours in the attempt to evade huge losses from their excessive inventory. *Mei huo* retain some potential for partial profit, since they still signify some degree of iconic meaning by leaving traces of a downward-dipping fashion cycle. As street hawkers, these migrant entrepreneurs become what local Guangzhou residents call *zou gui* or "fleeing ghosts," who sell commodities such as food, novelties, gadgets, clothes, and accessories without a license on the city streets. In order to curb tax evasion among street vendors, municipal governments have prohibited acts of selling items on the street without a license. The *cheng guan*, or city police, patrol the streets in search of these illegal street vendors. Their primary duty is to govern (and sometimes extort money from) their commercial activities. Oftentimes, street vendors will warn other sellers by announcing the presence of a *cheng guan* officer with a secret sound or signal, like a flick of a light switch. Thus alerted, the vendors—who risk heavy fines and confiscation of their inventory—will immediately leap up from their sitting or standing positions and stealthily round up their goods in their tarps so as to avoid confrontations with officers.

Finally, sellers describe unsold, off-season merchandise as *si huo*, or dead goods, garments that merely retain the material features of an original sample (index) but that fail to demand consumer desire throughout the

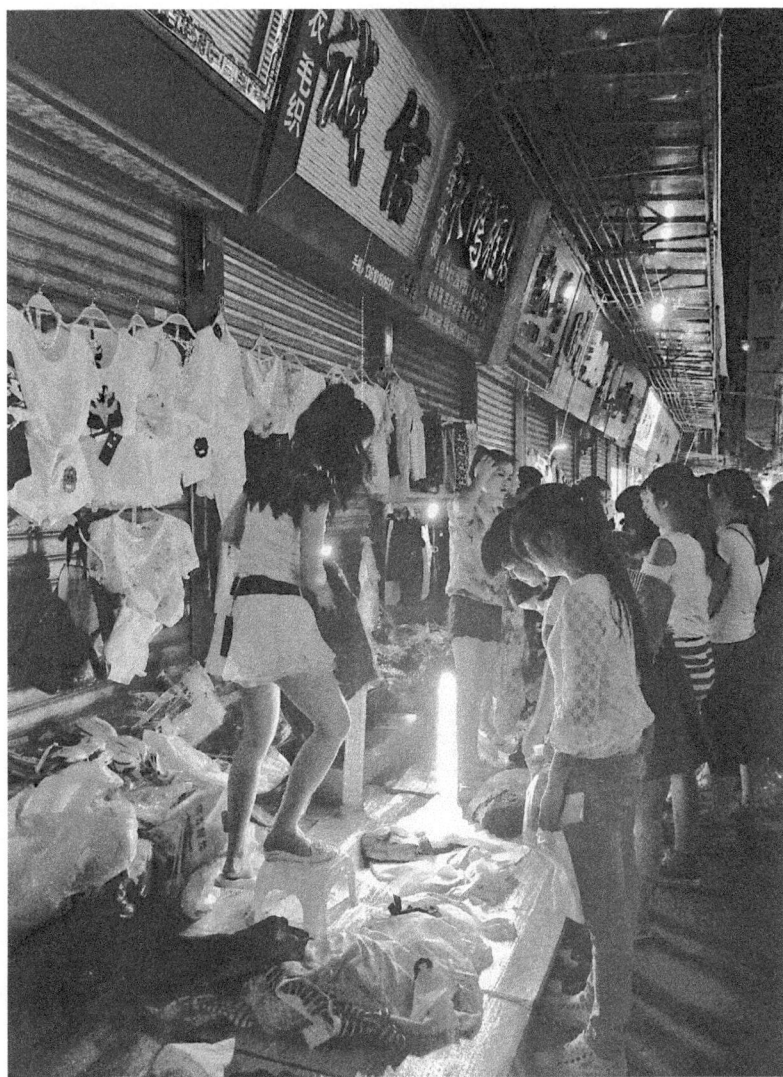

4.3 Crowds of women gather in a night market in Guangzhou, 2016. Photo by Nellie Chu.

short-lived fashion cycle. In the eyes of the wholesalers, these clothes, which are often the leftover pieces of a collection, represent commodities that failed to be converted back to money or liquid capital, so they are often discounted below cost. These goods often represent misjudgment or poor taste on the part of the wholesaler in accurately predicting, during the last fashion wave, the styles that consumers would desire. Alternatively, these goods may also have been heavily copied and reproduced by other competitors within the market, which subsequently caused an overflow of similar goods on the market floors. These commodities are frequently found wrinkled and scattered in loose piles by the front doors of showrooms under makeshift signs with scribbles advertising 10 to 20 RMB for each item. These goods, along with other unwanted garments, are haphazardly tossed about instead of hanging formally along the walls or around the front of display areas. *Si huo* are frequently sold well below cost to other wholesalers or intermediary buyers from second-tier or third-tier cities outside of Guangzhou. Because the clientele in these regions tends to be poorer and less cosmopolitan, regionally based bosses can take advantage of the lower price tags of *si huo* goods in order to make a marginal profit.

The terms, *ya huo, mei huo,* or *si huo,* shed light on the migrant bosses' conceptions of fast fashion markets as temporal lifecycles of money and designer-inspired objects that move amid unbridled real estate speculation and regulation. Wholesalers mark categories of production time and costs, while they exploit differentials in commodity prices and qualities across various markets. As the key agents of arbitrage across the supply chains, one of the primary roles of wholesalers is to move fashion garments and commodities into and out of warehouses, wholesale markets, and even city streets in order to sustain the production of new garment styles. As Lisa Adkins (2009) argues, time itself has become an object of competition, contestation, and value. As fashion seasons wind down only to restart again, sellers rush to sell off their remaining goods to secure a source of liquid capital. This money is used to reinvest in future projects. Thus, fast fashion's incessant speculative dynamics are exemplified by the forecasting of upcoming trends, the search for new styles, and the creation of new fashions critically depend on the outflows of static, unsold merchandise in order to maintain steady inflows of money and other forms of liquid capital, which in turn are used to produce additional commodities. These intersecting flows are critically linked to the inflationary pressures of renting commercial spaces in the Xi Fang Hang building.

OVERSATURATION OF COPY-DESIGNS AND
SPECULATIVE ENTREPRENEURSHIP

Wholesalers are less concerned with the authenticity of a brand logo or style per se than they are with their aspirations to stay financially afloat, to accumulate wealth, and to eventually claim legitimacy as boss. They hope to develop their line of original designs once they can afford to take the financial risks. For the time being, they must engage in design-copying and various forms of flexible appropriation to accumulate passive income and to wait until market conditions are ripe to experiment with their own designs. Flexible appropriation entails manipulating the categorical spectrum of the real and the fake to scale up or "flip" the value of fashion objects. The aims of flipping, retagging, and reselling are to conceal the source of a garment's design and to dodge accusations of copying by building managers. Wholesalers do so to temporally and spatially circumnavigate the rotation of uniformed officers and property managers that pass through the marketplace's hallways.

The fast fashion bosses' attempts to dodge extraction, to speculate on profits, and to hedge risk, while economically reasonable from the point of view of the individual entrepreneur, have paradoxically worsened the accessibility of the Xi Fang Hang marketplace by generating an oversaturation of similar styles. The excessive inventory of similar designs, along with rising rents, has undercut the stability and vibrancy of market relations as a whole. Sophie explained to me that with the limited number of unique styles to choose from, clients were increasingly turning to wholesale outlets online rather than visiting the market. She admitted that design appropriation, resulting in nearly identical garments being sold by competing wholesalers, was a pervasive practice; and she speculated that flipping and retagging garments on a mass scale would eventually hurt the larger group of competing business owners. In her view, this form of appropriation intensified the competitive atmosphere among wholesalers, while clients were being offered fewer choices of lower quality. As Sophie noted, the extensive reselling of similar garment designs without obvious modifications was more common when business declined. The rising costs of cotton and other raw materials since 2010 also thwarted sellers' abilities to provide desirable, high-quality garments. As a means of evading these economic risks, increasing numbers of sellers in the highly competitive Xi Fang Hang market resorted to directly copying competitors' designs (with minimal to no modification) to stay financially afloat, thus further exacerbating the fast fashion bosses' conditions of precariousness and stalled mobility.

For instance, Edwin (originally from Shenzhen), a former migrant wholesaler at Xi Fang Hang, relied on design-copying to sustain his businesses, since design-copying was pervasive. He explained that once business owners became privy to a certain style or design that sold well, competitors would quickly copy the exact design within two to three days. They would either directly copy an entire look with minor modifications or simply purchase garment pieces from a competitor and retag them as their own. By then, one could see that several storeowners had already sold that very same design. Migrant entrepreneurs like him must then constantly create new styles to remain competitive. For Edwin, the fact that a competitor copied his design implied that he had achieved a level of success and admiration from his competitors. His statement seemed to suggest that copying was advantageous to wholesalers, because in many ways the practice of design-copying signaled public recognition, even if the object was not directly attributed to the creator. In his view, legitimacy as a successful entrepreneur was secured by eliciting acceptance and admiration from others. For Edwin, copying was the sincerest form of flattery.

Edwin further reasoned that the preponderance of copying among local markets bore witness to the fact that the wholesale niche should nonetheless facilitate a slower, reflective response to the market. The volume of new fashions that rotated into and out of the wholesale markets moved too quickly to nurture and facilitate the necessary time and creative space for sellers to reflect upon the changes in the market and to respond accordingly with new designs. Even retailers, the clients of the wholesalers that I discuss here, often complained about neighboring competitors who attempted to copy their designs by choosing the same merchandise to sell. I once overheard a young seller in a retail market complaining about her neighbor in the next stall. She said, "Now if you compare her clothes with mine, what differences are there? She had explicitly promised me to not worry because she wouldn't pick up *my* style and taste." Her sympathetic friend expressed her support for the distressed woman by saying, "Yes, the clothes that you picked up depend on your discerning eye and *feel* for fashion," as if creativity was endowed as a talent or skill cultivated by years of learning and experience. Their exchange unveiled the contentious discourse around copying and the painstaking efforts among industry participants in claiming and authenticating their own creativity as purveyors of fashion.

Indeed, not all wholesalers share Edwin's enthusiasm for copying. When I asked Sophie whether she personally experienced someone copying from her, she recounted a time when a friend of hers, a wealthy local boss who operated a boutique on one of the upper floors of the market, introduced Sophie to a younger cousin of hers. The boss asked her to show this younger relative the ropes of the fashion trade. Sophie agreed and added this young woman as one of her employees. Over the course of six months, the young woman learned most, if not all of Sophie's business secrets, including her aesthetic style, design strategies, and business contacts, and she then opened a competing stall directly next to Sophie's (before Sophie closed her business), using her relative's money. To Sophie's dismay, her stall mirrored most, if not all, of her own garment styles and fashion aesthetic, including the interior decorations of her stall. When Sophie confronted the woman and the wealthy boss, they simply claimed that their "look" was uniquely original. Since the young woman claimed to have studied fashion design before, her assertion of originality seemed more credible to other wholesalers and clients at the time. With fewer capital and resources at hand, Sophie conceded, "What can you do? Business is business. By the time, someone copies you, the styles would have already changed anyways."

In short, the practices of flexible appropriation in Guangzhou's fast fashion markets impede the efforts of migrant bosses to minimize market risks, evade surveillance, and extortion by building managers, and to pass those risks onto rival competitors. As competitors flood the market with copy-designs, consumer demand stalls and plateaus, forcing bosses to close shop and allowing eager newcomers to take their place. The ongoing flows of commodities and migrant entrepreneurs entering and exiting this market illustrate how transnational fast fashion exchange is implicated within a larger economy of collusion and extraction based on accumulation via real estate speculation. The cyclical exchanges of fast fashion and rental properties underscore how the rhythms of creative destruction that animate this market directly undermine the accumulative interests of small-scale migrant entrepreneurs who remain constantly exposed to the predatory demands of the local landlords and property managers (Schumpeter 1994). Fast fashion production is thus indelibly tied to the fluctuations of the place-based real estate market that is occupied by wealthier, more powerful bosses across the supply chain.

5 Transnational Migrant Bosshood

"Look, the American market is hot right now. All my friends in the logistics business have been making deals with American companies since the COVID-19 outbreak. You must help me make a deal. I'm missing out on an enormous opportunity!" exclaimed Tina, a *Chaoxianzu* (Korean Chinese) migrant entrepreneur whom I visited in Guangzhou in July 2021. I had met her through the Senegalese migrant Sylvianne, whom I described in chapter 3. Years ago, Tina had worked for Sylvianne's father, helping to manage clients and to coordinate the administrative side of his family-run shipping company. Since then, Tina and Sylvianne had become close friends; and after Sylvianne's father returned to Senegal, Tina branched out and began her own small-scale logistics company that arranged shipping containers for West African clients who traveled between China, Europe, and countries across West Africa. These containers shipped fast fashions and other types of clothing and accessories as well as household items, furniture, motorcycles, and other consumer goods. That day, I was shocked to have discovered that nearly every single office space once occupied by competing logistics companies that served Africa, Europe, and the Middle East had become completely vacant. The feelings of insecurity and ambivalence among migrant bosses who engaged in precarious accumulation across the fast fashion supply chains had never been more palpable.

I became acutely aware of the dynamics of uncertainty and ambivalence that afternoon when I was sitting in Tina's office in Guangzhou's Xiaobei district catching up on how the COVID-19 pandemic had impacted her business. Tina's company, H. K. Holdings, was the only business that remained in operation on the entire floor of the building. All the other businesses along the hallway had vanished, leaving no trace of their existence except for post-it notes with the former bosses' names and phone numbers stuck onto dusty glass doors. Relieved to discover that Tina's company was still around, I inquired about the current and future state of her business. She replied quite matter-of-factly that in the five years that her company had been in business, profits had dramatically declined. Scores of African migrants had left Guangzhou or China altogether. While most were forced out of the country due to evictions, detentions, and deportations, many African traders chose to move to cities in Southeast Asia, where they searched for economic growth opportunities despite the overall slowdown of the global economy. The price of a shipping container during the pandemic skyrocketed to over ten times its pre-COVID-19 cost. Since most African migrants had left Xiaobei and Guangzhou, Tina had no option but to rely on her existing clients, including Sylvianne's father. That day, Tina was assisting Sylvianne's father in shipping medicine from Thailand to the Congo because of the dire COVID-19 situation there.

Unlike the exorbitant cost of exports from China to Africa, American demand for China-made goods, including medical supplies, medicines, and household goods, outpaced the costs of shipping to the United States. Tina continued, "What I need right now are connections to the US, someone to cosign a bill of lading with me, so that I can export goods directly to there. All my friends and colleagues have someone to cosign with them. They have shared all kinds of valuable information with me. But I can't ask for their help to find a trading partner in the US. After all, they are my competitors. I just can't do that." I was surprised by Tina's desperate plea for my assistance, and I frankly felt awkward. With no business knowledge or connections, I felt helpless in fulfilling Tina's request. And yet, I empathized with her worries about the future of her enterprise as well as with her feeling that a once-in-a-lifetime opportunity was passing her by.

Tina's feelings of lament and disappointment for missing out on a lucrative business opportunity illustrate the conditions of anticipation and deferment that undergird entrepreneurial self-enterprise, whereby migrant bosses like her are left to continuously search for pathways to accumulative expansion, growth, or means of leveraging of their entrepreneurial investments. Like the Wongs and many other migrant bosses in Guangzhou's fast fashion industry, Tina's business had survived, thanks to intermittent orders that she received from her West African clients here and there. Tina knew that a critical aspect of entrepreneurship was finding or creating new possibilities for ongoing accumulation, but she lacked the personal connections to bring those opportunities to fruition. The trickling in of these profits was enough to make ends meet, but it did not guarantee a desirable or secure future.

In recent years, the West African–South Korean supply chains in Guangzhou have been unexpectedly disrupted by nationalistic and anti-foreigner movements across Chinese cities. The start of the COVID-19 pandemic accelerated these dynamics, gradually erasing these once-thriving transnational migrant communities in Guangzhou. Indeed, a major reason for the dramatic downturn in businesses in Xiaobei during the height of the COVID-19 pandemic was that the regulations and surveillance that migrants encountered intensified, primarily due to their status as foreign traders. These experiences exacerbated their conditions of deferment and stalled mobility. Government crackdowns on religious congregations across China also intensified beginning in 2017, closing many licensed and unlicensed churches, and forcing many faith-based communities to go underground. Moreover, scores of West African migrants were evicted from their apartments in Xiaobei during the initial COVID-19 lockdowns in 2020, forcing many to sleep on the streets before departing to other more religiously tolerant and foreigner-friendly cities across China and Asia. Many transnational migrants were thus forced to venture out to distant regions in Southeast Asia, Africa, and Latin America to continue to pursue their luck in entrepreneurial self-enterprise.

In light of these moments of displacement and dispossession, this chapter takes a look back at the years before the COVID-19 pandemic to examine how spatial imaginations of Guangzhou, China, and the world, as well as migrants' abilities to move across them, shaped migrant bosses' sensibilities and imaginations of the world and their place in it (N. Chu 2019). I pay particular attention to transnational bosses, namely West African and South Korean migrants, and how they imagined both China's place in the fast fashion worlds created by the global Made in China label as well as their own positions within these worlds. West African migrants forged religious and otherworldly ties with God while they imagined China as a space of capitalist and spiritual accumulation. At the same time, Korean Chinese and South Korean bosses recreated diasporic and ethnic-based migratory chains and trade relations that exceeded national boundaries by testing the limits of their entrepreneurial fates and destiny. Transnational migrants' spatial imaginations of China and the world were connected to their engagements with the socioeconomic structures and order brought about by the materials conditions of late capitalism, which in the case of the migrant bosses, were specifically tied to fast fashion and supply chain capitalism (Jameson 1990; Tsing 2009). Aspiration, desires, and fears of economic loss and exploitation emerged through the migrants' spatial imaginations and engagements with bosshood, informing their senses of self in an increasingly unequal and uncertain world (Tally 1996; N. Chu 2019).

CHINA AS A SPATIAL IMAGINARY FOR GLOBAL BOSSHOOD AND FAST FASHION

While Chinese rural migrants view Guangzhou as a platform for transnational capital and cross-cultural exchange—ways of "going out" (*zou xiang shiji*) economically into the world—foreign migrants view China as a stage for worldly and otherworldly forms of ethnic and faith-based accumulation. Thus, West African and South Korean migrant entrepreneurs experience similar dynamics of stalled mobility as Chinese rural migrants experience, yet on different spatial scales of mobility and immobility. This is evidenced in the ways West African and South Korean migrants imagine Guangzhou and China as key sites for accumulation. For domestic and transnational migrants, the forms of dispossession and constraint they experienced shapes their different imaginations of Guangzhou and China at large.

For the Chinese rural migrants, "going out to the world" has become a symbol of cosmopolitanism, social mobility, and cultural capital. Confined to their sites of labor, rural migrants across the fast fashion supply chains experience a sense of cosmopolitanism directly through their participation in manufacture and exchange of fashion, gaining cultural fluidity, transnational experiences, and business acumen through their connections with their globe-trotting clients. The Wongs, for example, take pride in the fact that their clients come from all corners of the world and that their garments are sent to places to which they have never been. Their socioeconomic ties with their clients allow rural migrants to live vicariously through their clients' transnational travels and entrepreneurial endeavors. In many ways, their clients' worldly experiences serve as imaginary narratives of the kinds of bosses the migrants can never become, given their socioeconomic status.

Their social and economic connections via the transnational supply chains nonetheless enabled the Wongs to extend their social worlds beyond the everyday confines of their factory. Mrs. Wong described every country of the world to which the garments they manufacture were sent, and she imagined what traveling to these places would be like. She often asked me what flying in an airplane feels like, or how long an airplane ride from China to the United States takes, demonstrating her curiosity about seeing and experiencing a wider world outside the confines of her workshop. As a witness to the rise of her clients' expanding business ventures, Mrs. Wong imagined herself as a participant in her clients' worldly exchanges.

Indeed, the passing of globe-trotting clients across the shop floor, along with the transnational circulation of fabrics and garments into and out of the factories and market stalls shapes how Chinese rural migrants like the Wongs position themselves within the transnational circuits of fashion production and exchange. By discursively positioning their garment workshop as part of a wider chain of transnational enterprise and exchange, rural migrant laborers across the fast fashion supply chains paradoxically acknowledge their displaced positions along the garment production hierarchy while using their skilled labor, hard work, and client networks to connect themselves with these transnational circuits of garments and fashion. During the two years that I visited garment factories and household workshops across the Pearl River Delta region, Chinese migrant factory bosses and wholesalers gave me countless samples of their work for me to bring back to America and show to my peers. Aside from their immeasurable generosity, migrant laborers in China pride themselves on the fact that the products of their unwavering dedication and hard work are gifted to and displayed in faraway worlds beyond the spatial limits of the factory and beyond their emplaced roles as garment manufacturers and stall keepers. Through their everyday encounters with traveling clients, garments, and designs that float into and out of the stalls and factory spaces, Chinese rural migrants embody the discourse and practices of garment production and fashion-making in order to imagine and construct themselves as part of a wider world.

By contrast, West African Christians' experiences of war, debt, and unemployment in their home countries lead them to view Guangzhou as God's otherworldly kingdom, a site of religious conversion and faith-based accumulation. They engage in precarious accumulation that bridges their religious faith with their profit-driven desires for wealth and prosperity via the prosperity doctrine. Meanwhile, Korean Chinese and South Korean migrants view Guangzhou as a global platform for ethnic-diasporic migratory and capital flows beyond the limitations posed by national borders, citizenship, and belonging. More specifically, South Korean migrants forge ties with Korean Chinese (*Chaoxianzu*) ethnic communities in Guangzhou by drawing upon their collective histories of transnational separation and divided national affiliations to suture business and friendship ties that cross ethnic and national boundaries. Thus, the transnational migrants' religious faith and ethnic identification lead them to pursue precarious accumulation based on these affiliations. However, as I will argue, these very same religious and ethnic affiliations eventually lead to the migrants' departure from China. The uncertain futures and experiences of dispossession in China compel West African and South Korean migrant bosses to view China as a *temporary* site of economic accumulation and religious conversion before they seek opportunities elsewhere.

To be sure, their status as foreign migrants in Guangzhou leads them to occupy positions along the fast fashion supply chains that are different from those of Chinese rural migrants. Residents and government officials in Guangzhou widely recognize that foreign traders bring with them invaluable cultural knowledge, skills, and transnational business networks to create the South Korean–West African–Chinese links that comprise the city's fast fashion exchange. However, these traders, including West African and South Korean migrant bosses across the fast fashion supply chains in China, often take financial and social risks that are distinct from those faced by Chinese rural migrants. Foreign bosses must make significant investments in bridging economic and cultural links to overseas markets. This includes investing the time and effort to forge ties with Chinese translators and other cultural/linguistic intermediaries who assist them in renting commercial and residential spaces and in building local client bases to grow their businesses in Guangzhou. At the same time, these transnational migrants often lack the local connections and legal protections to offset the surveillance and other regulatory practices that they encounter based on their status as non-Chinese foreigners, a point I elaborated in chapter 3. The restrictions that emerge from these surveillance and regulatory practices present potential dangers as well as challenges for West African and South Korean migrant bosses who wish to settle in China and to achieve meaningful and long-term accumulation there.

In the sections that follow, I take the readers out of the factories and wholesale markets and bring them into the underground churches and fashion showrooms that are occupied by West African and South Korean migrants in Guangzhou's fast fashion sector. Specifically, I present ethnographic analyses to illustrate how, in the years before the COVID-19 pandemic, West African, South Korean, and Korean Chinese migrant bosses labored across the supply chains of fast fashion. These migrant bosses are initially drawn into the supply chains as migrant bosses in China based on their religious, ethnic, and nationalist identifications (Tsing 2009). Upon their arrival in China, however, these very same religious, ethnic, and national identifications lead to their expulsions from the chains and their eventual departure from China.

My ethnographic analyses illustrate a range of spatial imaginations of China and the world based on West African and South Korean experiences of migrant bosshood in Guangzhou. The descriptions below are not exhaustive of the full range and diversity of transnational migrant entrepreneurship. The aim in this chapter is not to essentialize or to encapsulate in a few ethnographic vignettes the full diversity of bosshood based merely based on migrants' ethnic, racial, and/or religious identifications. Rather, my aim is to draw out comparative and overlapping dynamics of bosshood that eventually conflict with the rising tides of capitalistic competition, religious surveillance, and ethno-nationalism in China and across the global supply chains.

GOD AS "BOSS": THE PROSPERITY DOCTRINE IN CHINA

For members of the West African Christian community in Guangzhou, migrant bosshood is experienced as a transactional relationship with God, as guided by the prosperity doctrine. In Xiaobei, thousands of migrants from different regions across West Africa, including the Ivory Coast, Liberia, Nigeria, Guinea, and Gambia, regularly assembled in a compact office room on the thirty-first floor of a semidilapidated building, where weekly services for the Global Pentecostal Living Faith Fellowship (GPLFF) took place. From 2011 to 2014, the GPLFF was an underground church in Guangzhou. This fellowship constituted one of numerous licensed and unlicensed Christian churches that served Guangzhou's transnational and multilingual diasporic communities.

At the time of my research, Christian congregations, along with other faith-based organizations, were tightly controlled by the government. They were generally divided between those that served local Chinese and those that served foreigners. At the time, Chinese congregants had to be over the age of eighteen and officially registered with one of the following three state-sanctioned groups: (1) Catholic Patriotic Church, (2) China Christian Council, and (3) the Protestant Three-Self Church.[1] Many more Chinese and foreigner congregants gathered (and possibly continue to gather) in unregistered and underground churches across China. Although regulation varied according to region and religion, state surveillance and control over faith-based activities across the nation has intensified, as the following sections of this chapter explain.

Within the physical space of GPLFF, rich purple velvet curtains draped all four walls, including all windows of the room, while black and white linoleum flooring contrasted with the burgundy velvet chairs that spanned the space. On one side of the room, a keyboardist and a singer faced the audience, while the congregation collectively sang songs of prayer and praise. With their heads bowed and their eyes firmly closed, parents, children, and young couples in the crowded audience sang songs in French and English, which they had learned in their countries of origin far away. Dressed in their Sunday finest, congregants reflected on the sermons led by Pastor Thomas, a charismatic leader from the Congo, and by Pastor Johnson, a preacher-in-training from Liberia.

Like Pastor Thomas and Pastor Johnson, many congregants in this underground fellowship were itinerant traders who exported commodities in relatively small volumes to retailers and wholesalers in all regions of Africa. For these West African pastors and congregants, their faith-based and profit-driven endeavors served as key nodes through which transnational Christianity and business networks articulated with practices of capitalist accumulation and religious conversion in southern China. Their market activities across the fast fashion supply chains represented more than the mere pursuit of profits in the secular world. They were also actions that demonstrated their faith in God as a higher authority (their "boss" in the faith-based world), which granted grace and prosperity upon those who successfully accumulated his blessings and grace.

As a case in point, one Sunday, Pastor Thomas approached the podium to lead the day's sermon. As he delivered his sermon in French, his wife, Christina, stood next to him, translating his lecture word-for-word into English. In his sermon, he explained how congregants' journeys of becoming faith-based entrepreneurs in China started with the initial realization of their otherworldly potential. A central theme that Pastor Thomas often highlighted in his sermons on the prosperity doctrine was the role of self-transformation in fulfilling one's prophetic destiny as directed by God. He declared that the way in which congregants could serve God's will was through entrepreneurship. He stated, "A man must have a vision, a higher goal. Dreams and aspirations are what separate human beings from animals. Lofty visions unite us as moneyed traders and self-made entrepreneurs who are predestined by God to carry out His message." Pastor Thomas thus reminded his congregants that money alone could not yield a deeper sense of meaning in life, yet the spread of God's message would not be possible without financial success. Money, in and of itself, held no intrinsic value if one did not possess faith in God. Without money, however, worldly projects of faith-based conversion would not be possible.

The prosperity doctrine, otherwise known as the prosperity gospel, preaches that faith in and devotion to God ensure health and prosperity in the bodily world. According to the prosperity gospel, modest monetary contributions are given as seed offerings by followers to God in exchange for bountiful health and wealth (Haynes 2013). Believers discursively link their interpretation of the prosperity doctrine to what Max Weber (2002) calls a spiritual calling, or *Beruf*. They cultivate a sense of entrepreneurial personhood through the actualization of their personal desires while accumulating God's graces to attain eternal salvation. For pastors and congregants in GPLFF, the entrepreneurial self became actualized through the enactment of their profit-driven desires in the human-centered, material world, thereby also accumulating God's graces to attain eternal salvation. Through these actions, believers accumulated God's graces in the face of ongoing uncertainty as to whether they were among God's chosen people or not. These ongoing acts of asking and receiving involved the dialectical processes of uncertainty, action, and devotional renewal, a process frequently epitomized by the maxim, "God helps those who help themselves."

West African migrants' experiences of worldly travel and small-scale entrepreneurship in China cast faith not simply as a given totality that the congregants may or may not possess. The migrants' experiences of bosshood entailed the ongoing transactional exchange—often characterized by faith, dependency, and uncertainty—between a believer and God. West African pastors and congregants expressed their faith through the discursive constructions of desire and freedom while they negotiated their encounters with racial discrimination, policing, debt, and theft in China.

West African migrants' journeys of migrant bosshood thus deepen Weber's analysis of the Protestant *spirit* of capitalism by practicing faith as transactional exchanges with God, wherein followers amass wealth in the bodily world in exchange for the accumulation of God's graces in the afterlife. As Weber (2002) writes, certain ethical values and dispositions exemplified by followers of Protestantism, such as asceticism, hard work, and modesty, compel believers of the prosperity doctrine to strive for entrepreneurial success in modern capitalist activities. In Weber's view, faith, rather than rationality and calculation, serves as the key aspect of profit-driven, capitalist motivation.

According to the West African migrants' worldviews, pathways to self-liberation thus entail the recreation of oneself as a worldly entrepreneurial subject, one that is mobile and endowed with money. The pastors' sermons not only convey messages of spiritual empowerment and uplift; they also demonstrate how congregants, the majority of whom are small-scale itinerant traders, learn to become proper entrepreneurial subjects through a business management mindset, so as to serve as personal manifestations of God's Word. For the West African Christian migrants, bosshood involves journeys and faith-based conversions that are driven and accompanied by a personal sense of self-transformation and devotional renewal. Wealth and prosperity are thus closely enjoined with devotion and religious conversion.

Pastor Thomas, for instance, recalled his first journey to China when, as a youth, he rode on a boat passing through the Ivory Coast to Sierra Leone. At that time, a long-standing civil war was raging through the region, leaving thousands of people dead and millions displaced. Thomas's boat suddenly came to a halt in the middle of the river. Several armed soldiers unexpectedly approached the stranded boat, pointing their rifles directly at him and demanding a toll fee. Moments later, gunshots ripped through the sky, leaving Thomas stricken with fear. He ducked down and thought for a second that he was dead. When he finally found the courage to open his eyes, he realized that the soldiers merely demanded a small payment and had no intention of killing him. After the young Thomas paid the fee, he proceeded onward with his journey. In that instance, as Pastor Thomas recalled, he realized that the tokens of his prosperity, including his youth, health, and survival, were given by God to fulfill his personal mission of creating a Christian fellowship in China.

Similarly, Pastor Johnson shared experiences from his childhood during the late 1980s and early 1990s in the war-torn country of Liberia. As a son of a relatively well-off businessman, he managed to escape spaces of heavy conflict incited by two civil wars by retreating from the city of Monrovia and escaping into the countryside. As a child, Johnson was raised by his paternal grandmother, who was one of four wives; and he grew up surrounded by his forty cousins. His father ran his business from home, and young Johnson remained mostly in the countryside until his teenage years. Since schools were, for the most part, closed during the two long-standing conflicts, Johnson was home-schooled. He learned to write and read by reciting passages from the Bible with his grandmother. He also picked up his business acumen from his father. Influenced by his family's faith in Christianity, the teenage Johnson decided to visit China in his search for economic and religious opportunity. With a modest amount of capital saved by his relatives at home, Johnson left Liberia through informal smuggling networks by way of Sierra Leone. He worked for a friend of his father's in Dubai for a few years to accumulate some personal savings, before he arrived in China on a one-month tourist visa in 2009. He eventually enrolled as a university student in a business college in Guangzhou to maintain his resident visa in China. Meanwhile, he taught English part-time to Chinese youths, while he struggled to grow his export business. When he met Pastor Thomas through a business exchange that year, Johnson was overwhelmed by the pastor's devotion to God, and he decided to train as a preacher under Thomas's guidance.

Migrant bosses' transoceanic journeys in search of material wealth and eternal salvation deepened their faith in God. Much like the heterogeneous processes of "imaginative world-making," as described by Carlos Rojas and Lisa Rofel (2022), African migrants' worldly pathways to self-discovery as followers of the Christian faith were punctuated by disruptions and displacements, followed by devotional renewal. In this exchange, the believer must demonstrate their devotion in God through the enactment of particular actions and qualities in this world, even though the majority of believers might not be saved.

CHINA AS AN IMAGINED SITE OF RELIGIOUS AND CAPITALIST ACCUMULATION

For many West African migrant bosses, their experiences of migration and dispossession shaped their imagination of China's place in the world of religious and capital accumulation. Once they arrived in Guangzhou, tests to their faiths materialized through their encounters with racial and religious profiling and other forms of discrimination across the fast fashion supply chains. Their experiences brewed a sense of distrust toward Chinese migrant bosses, particularly those who were not religious and had not shown active support of their own (Chinese) faith-based communities. Such distrust left some African groups isolated from Chinese communities in Xiaobei. Tensions such as these, which oftentimes characterized this neighborhood, thus colored migrants' experiences of religious and entrepreneurial life across the fast fashion supply chains in Guangzhou. The uncertain futures of West African migrants increasingly induced these itinerant traders to view China as a temporary site of economic accumulation and religious conversion.

West African migrants' journeys of precarious accumulation as migrant bosses involved uneven, dialectical transformations of personhood. More specifically, these journeys toward otherworldly salvation entailed ongoing uncertainty, divergence, and reaffirmation. Some African migrants, for example, viewed their experiences of racism and structural violence in Guangzhou as obstacles in adapting to the world of transnational subcontracting in China and on the global stage. As my preceding chapters have shown, many African migrants felt anger, disappointment, and frustration with the institutional challenges they faced here. For those who had already faced financial debt and bankruptcy, the policing and racial discrimination they encountered in Guangzhou became part and parcel of the enormous risks in attaining the health and wealth that were promised to them by the prosperity doctrine.

For example, during one Sunday service, a slim, thirty-something-year-old man from Nigeria, Peter, stood up to give the audience his testimonial. Wearing a beige button-up shirt and a matching tie, he walked up to the front of the room and stood facing the congregants. After a brief pause, he told the story of his first encounter with a Chinese customs inspector in Guangzhou. According to his testimony, as he was preparing to ship his cargo of DVDs, furniture, clothing, and household supplies overseas, an inspector halted his shipment, charging him of illegally shipping counterfeit, or "copy" goods. As he retold his story to the congregation, Peter raised his arms mimicking the sense of panic and desperation he felt as he tried to reason with the inspector. Nearly everyone in the room remained silent as Peter told his story. Perhaps they were thereby acknowledging the fact that the inspector's accusation was a mere attempt to solicit some form of monetary kickback from Peter, one that could potentially pose a large financial setback for him as a self-employed and small-scale trader. Shipping counterfeit goods served as a reason for custom officers to inspect his goods and, possibly, to charge him a fee or send him to jail.

After a long process of negotiation, the inspector eventually released Peter, free of any debt or criminal charge. As he brought his story to a close, he declared to the congregation his indebtedness to God's divine intervention in bringing a resolution to his dilemma. "I have witnessed God's grace," Thomas announced with an air of conviction, "and thanks to Him, I have been able to conduct my business here (in China). It is by the grace of God that I have my life and my livelihood here!"

In his narration of his interactions with the customs inspector, Peter conveyed the sense of helplessness he felt during his encounter. In the end, however, Peter believed that a divine intervention from God freed him from the accusations of the customs agents. Peter's testimony underscored the ways in which the accumulative practices of these West African migrants remained vulnerable to interventions by both God and the municipal state in Guangzhou. At times, divine intervention served to save the migrant bosses from debt, bankruptcy, and detainment. At other times, however, these migrant bosses were left indebted to both powers. For this reason, through their faith in God, they sought protection from the spiritual and economic risks of transnational migrant bosshood in China.

Pastor Johnson viewed such encounters with the local officials in Guangzhou as ongoing tests migrants faced in fulfilling their entrepreneurial and spiritual destinies. He explained,

> Many African migrants are foolish not to follow the rules of the administrative game here. They either don't register (with the police or the foreign visitors' bureau as required by law) or they simply throw away their passports. They merely see China as a temporary place to make money. Fast money does not exist. The world is unequal and will always be. Wealth without God are merely possessions. You must be patient and humble in the eyes of God order to succeed with Him. That is the ultimate test. God is our Provider. Business is not possible without God!

In other words, entrepreneurship, along with the promises of hope and opportunity it provided, are not possible without faith in God. Thus, the obstacles that African Christian migrants encountered did not necessarily hinder what some migrants believed to be the pathways to prosperity through God's graces. In turn, these graces were made possible by their journey to China. Congregants frequently drew comparisons between China and the rest of the world, emphasizing the number of unique business opportunities they found here, which would not be possible anywhere else. In one instance, John, a thirty-six-year-old migrant from Nigeria, narrated his experiences of living and working in Michigan for five years before moving to Guangzhou. During his time in the United States, he juggled two minimum-wage jobs, one as a bouncer in a nightclub and other as a server in a fast-food restaurant, to make ends meet. When a relative of his invited him to invest in a small import-export business in Guangzhou, John jumped at the chance to start his own business. After four years of living in Guangzhou, John continued to run a modestly successful business out of his living room in Xiaobei. He exclaimed to me, "China is the land of money and opportunity. In the US, all I could do was work as an employee. Here, I am boss!"

Believers view economic risk as an ongoing renewal of faith in their transactional exchanges with God. Taking on risk, whether economic or spiritual, is a devotional act that reinforces God's position as their boss, which is particularly significant as they imagine China as a platform upon which they could fulfill their religious and economic endeavors. For instance, Pastor Thomas once explained to me, "Anyone can be a boss in China. Most of the world's commodities are sourced here, and the cost of goods is low enough that almost anyone can buy and own branded goods. In Africa, consumers want brand names for the 'look.' They want to look like celebrities for a cheap price." He then extended his role as an entrepreneurial broker into his religious life. "In China, you can fulfill your holy destiny determined by God. But God is our boss, our provider. He comes before business. No business is possible without God. If money grows on trees, then God nurtures those trees."

Pastors Johnson and Thomas also believed that China's rise onto the world stage offered them the freedom, mobility, and possibility to manifest their faith-based potential as directed by God. Specifically, they defined themselves through the discourse of *entrepreneurial becoming*. They viewed themselves as emerging bosses and leaders, chosen from among the poor and endowed with increasing mobility and access to worlds of communication and financial abundance across Africa, China, and beyond. Their arrival in China appealed to a particular sense of being in the world where the self always emerged in relation to God. As a case in point, when I asked Pastor Johnson about his journey to China, he responded,

> Living in China has opened my mind to people of different religious backgrounds. I've expanded my awareness and understanding of the world. I now have a larger purpose, a mission. Even though the Chinese (government) presents setbacks, I am always reminded that being in China is a privilege and not a right. . . . Here, Africans, for the most part, have been misunderstood. We have always seen ourselves as people of the world despite the poverty, wars, and violence we've experienced. That is why man needs his money, family, and health to stay connected in this world. It is a matter of life and death.

The emphasis on China as a place of economic possibility was affirmed to many other African migrants in 2014, when news of Ebola-related sickness and deaths among friends and loved ones spread throughout African communities in Xiaobei. Curfews, quarantines, and closing of borders to people, money, and goods across West Africa disrupted many congregants' businesses in China to such an extent that many had to temporarily suspend their businesses. For example, Pastor Johnson relied on his part-time work as an English teacher as an alternative source of income, and congregants turned to alternative trading connections in countries across North America, the Middle East, and Southeast Asia. In this way, their experiences of dealing with the Ebola virus in Africa in 2014 foreshadowed their experiences of the COVID-19 virus in 2019–20.

The West African migrants' experiences of widespread discrimination and eviction due to COVID-related lockdowns, mass testing, and other regulations in Xiaobei in 2020, however, were quite different from their experiences of the Ebola-related lockdowns in Africa years prior. West African migrants, including Pastor Johnson, had favorable impressions of China's assistance to West African countries during the Ebola outbreak in 2014, yet these impressions changed in 2020. In my private conversations with Pastor Johnson in 2014, he frequently emphasized China's role in donating money and research efforts to aid in the Ebola crisis. At that time, congregants often stressed to me that China–Africa relations were rising in political and economic importance on the world stage. The Ebola crisis had once confirmed this belief, only for the COVID-19 outbreak to reverse it.

Though Pastors Thomas and Johnson subscribed to a future-oriented view of economic progress and eternal salvation in their financial and spiritual trajectories, their jointly held notion of development was not tied merely to the unpredictable actions of the state or to the uncertainties of the market. Rather, their financial and faith-based futures were also tied to their evangelical actions in China as stepping-stones to a global platform and to the afterlife. For them, China served as a growing church, and the body of that church symbolized the body of Christ. In expanding their evangelical and profit-driven pursuits in China, pastors and congregants followed the principles of religious and capitalist expansion, akin to the imaginations of American manifest destiny, where individuals could become "kings" of their land and of their fates.

WORLDING CHINA: LINKING CHINA WITH THE GLOBE VIA THE PROSPERITY DOCTRINE

According to the pastors of GPLFF, their experiences of transnational migration led them to view their roles as religious and entrepreneurial intermediaries in China who brokered between God and the Chinese people by negotiating financial deals while spreading God's Word. The discourse of territorialization often echoed the religious leaders' motivations to accumulate wealth and to extend the geographic boundaries of global Christianity. For example, one of the flyers advertising their Sunday services displayed the message, "Expand God's Territory." In the pastors' view, China's expansive land, its dense atheist population, and its emergence on the global stage facilitated the pastors' shared visions of evangelical conversion and economic accumulation. As Pastor Johnson once explained to me, "China is for business. China is the world." For Pastors Thomas and Johnson, China served as a growing church, and the body of that church symbolized the body of Christ. Following this belief, the pastors often echoed the following catchphrases to their congregants, "China is the Kingdom, and You are the Kingship. Expand your Territory!"

While the faith-based, transoceanic journeys of Pastors Thomas and Johnson were intimately shaped by their experiences of crossing transnational and oceanic boundaries, these pastor-entrepreneurs encountered constraints to their transnational and evangelical pursuits. These constraints were defined by governmental policies that regulate religious practices within the strict limits of the nation-state. Church members, for example, often remained vulnerable to the racial profiling, the heavy policing, and the various rent-seeking activities that regularly plagued the migrant district of Xiaobei. Congregants would find themselves sitting through service in the dark whenever the landlords decided to cut off their electricity because of late rent or unpaid bills. Ultimately, the pressures of surveillance and harassment forced pastors of this congregation to close their doors in 2014, a year during which African communities in Xiaobei faced even tighter restrictions by the police and other law enforcement officials in Guangzhou. As Pastors Thomas's and Johnson's sermons illustrate, bosshood was characterized by a dual dynamic that pushed migrant bosses to expand the territories of evangelical entrepreneurship across China and beyond, yet it pulled them back from achieving this vision when they, as bosses, encountered constraints placed upon their evangelical and accumulative pursuits.

While some scholars have argued that the prosperity doctrine offers believers a sense of hope in sustaining their lifelong search for health and wealth, West African migrants' understanding of the doctrine exceeded a mere functionalist approach. Rather, their life histories of transnational migration, cross-cultural encounters, and economic successes and failures provided a language and mode of action through which they could imagine themselves as part of a transnational, profit-driven, and God-fearing kingdom in which they served as "boss." While both pastors and congregants at GPLFF believed that they were divinely chosen by God to leave their native countries in West Africa, their search for health, wealth, and eternal salvation in the face of violence, racism, and poverty remained a continuous process of spiritual and entrepreneurial transformation that remained extremely risky and volatile.

For the pastor-entrepreneurs, the possibility for health and wealth were colored by risk, uncertainty, and the unknown on a global platform, which exceeded the physical territories of the nation-state. Faced with structural poverty in their home countries, as well as with structural violence and racism in China, their presence in China conjured a certain sense of being in the world, one that was tied to a particular cosmopolitan identity as well as to a universalistic belief in expanding the territories of God. For example, during another sermon, Pastor Thomas narrated a story about a salamander climbing up a tree as a story of self-empowerment in light of widespread debt, poverty, and disease. In using this metaphor, the pastor related the congregants' roles in China as God's chosen people in helping to spread the gospel. While China was described as their Kingdom in the spiritual sense, the congregants' transformations as entrepreneurial subjects and as faith-driven subjects always developed in relation to God—the ultimate "boss."

CHANGING FLOWS OF FATE AND DESTINY ACROSS THE CHINA-SOUTH KOREA BORDER

While West African Christians found meaning in migrant bosshood via the prosperity gospel, with God as the ultimate "boss" or guarantor of their health and wealth, South Korean migrants and the *Chaoxianzu* (Korean Chinese) ethnic minority experience precarious accumulation by drawing upon their ethnic ties to perform their specific roles as intermediaries of larger foreign companies across the global fast fashion supply chains. As jobbers and as logistics agents, South Korean bosses shadow the flows of commodities and capital around the globe and set up their livelihoods across these geographical regions. They take up the risks of market failures, including capital flight, labor disputes, and border restrictions.

As jobbers, they arrange to ship the finished goods to Guatemala or other destinations before they are redistributed to the United States. For this reason, companies rely on the work of subcontractors so that goods can pass through multiple ports and customs agents in regions across the world, including Mexico (to avoid import taxes through the North American Free Trade Agreement [NAFTA], before they arrived in the United States). Jobbers do this to help companies evade various importation and tax regulations posed by different countries. Jobbers must continuously check on the political economic conditions of countries, particularly in the developing world, since government officials often change their importation procedures and requirements unexpectedly.

Since the introduction of market reforms in China, the transnational supply chains of fast fashion manufacture and exchange have historically been driven by the entrepreneurial activities of the South Korean diasporic community in Guangzhou. Their diasporic business networks extend across East and Southeast Asia as well as across Latin America (Moon 2014, 2016). The South Korean bosses in Guangzhou rely heavily on the work of the *Chaoxianzu* as cultural and linguistic intermediaries. The *Chaoxianzu* are an officially recognized ethnic minority in China; the term refers to populations of ethnic Korean descent primarily from the regions of Yanbian Korean Autonomous Prefecture in Jilin as well as from the provinces of Heilongjiang and Liaoning. Since the early 1990s, an influx of Korean Chinese migrants from the northern region of Dongbei arrived in Guangzhou to work as small-scale entrepreneurs—mainly as intermediary agents in the emerging fashion trade. Many Korean Chinese left their homes in northern China to try their luck in entrepreneurship by collaborating with South Korean migrants, who had previously worked in Seoul's Dongdaemun fashion market and now settled in Guangzhou to take part in the burgeoning fashion industry.

The social status of the *Chaoxianzu* within the global South Korean communities remains subordinate to that of their South Korean bosses since their national affiliations and affective ties remain historically outside of South Korea. The *Chaoxianzu* often come from poorer regions of northern China and have no legal claims to state-sponsored welfare, including housing, childcare, and health care, in Guangzhou or other Chinese cities. As ethnic intermediaries, they have cultural-linguistic access to the world markets of fast fashion through their connections to South Korean traders, though these links are often short-term, unreliable, and even exploitative. This notion of ethnic and national inferiority leaves the *Chaoxianzu* in Guangzhou subject to labor exploitation, economic struggles, familial separation, and social isolation.

Despite the challenges they face, members of the *Chaoxianzu* ethnic minority who engage in fast fashion exchange tend to view the uncertainty of their socioeconomic statuses as opportunities to change the flow of their life course. Moving back and forth between China and Korea, they insert themselves into the commodity chains in order to seize whatever entrepreneurial opportunities they can. They describe this act as an attempt to "break out" (*chuang*) out of their fate in the global capitalist economy, as they struggle to exceed the limitations of their national affiliations. Migrant bosshood entails waiting until fate or destiny befalls them. As they wait, they try every opportunity to test their luck, just in case their moment to *chuang* arrives.

The enactments of *chuang* as a business-oriented means of "breaking out" of their fates and destinies materialize precisely from the folds between the future and the present as well as from the gaps between desires and reality. In this way, this *chuang* differs from what anthropologist Yang Zhan (2022) in her study of migrant laborers in Beijing observes, which describes how Chinese migrants enact *chuang* as a form of "venturing out," a mode of migratory living and labor mobility that entails frequent relocation, unpredictable economic risks, and (re)mapping personal futures so as to push on the existing boundaries of entrepreneurship and risky self-enterprise. While Zhan insightfully points out the gap between reality and Chinese migrants' desires for freedom and mobility, South Korean migrant bosses and the *Chaoxianzu* ethnic minority across Guangzhou's fast fashion sector regard bosshood as a means to redirect the course of their futures, via fate and destiny, beyond China's national boundaries, precisely through their ethnic and diasporic connections. These conditions of hope and deferment, which are mapped across transoceanic and diasporic ties, keep migrant bosses physically mobile yet experientially confined within the condition of stalled mobility, in hopes that fulfillment of their aspirations might materialize at any unforeseen moment.

THE CHAOXIANZU CULTURAL AND LINGUISTIC LINKS
ACROSS GUANGZHOU'S FAST FASHION SUPPLY CHAINS

The participation of the *Chaoxianzu* intermediaries across the transnational supply chains for fast fashion enables these cross-cultural migrants to straddle and thus to occupy multiple worlds of cultural identity, fashion, capital, and exchange so as to forge unique market niches as intermediary agents, linguistic translators, and cultural brokers. By asserting their partial, multiple, and overlapping cultural affiliations through transnational encounters, the *Chaoxianzu* emphasize their differentiated and, at times, fragmented identities across the boundaries of China, South Korea, and countries across Latin America as well as across multiple dimensions of material and spiritual worlds. As ethnic and economic intermediaries, the *Chaoxianzu* occupy a unique position in the global division of labor and exchange, one that is characterized by ambivalence and ambiguity. Since they bridge and straddle the worlds of South Korean beauty and fashion, they claim a limited degree of social capital in the worlds of fast fashion and popular cultures in Guangzhou, primarily because of their linguistic and cultural connections to the South Korean diaspora which have given rise to the global K-pop and fast fashion industries (Moon 2016, 2020).

During my research on the fast fashion supply chain in Guangzhou, for instance, I came across several intermediary agents who operated as linguistic translators and brokers for South Korean jobbers in China. Many of these Korean Chinese agents were in their twenties and thirties, young adults who had forfeited the comforts of their homes and their chances of a university education in search of profits in Guangzhou's fast fashion sector. As I became acquainted with these Korean Chinese intermediaries, I learned about their struggles with employment, migration, and familial separation. They often recalled the long and difficult train ride from China's Dongbei region to Guangzhou, where they arrived with few belongings. Some *Chaoxianzu* migrants recalled arriving in Guangzhou without contacts and without any extra clothes. They often relied on employment agencies that were unreliable or even dishonest about the employment conditions they offered. Many migrants would take up low-paying wage employment in factories, logistics companies, and wholesale markets as they struggled to forge their new lives away from home.

Sun, for example, was a forty-year-old Guangzhou resident of ethnic Korean Chinese (*Chaoxian*) descent. Sun was a good friend of Tina's. Sun and I discussed the intricacies and challenges of the fast fashion industry in Guangzhou. In 2016, at the time of our meeting, Sun worked as a jobber for South Korean clients who operated corporate-sized garment wholesale businesses and factories in Guatemala. His role as a jobber was to facilitate business partnerships between his South Korean clients and local Chinese manufacturers. His ethnic-linguistic background provided him with the necessary skills to function as a cultural translator in Guangzhou. As Sun explained to me, Guatemala and Nicaragua were important distribution hubs for finished clothing in the American markets. Fast fashion commodities were shipped from Guatemala to other wholesale markets across Central and Latin America. His Korean clients from Guatemala would visit Guangzhou at least twice a year to purchase samples and to coordinate supplies and raw materials. They would come in February or March to prepare for the spring season, and they would return in July or August to prepare for the winter season. Some of Sun's clients operated as Original Equipment Manufacturers (OEMs) for Zara and other fast fashion brands based in the United States or in Europe. In addition to their work as OEMs, they also owned and ran independent stalls in garment wholesale markets in Guatemala (K. Thomas 2016).

Sun's personal history and involvement in the global fast fashion industry was mired in complication and heartbreak, leaving him to continuously defer his aspirations for successful entrepreneurship. He recounted a time when he was a child in Heilongjiang, when he would travel to the China/Russia border and watch massive shipping containers pass by. This memory, in some way, foreshadowed his involvement in the jobbing/logistics industry. In the 1950s, his maternal grandfather swam from what is today South Korea to Jilin, China, during the Korean war. From there, he had walked and hitchhiked north to Heilongjiang, where he settled there as a farmer. He eventually married a Chinese woman and together they had Sun. After Sun was born, his parents moved from Heilongjiang back to South Korea to escape poverty. They left Sun and his brother behind in the care of his paternal grandmother.

Growing up, Sun rarely saw his grandmother or his parents, since he attended a local boarding school. As a teenager, he dropped out of school and took odd jobs in construction. With his modest savings, Sun later moved to South Korea to reunite with his family who had built a business in interior design. Unfortunately, his entry and stay in South Korea was not through legal means. Bad luck befell him when authorities in South Korea eventually found out and deported Sun back to China in 2008. His family remained in South Korea. In the course of narrating his life story, Sun remarked that, like him, most *Chaoxianzu* in China had broken family ties due to the strain of migration, including exclusions in citizenship and geographical distances. To this day, Sun and his family remain separated because of their different citizenship statuses. As escapees from China, his family members thought about returning to China. However, if they were to do so, they could not leave China again. They instead preferred to stay in South Korea, where they were accustomed to their new way of life. Determined to return and reunite with his family in South Korea, Sun chose to invest the savings that were entrusted to him by his relatives to buy a house. Unfortunately, he lost his investments in the stock market in the 2008 financial crisis. His parents cut off communications with him as a result.

Though Sun often attributed the course of his fate to bad timing or bad luck, his financial losses were clearly linked to the timing of global events that were linked to the worldwide financialization of capital. His entry into the fast fashion market was, in fact, tied to the global neoliberalization and intensification of finance capital as well as to the large-scale restructuring of labor markets across Asia. Sun explained that he entered the fashion markets in southern China when Guangzhou replaced the Dongdaemun market in Seoul as the hub of trendy, low-cost clothing. The rise of wages in Seoul, along with growing labor unrest, coincided with the introduction of China's economic reforms in the early 1980s. During this time, South Korean workers and entrepreneurs emigrated to the United States, Guatemala, Nicaragua, Argentina, and countries in Southeast Asia to open garment factories and wholesale markets. South Koreans, along with Middle Eastern, Southeast Asian, Japanese, and Russian traders flocked to Guangzhou to purchase fashion goods. Sun tried to capitalize on his cultural and linguistic ties and established a business assisting South Korean clients in Guangzhou.

Testing the flows of his fortune thus seemed to be central to Sun's work as a jobber. He was in constant search of new clients and new markets in which they could operate. When the timing of the market was right, Sun recognized that he must take the risk and boldly invest in new business ventures or aggressively claim access to new markets for shipping and imports. For Sun and for the *Chaoxianzu* generally, moving across the supply chains for fast fashion as well as across the border between China and South Korea, were acts of waiting until prosperity struck. For this reason, for the *Chaoxianzu*, migrant bosshood was imagined, practiced, and calculated on a transnational scale, beyond the geographic and political boundaries of nation-state. Yet, Sun paradoxically encountered ongoing limitations and deferment of his global ambitions in the form of national laws and citizenship restrictions. Bosshood thus served as a means through which migrants like Sun attempted to redraw the flows of their fates along national boundaries of inclusion and exclusion through their engagements in the global capitalist economy. Members of the *Chaoxianzu* community in Guangzhou's fast fashion industry thus appropriated the notion of predestined, transnational encounters as a means of changing the cross-regional flows of their fates and fortunes, which unfortunately were often defined and limited by boundaries of the nation-state.[2]

ENTREPRENEURIAL WAITING: TRANSNATIONAL DESTINIES AND ETHNIC MEDIATIONS

As jobbers and logistics agents, Sun and Tina had to check on the political economic conditions of countries continuously and gauge their risks accordingly. In a way, their calculations of risk involved a spatial mapping of various importation procedures and tax requirements around the globe. For example, Tina informed us one evening over dinner that she had heard a rumor that the Philippines no longer accepted imports of certain gems and fabrics from China. Consequently, she quickly had to find another warehouse in which to store her clients' goods. She was considering somewhere in West Africa, since many of her clients were from that region. Before she found a warehouse, she explained, she must look for someone who would sign contracts (bills of lading) for her in French, since she was interested in finding more clients and thus shipping more goods to French-speaking countries. She asked Jackie (another mutual friend) and Sun about the risks involved in storing her clients' goods in posts across West Africa. Implicitly, she was asking Jackie and Sun whether they knew anyone in the region whom they could bribe to get the goods through customs inspection. The sum of bribes and terms of exchange, as Jackie and Sun elaborated, depended on the destination and types of goods that were being shipped. Logistics agents often swapped RMB for local currency to avoid local taxes (*xiqian*, or "wash money"). Agents would also hire mules (*hei gui*) to assist traders in carrying goods illegally across national borders.

At that point of the conversation, Sun then turned to me and explained that *guanxi*, or intimate ties and relationships, along with quickness and boldness in one's entrepreneurial mindset, were the most important assets in running a logistics business, since global logistics empires would not be possible without breaking the law (Nordstrom 2007). These cross-border trades critically relied on bribery and other illegal strategies to move goods from region to region. Though often seen as an illicit and risky act, bribery served as a means of mitigating the risks involved in the unpredictable fluctuations of the global economy. For instance, if Tina could not find an alternative location to store her clients' goods, she could potentially lose her client's business.

In short, chance, fate, and market timing were critical aspects of boss-hood among the *Chaoxianzu* migrant bosses, since trade laws and customs agents with whom they had cushy relationships changed frequently. In the jobbers' view, this practice involved testing their luck in meeting the right people at the right time. When we met, Sun was looking to establish partnerships in Luxembourg, the Congo, and the United States. To achieve this, he looked to his close friendship networks, including me, as potential business connections. He also traveled to the Congo in 2016 to meet potential business partners and to establish a more solid, trusting relationship with them. Additionally, he often asked about the economic and political climate in regions around the world. For instance, Sun asked Tina whether Russia would be a good market into which to transport fast fashions. Tina then advised Sun to abstain from investing in Russian markets, since customs agents expected too many bribes. For these jobbers, business partnerships there would simply be too costly. To this day, Sun was still testing the boundaries of his fate and destiny.

While the ethnographic vignettes above narrate the stories of Tina and Sun, migrant bosses of a *Chaoxianzu* ethnic background who attempted to sync their entrepreneurial ambitions to the fluctuations of the global fast fashion industry, the experiences of migrant bosshood among South Korean migrants to China, by contrast, were shaped by their gendered and class-based positions across the commodity chains. Much like the experiences of rural Chinese bosses, the everyday intimacies of labor and exchange between South Korean business partners capture the vivid moments in which migrant bosses' experiences hinge precariously upon relations with *other* migrant bosses across the commodity chain. However, unlike Chinese bosses, transnational bosses, including South Korean and West African migrants, must negotiate the boundaries of competition and dependence as they attempt to navigate the cultural and linguistic worlds in China. At the same time, these bosses' ability to strike out on a business opportunity at the precise fateful moment determines their successes in adequately performing the gendered role of the risk-taking masculine "boss."

Here, I turn to performances of masculinity that are made possible by migrant bosshood, even though they rely critically upon the intimate acts of *mutual dependencies* that sustain the transnational supply chains of fast fashion. Such relations draw upon human intimacies in which care, reliance, trust, and vulnerability punctuate migrants' experiences of bosshood. Because of various linguistic and cultural differences between South

Koreans and Chinese in Guangzhou, migrant bosses from South Korea rely heavily on the *Chaoxianzu* as cultural translators who help them navigate the complex worlds of bureaucracy and self-enterprise in China. Place-based *guanxi* are essential to getting a foot in the door or establishing oneself in Guangzhou's fast fashion industry. Those who lack the deep cultural ties to local Chinese officials, suppliers, and other entrepreneurs are vulnerable to nationalist tensions, jealousy, cultural misunderstandings, and distrust.

More specifically, South Korean bosses must constantly negotiate the fine line between dependency and distrust when they deal with their Chinese employees, their transnational clients, and local Chinese manufacturers. On the one hand, migrant entrepreneurs from South Korea rely on other South Korean bosses and local *Chaoxianzu* employees for linguistic and cultural translation. *Chaoxianzu* employees become especially important when the bosses need to build political connections or to request special requests from local Chinese officials. On the other hand, however, the bosses' cultural dependency becomes a source of distrust when these dealings are not transparent, causing South Korean bosses to feel they are losing a certain degree of leverage.

PERFORMING THE MASCULINE "BOSS"

The dynamics of dependency and distrust became apparent to me when in 2016, I met Mr. Jin, a South Korean jobber in Guangzhou. Mr. Jin was a soft-spoken man with a gentle, pleasant smile. I had become acquainted with him through a mutual friend who was a regular client of his shop in one of Sanyuanli's well-known wholesale markets. His wholesale outlet, CESS, sold sophisticated and functional women's contemporary clothing featuring straight cuts and minimalist colors. His label gave sporty chic a fresh new look by combining refined cuts with casual flair. That day, we met in his private office on Yuanjinglu, a street lined with Korean cafes, restaurants, and commercial offices frequented by South Koreans and ethnic Korean Chinese residents in Guangzhou. When I arrived at his office, I introduced myself and explained to him the details of my research project. Mr. Jin then began to describe his entry into the fast fashion markets in Guangzhou.

Mr. Jin shared with me his vivid memories of growing up in the countryside, not far from Seoul, where he moved after his high school graduation. As a child he had witnessed the emergence of the North/South division in Korea, and he described the flood of migrants from Korea's northern regions into Seoul as low-wage workers. He recalled his childhood fondly, though he admitted he was a relatively bad student. While many of his friends entered the professional classes by studying law, economics, medicine, and engineering, Mr. Jin achieved a modest degree of social mobility by enrolling in a professional program in textile science in Seoul. Textile science was a relatively new and expanding field at the time, one in which he thrived.

The post-1970s market liberalization and subsequent expansion of textile and garment exports from South Korea paved the way for Mr. Jin's entry into the global fast fashion industry. During these decades of economic restructuring, Mr. Jin participated firsthand in the rise and eventual fall of the Dongdaemun market in Seoul as the global export hub for stylish and low-cost Korean fashion. After graduation, he worked in several apprenticeships, which allowed him to perfect his skills in garment-making and design. Mr. Jin then opened a small boutique in the Dongdaemun market, which, at that time, served as the global export hub for Korean fast fashion. He used his family savings to export clothing to China, the United States, Canada, and Europe under his own local brand. A decade later, he expanded his company's client base internationally by collaborating with jobbers from around the world, who would purchase his company's clothing and resell them under other brands.

Despite the growth of his business over the years, Mr. Jin found that the high cost of rent in Seoul was becoming unmanageable. To continue running his wholesale outlet in Seoul's Dongdeamun market, he had to pay at least 500,000 RMB ($77,000 USD) in annual capital or what he called "key money." On top of that, he spent 50,000 RMB ($7,700 USD) on the first month's rent and 100,000 RMB ($15,800 USD) per month subsequently for the duration of his lease. After the 1997 Asian financial crisis, he and his colleagues experienced huge financial losses, which he managed to cover by informally borrowing from family and friends. By 2000, Mr. Jin still teetered on the brink of bankruptcy, so he was eager to find alternatives to the Dongdeamun market. He learned about Guangzhou's growing status in the global fast fashion industry through clients whom he met at the annual Magic Trade Show for jewelry and fashion in Las Vegas. On his trips to Las Vegas, he would purchase samples and recruit transnational clients for his company. He began to gradually establish connections with Chinese manufacturers through his clients, who had hired factory owners in China to assist them in producing inexpensive samples for the trade show.

When he arrived in China to start his business in 2005, he encountered challenges in getting his company started. He relied heavily on existing South Korean Christian associations in Guangzhou as well as on networks within the *Chaoxianzu* migrant community. Most of the client traffic that he received was through the internet, though he found that initiating new partnerships with unfamiliar clients carried many risks. For instance, when the economy weakened, many of his clients absconded without picking up their orders or paying for their goods. One client in the Philippines submitted an order of clothing but didn't return to pick up his goods for more than one year. Mr. Jin would then have to sell his extra inventory at discounted prices. After encountering these and other financial losses, Mr. Jin required that his clients pay a 10 percent deposit on their orders before manufacturing would begin.

Despite these challenges, Mr. Jin successfully gained a foothold in the industry. He arrived in China just as the import of Korean styles in fashion, beauty, and pop culture caught hold of Chinese consumer youths. While his business in Guangzhou slowly grew, Mr. Jin ventured out to start his own design label, an aspiration of his that he believed would allow him to exert more control over the design and production processes. Even though he maintained his business as a third-party agent who served clients across the Seoul and Los Angeles supply chains, he worked part-time as an independent designer, drawing samples and creating unique designs under his own brand. As a third-party agent, he would subcontract from other agents. He would bring samples in from abroad and coordinate their mass manufacture with a local factory owner. By contrast, as a designer, he would alter minor designs he found in the Zhaocun fabric market or the Xi Fang Hang wholesale market and use them as samples under his own brand. His dual roles as agent and designer led him to switch easily between boss and subcontractor, which made good financial sense, since his employment as an agent helped to financially support his venture as an independent design label. He aspired to operate an independent boutique label full time, since he enjoyed the creative aspects of his work as a designer. By developing his own fashion line, he would find more opportunity to extend to other markets around the world.

Mr. Jin's trajectory in scaling up his labor from a subcontractor to a designer with his own creative label fits the conventional figure of the masculine entrepreneur, who *chuang*, or seized upon economic opportunity when the moment arose, despite the financial risks that were involved. At the time of our meeting, Mr. Jin was on the cusp of expanding his own independent label, CESS. The world of Korean-influenced athleisure wear was rising in popularity. He was able to display his entrepreneurial successes by establishing his reputation as a church and family man in his local Christian community. The collaborations that Mr. Jin forged based on ethnic and national ties across Guangzhou and Seoul, however, ultimately became challenges to other South Korean men's perceived roles as masculine figures of accumulation.

A CHAIN OF UNCERTAIN MASCULINITIES

A look back at Mr. Jin's entrepreneurial rise as a South Korean contractor and designer in Guangzhou is instructive of the cultural significance that migrants invest in their inclusion and participation in the global supply chains of fast fashion. As I will show, the elevation of his labor into the ranks of bosshood secured Mr. Jin's role as a family man and community leader. His advancement, however, set barriers for the masculine performances of other ethnic Korean male bosses further down the South Korean–*Chaoxianzu* supply chains. The following case study of two Korean migrant bosses, Mr. Jin and Mr. Park, across the fast fashion supply chain in Guangzhou demonstrates how masculinity is affectively invested in and performed by migrant bosshood across the supply chains of fast fashion. Bosshood serves as a relational dynamic of capitalist accumulation, but much like supply chains themselves, these performances of gender are tenuously constructed and ultimately destabilized if they cross class and ethnic lines.

Later in the afternoon on the day of our meeting, Mr. Jin took me a café on Yuanjinglu to meet his former employee, another South Korean jobber, Mr. Park. He was an older, plumper man with an outgoing and gregarious personality. My first impression of the two men was that they were close business associates and good friends. Mr. Park explained that they spent their weekends playing golf near Baiyuan park and would like to take me along on their next outing. Like Mr. Jin, Mr. Park owned and operated a garment wholesale company in Guangzhou, which supplied many big box chains across the United States and Europe. The two South Korean men had met a few years earlier at the LA Jobber Market when they collaborated on a purchase order for a department store chain. At the time I met the men, Mr. Park employed, at most, five Chinese workers. Mr. Park and Mr. Jin would receive production orders from their US-based clients, and they would find samples and accessories at the Zhaocun wholesale market, close to the Wongs' factory, before bringing the supplies to Chinese manufacturers. One of the primary tasks of the boss' role across the garment supply chains was to oversee the timing and quality of the mass-produced garments on behalf of their clients.

After our initial meeting that afternoon, I subsequently met Mr. Park independently a couple of times since he seemed quite open to sharing his experiences of working in Guangzhou. He had also lived and worked in LA for several years, so Mr. Jin thought that Mr. Park would be a useful contact for me in my research. In fact, Mr. Park's wife and children lived in LA at the time of our meeting. Mr. Park usually spent nearly half the year living with his family in LA, returning to Guangzhou only during the second half of the year to run his company.

When I spent more time with Mr. Park, I learned that as a young man he had served in the military in South Korea. However, he was eventually discharged when he was in his thirties, and he moved to LA to start a life with his wife and family there. When he lived in LA, he worked as a manager of a small Korean restaurant downtown, but he found the work to be grueling, and the profits were modest, at best. He had also experienced several racist encounters there, particularly in the wake of the LA riots in the 1990s.

Based on his experience running a small business in the United States, Mr. Park often asserted his sense of South Korean national belonging as critical to his identity as a boss in China. During our meals, he would repeatedly show us the "Korean style" of eating and drinking. He openly stated that he felt "free" in China, but he did not seem to like America or the American way of life. In fact, he once stated that he trusted the Chinese government more than the US government. To be sure, he felt more free working as his own boss than as a manager of a small restaurant in LA. Throughout our conversations, he would assert himself as a "man" (as a performance of masculinity) by suggesting that he took his role as a self-made entrepreneur as seriously as when he served in the South Korean military. As the breadwinner of his family and as an independent contractor, bosshood was one way of performing his masculinity. His assertions of masculinity show his attempts to resolve his sense of relative uneasiness and, to some extent, powerlessness in his role as a boss in China.

According to Mr. Park, fate had connected him with Mr. Jin. As he was in close proximity to the LA Jobber Market, Mr. Park learned about the garment trade through extended relatives, and it was through some family connections that he found Mr. Jin, who assisted him in starting his own business in Guangzhou. Initially, at their first meeting, Mr. Jin had provided Mr. Park with some limited contacts to establish his company in Guangzhou. This included information on acquiring a business visa and an apartment and several contacts to Chinese manufacturers, and so on. However, in recounting his arrival in Guangzhou, Mr. Park explained that one day, Mr. Jin abruptly began ignoring Mr. Park. This was probably out of fear of competition. Mr. Park then explained, "In the beginning while I was still employed by Mr. Jin, I relied quite a bit on him for key business information in Guangzhou. However, I knew that he wanted to remain distant from me. There were many times when I first started my business that I wanted to ask him questions, but I refrained. I didn't want to bother him too much." It was clear that the relationship between Mr. Jin and Mr. Park was peppered with jealousy, distrust, and competition, even though Mr. Park had depended on Mr. Jin in establishing his business in Guangzhou.

This uneasy relationship seemed to have set the tone for Mr. Park's other professional relationships in his company. This unease crossed gender and ethnic relations, which played significant roles in Mr. Park's experiences and understanding of bosshood in Guangzhou. To my surprise, Mr. Park elaborated that he still did not trust most of his own employees, because he did not seem to feel comfortable being a foreign boss in China. He remained distant from his local Chinese and *Chaoxianzu* employees. Since Mr. Park did not speak the language of his employees, he feared that they would steal his profits as well as his professional contacts. And because Mr. Park feared that he would anger one of his employees, he remained silent about his various misgivings.

Mr. Jin's financial struggles in Seoul after the global financial crisis ultimately contributed to Mr. Park's sense of displacement along nationalistic, religious, and linguistic divides. Mr. Jin arrived in China hoping to build his subcontracting business from the ground up before experimenting in his own creative design label. His life history resonated, in many ways, with the conventional trajectory of an upwardly mobile migrant entrepreneur in China. His reputation as a respected family man elevated his standing in the South Korean Christian community, endowing him with both economic and social capital. As a member of the diasporic community in Guangzhou, Mr. Jin achieved relative success in translating his technical skills, business experience, and clientele from South Korea and the United States to China. His successes enabled him to accumulate a certain level of wealth and standing in Guangzhou. Mr. Jin's personification of masculinity thus hinged upon his economic productivity and accumulation, as demonstrated by his ability to leverage and convert family savings into transnational wealth.

By contrast, Mr. Park's inability to live up to the masculine figure of self-enterprising businessman left him in a position of relative vulnerability vis-à-vis Mr. Jin. Though he was also a transnational contractor with clients in the United States and across South America, Mr. Park could not accumulate the necessary social and monetary capital to perform the image of a reputable family man with social networks within the diasporic community. This left him feeling isolated and lonely in China. Without a linguistic ability in Chinese and without membership in the religious community in Guangzhou, Mr. Park remained distrustful of his fellow South Korean business partners and his Chinese and *Chaoxianzu* employees. The contrast of self-perceived success between the two men highlights the ways in which the performance of the masculine, self-enterprising, globetrotting entrepreneur rests upon uneven and unstable terrain.

Despite their similar ambitions, their experiences of waiting to seize business opportunities and to change the flows of their entrepreneurial fates entailed negotiating the fine line between masculine competition as self-enterprising "bosses" and friendly collaborators. The uncertainty of their trust in and bond with one another thus left the status of their personal friendship and business collaboration in a state of waiting and deferment. Mr. Park's successes in performing the role of the risk-taking, masculine entrepreneur depended on his relationship with Mr. Jin, who had provided the key contacts for Mr. Park needed to establish a foothold in the fast fashion industry in Guangzhou. In turn, Mr. Jin needed Mr. Park's dependence upon him to reinforce his own status as a modestly established and successful South Korean boss in China. Ironically, both migrant bosses were testing their economic fates and continuously looking for new business opportunities both in China and across the globe.

None of us could have known that, one year later, the South Korean men's marketing and self-identification as purveyors of the global K-pop scene paved the way for the closing of their businesses in Guangzhou and their eventual departure from China. In 2017, scores of nationalistically driven demonstrators publicly organized across Chinese cities to protest the US-backed THAAD anti-ballistic missile system in South Korea, calling for the boycott of Korean consumer goods.[3] This anti-Korean backlash (*xianhan*) led to a sudden and unexpected drop in the number of South Korean–run businesses, as Chinese clients cancelled production orders, landlords broke contracts by raising rents, and walk-in clients boycotted Mr. Jin's clothing.

Caught in the crossfire of fervent nationalism in China, global consumer movements, and changing military alignments across the Yellow Sea, Mr. Jin's and Mr. Park's embodiments of ethnic and national identifications that once secured their modest rise to the ranks of bosshood in Guangzhou turned into liabilities. The nationalistic divisions that emerged since China intensified its participation in the global economy could not also sustain the global reach and the staying power of the Korean Wave in China's fast fashion circles. Both men eventually left China to search for new business ventures elsewhere. Yet, even when they had achieved modest economic gains as bosses of their own fates and destinies in Guangzhou, their successes remained precarious and uncertain. Like many of their South Korean friends, business partners, and colleagues in Guangzhou, Mr. Jin and Mr. Park left Guangzhou to venture and territorialize other fashion markets in Southeast Asia. After a few months, I had never heard back from Mr. Jin or Mr. Park, leaving me to wonder whether they and the second wave of K-pop fandom fashion and sensibility would ever return to Guangzhou.

DISILLUSIONMENTS AND DEPARTURES

Straddling the worlds of labor and capital led these transnational migrant bosses to negotiate intersecting cultural and geographic divides on a global scale. Their experiences of migrant bosshood were unique from those of Chinese rural migrants in that they had to negotiate the possibilities and limitations of their entrepreneurial aspirations that crossed ethnic, religious, and national boundaries. Through their experiences of cross-racial and cross-ethnic encounters, they imagined Guangzhou and China as platforms of religious and ethnic accumulation that, in turn, were determined by nationalism and national belonging. The notion of "straddling" is particularly useful in characterizing the intersection of multiple life-generating projects that collide, connect, and eventually disconnect across transnational supply chains (Roitman 1990), since migrants must constantly negotiate and reassess their own identities, worldviews, and obligations when they engage with other migrant bosses across the supply chains. These transnational and transregional divides embed global supply chains within China's contemporary moments of post-socialist transformation.

For the West African and South Korean migrants in Guangzhou, migrant bosshood entailed the strategic navigation and transformation of one's fate and destiny when the opportunity struck. West African Christians attempted to secure their status as those who were chosen by God in the otherworldly realms of faith and redemption through actions taken in the bodily world. They demonstrated their beliefs by establishing licensed and underground congregations and by preaching the word of God, the "boss" of faith and salvation. South Korean migrants altered the flows of fortunes and prosperity by actively seeking new business partners and new hubs of capital around the globe, upon which they could anchor their entrepreneurial and gendered aspirations. The long-standing migration of friends and family between China and South Korea has facilitated the arrival of the Korean Wave as a worldwide cultural phenomenon, which in turn has led to the mushrooming of subcontractor relationships as personified by the masculine "boss." Ultimately, however, the transnational migrant "boss" as a figure of capitalist aspiration and accumulation in Guangzhou has become destabilized by the ethno-nationalist movements that underlie transnational supply chains.

The bridging of transnational supply chains across the borders of South Korea, Senegal, and China would not have been possible without the personal relationships among the West African, South Korean, and *Chaoxianzu* migrant bosses. The linking of these subjective and spatial divides across the supply chains, however, destabilizes other intersecting gendered, ethnic, and religious identifications, upon which labor mobilization across the supply chains depends. In effect, the same conditions that facilitate the formation of transnational supply chains ultimately set the stage for its eventual decoupling. After all, supply chains are constituted and are made possible by unstable contractual relationships and contingent arrangements (Tsing 2009).

The disillusionments and drawbacks of bosshood, as this chapter shows, become generative moments that reveal the contingencies and fragilities of capitalist accumulation. My ethnographic analyses engage with the subjective dimensions of capital flight, deindustrialization, and social abandonment as permanent states of being, particularly in the contemporary period of global neoliberalism (Biehl 2005; Bair and Werner 2011; Millar 2018; Finkelstein 2019; Steffan 2021), yet I push this literature further by detailing the ways in which participants across global supply chains confront their expulsions from the chains and their removal through forced, sometimes violent, exits.

For example, many of the transnational migrant bosses experienced pressure to leave China due to political campaigns that targeted their religious faiths. In recent years, the police and other state agents intensified the crackdowns on Chinese, West African, and South Korean religious congregations across Chinese cities (Hernandez 2018; Berlinger 2018; Mauldin 2020; A. Wang 2023). At the same time, intensified crackdowns on undocumented African migrants led many traders to close their businesses and to leave Guangzhou in favor of more religiously tolerant and business-friendly cities such as Yiwu in Zhejiang Province (Kohnert 2022; Olander 2016; G. Huang 2020; Kirton 2020; Vincent 2020). Unyielding surveillance and aggressive restrictions on mobility by the city police forced African church leaders and their congregants to go further underground, moving their sites of worship and limiting communication to individuals outside the congregation. The uncertain conditions of their religious and work lives demonstrated the enormous personal and economic risks that African traders took to establish their practices of profit-making and worship.

In this way, migrant bosses faced competing demands in their transnational evangelical and accumulative ambitions alongside the limits of those ambitions posed by the Chinese state. Rising ethno-nationalistic sentiments, as evidenced by national anti-THAAD protests in 2017, for instance, eventually shut down many Korean-owned businesses in China. The campaigns as well as the large-scale evictions and ensuing mass protests against African migrants in Guangzhou at the start of the COVID-19 pandemic shaped the migrant bosses' worldly and otherworldly ambitions for capitalist accumulation. They also colored the transnational migrants' image of China as a temporary spatial imaginary of precarious accumulation.

By nature of its tenuousness and diversity, migrant participation in transnational supply chains is inherently disruptive, unstable, and contingent. Indeed, global supply chains are created to ultimately de-link and transform into another configuration of labor and production as market participants continuously look to alternative frontiers of capitalist expansion and accumulation. Migrant bosses become entangled with the processes of linking and de-linking of supply chains as they confront failures in capital accumulation via disruptions of their gendered, ethnic, nationalistic, and kin-based performances and relations. The *unmaking* of their class, racial, gendered, and kin-based affiliations ultimately leads them to disengage from the chains before they venture for the next profit-driven opportunity. They then continue to stake their claims in precarious accumulation, albeit with ambivalence.

Conclusion

In July 2021, long after the departure from Guangzhou of my West African and South Korean friends and interlocutors, I spent an afternoon wandering through the store-lined streets that constituted the district of Xiaobei. I was curious to see what transformations the COVID-19 pandemic had brought to this neighborhood. To my surprise, Xiaobei had become a ghost town. By 2021, I had lost contact with members of the West African and South Korean communities in Xiaobei and Sanyuanli. Economic life, including the residents, shopkeepers, and visitors who once animated the streets with vibrant sights, sounds, and smells, had completely vanished, leaving shops boarded up and even entire buildings vacant and abandoned. In place of boisterous and crowded storefronts, silence pervaded nearly every corner of the neighborhood.

Large poster-sized propaganda banners depicting dancers waving their hands, wide-eyed and smiling, and dressed in traditional ethnic outfits covered the walls along the main thoroughfare of the neighborhood. In contrast to the silence and lifelessness of the streets, even in broad daylight, the propaganda banners awkwardly asserted a bold, somewhat aggressive presence to an absent audience. In bright red characters, one poster declared, "The Chinese Race/Nation (*Zhonghua*) as One Family, Unified in Heart Pursue the Chinese Dream!" Meanwhile, a police station and a pedestrian checkpoint were positioned directly across from the posters. They served as the material symbols of the continued and ever-pervasive threat of police regulation over the flows of people, cash, and commodities that once brought life to Xiaobei; the police presence persisted, even after the erasure of these flows following the start of the pandemic. Standing in the middle of an empty and lifeless street, I had wondered whether the

C.1 A propaganda poster featuring a group of ethnic minorities in China, 2021. Photo by Nellie Chu.

posters were placed there to cover up the fact that one year prior to my visit, scores of African migrants were forcibly evicted out of Xiaobei due to rising ethno-nationalism and xenophobia, which by then had become quite open. Consequently, city life in Xiaobei came to an abrupt stop, as village land-lords waited in hopes that Chinese migrants would one day occupy their apartments and storefronts in place of their previous tenants.

THE CHAINS OF PRECARITY, THE CHAINS OF MIGRANT BOSSHOOD IN THE URBAN VILLAGES

For the Wongs, the looming threat of eviction from the urban village, along with the economic slowdown across the supply chains, forced them to leave the garment district but not to abandon their participation in Guangzhou's supply chains entirely. In fact, their ability to sustain their small-scale workshop, or *jiagongchang*, in Guangzhou despite the economic downturn and tightened regulatory control over migrant populations in the urban villages, left the Wongs in heightened conditions of ambivalence

C.2 A police checkpoint at an intersection in the Xiaobei district of Guangzhou, 2021. Photo by Nellie Chu.

and stalled mobility. The boundaries between their limited entrepreneurial autonomy and undue exploitation were increasingly blurred and more difficult to differentiate.

After my tour around Xiaobei that afternoon, I paid a visit to the Wongs. It was two years since I had last seen them. Since the initial lockdown in Wuhan, Hubei Province in January 2020, the migrant couple and their younger son moved their *jiagongchang* out of the Zhaocun garment district and to another urban village approximately two miles away. The Wongs anticipated that the land on which the Zhaocun urban villages had been constructed would be transferred to the municipal government. Mrs. Wong informed me that they had moved to a different *jiagongchang* but had managed to stay within the city limits of Guangzhou. I naively assumed that the Wongs' business continued to thrive despite the pandemic, since rental costs for commercial spaces in Guangzhou had skyrocketed over the course of the intervening two years. When Mrs. Wong brought me to their new *jiagongchang* in the other urban village, however, I was surprised to see how their move had instead increased their isolation and precarity.

That afternoon, Mrs. Wong met me along a busy street lined with apartment complexes and grocery stores. The street was brimming with life and commercial activity. After we exchanged a warm greeting, she led me to the second floor of a dilapidated concrete building where their workshop was situated. The space occupied the entire second floor, which offered ample space, but it remained dark and musky throughout the day. Only a small window overlooking the rooftop of an adjacent building brought in a delicate ray of sunlight that illuminated the large cutting table the couple had moved from their former workspace.

Outside, a small grocery store blasted a piercing recording of a man's voice announcing the deals of the day in an endless loop. The sewing machines occupied the space to the right of the small window. Their younger son sat at a workstation with his head down working diligently on a production order of brightly colored fuchsia dresses. To the left of the window, the Wongs set up a twin-sized bed where the couple slept. The bed was immediately adjacent to the stove and bathroom where the family cooked, bathed, and washed their clothes. As I walked into the workshop, Mr. Wong greeted me at the stove, where he was preparing a scrumptious meal of assorted stir-fried dishes. As Mr. and Mrs. Wong set the table for us in the middle of the workshop, I looked around the large industrial room. Prominent, white Roman-style columns graced the back wall next to their son's sewing station. Jagged pieces of white and pink lace left hanging from the low ceiling swayed back and forth in front of the air conditioning unit. As I observed the decorations around me, I realized that the space formerly served as a bridal photography studio. The Wongs' *jiagongchang* seemed to have reclaimed the space of a former business that might have fallen victim to the economic downturn brought on by COVID-19.

As we sat down to eat lunch, the Wongs explained to me that they were in the process of finishing up a production order for an agent who was an overseas Chinese. Apparently, this agent handled orders exclusively for the African markets. The brightly colored fuchsia dresses strewn across the dingy concrete floor were for a production order placed by a Congolese client. While on the one hand, I was relieved to know that the Wongs had been able to sustain their business despite the pandemic, I realized, on the other hand, that their profits must have been shrinking. Mr. Wong explained that since they had moved into the new *jiagongchang*, they could no longer rely on walk-in clients, who once constituted a critical source of income and informal marketing when they occupied their former workshop. Also, the Wongs could no longer make quick and inexpensive stops to the fabric and accessories market since they had moved out of the garment district the previous year. Instead, the ordering and delivery of fabrics, accessories, and other raw materials imposed additional time and costs on their already tight production schedules and their meager profit margins. Additionally, their move away from the garment district made the Wongs' search for temporary workers difficult if it had to be done on a last-minute basis. Instead, the Wongs had to depend on their personal networks of friends and acquaintances to find help if it was available.

While we were chatting over stir-fried greens, black bean fish, and Hainanese chicken, Mr. and Mrs. Wong expressed a strong sense of ambivalence toward the state of their business. Mr. Wong explained that they still received production orders, which were keeping their *jiagongchang* afloat. However, the orders served almost exclusively African markets, which meant that their profit margins were exceedingly low, primarily because of the exorbitant costs of shipping goods to African markets amid the COVID-19 pandemic, and also because of the many intermediaries across the supply chains through which the commodities passed. (At that time, supply chains around the globe had been almost completely disrupted by the pandemic.) In the early years of their operation, the Wongs' strategy to minimize undue exploitation by their clients was to work almost exclusively with overseas agents. The pandemic, however, upended the world's fast fashion supply chains to such a degree that overseas orders from different regions around the globe became extremely difficult for the Wongs to secure. Mr. Wong expressed regret that their strategy of avoiding domestic orders no longer served them well.

With the Chinese border effectively closed, and with the dwindling of foreign presence in Guangzhou's fashion markets, many of the Wongs' competitors turned to the domestic markets to survive financially. Some contractors had the labor force and resources to manufacture garments extremely quickly, thus meeting the needs of just-in-time delivery in the domestic market. Others, however, had no choice but to take on the risks of encountering potential exploitation at the hands of domestic clients. By contrast, the Wongs refused to take on those risks in the slight hope that the overseas market would soon turn around. They thus extended their reliance on Chinese intermediaries who had overseas connections with clients in African markets to make ends meet.

This strategy, along with relocating to a new *jiagongchang*, had kept the Wongs in a seemingly endless condition of stalled mobility. On the one hand, the margins of profit that they received were fractions of what they earned before the pandemic. Yet, on the other hand, the trickling in of overseas production orders over the past two years had been enough to convince the Wongs to keep their business, to hang onto the hope that after the global economy recovered, they would once again receive lucrative orders from Japan, South Korea, and the United States. In the meantime, the Wongs worked longer hours for far fewer economic returns.

WORLDLY ASPIRATIONS, UNCERTAIN BOSSHOODS

Later that same afternoon, I learned that several factories in the area close to the Wongs' former *jiagongchang* had also closed. It seemed that these were the few remaining factories. I had recently learned that the fabric market would close in about three to five years and that it would move to the outer district of Qingyuan. I informed Mrs. Wong about this possibility, and she confirmed knowledge of this. I asked Mrs. Wong what she and Mr. Wong planned to do in the event the fabric market moved out of Zhaocun village and to the outskirts of the city. She replied that she did not know and that they would wait to see how their business developed in light of these changes. For the Wongs, moving to the Qingyuan district seemed to be a possibility, since they expected to continue their business in Guangzhou rather than in their home village in Guangxi Province. But they maintained they would also consider changing their line of work, perhaps switching to retailing or wholesaling, since Mr. Wong had contacts and experience in these industries.

I then asked Mrs. Wong whether they would base their factory business in Guigang, their hometown, since they had already built a factory space in their home. Surprisingly, Mrs. Wong replied no, indicating that their business decision to invest in the second factory had been a mistake. Mrs. Wong explained that if they moved their operations to Guigang, they would have to handle production orders from large corporations. "Whatever orders that are given to us, we must accept them under any condition. Whatever they [the corporate bosses] say, goes," explained Mrs. Wong. I interpreted her statement to mean that the Wongs would have more freedom (*ziyou*) if they continued to work for themselves. To my surprise, Mrs. Wong gave a more pragmatic answer. "It isn't simply a matter of *ziyou*. Perhaps you must be in the industry to fully understand. It's not about that. If the client orders thousands of pieces by the deadline, we have to do it. If they change the deadline at the last minute, we have to do it too. The boss can deduct us pay whenever they feel like it. By the end, we would make so little. It would force us out of business."

Mrs. Wong's rationale seemed logical and pragmatic to me at that time. I expected her to say that economic freedom and labor autonomy were the primary reasons for keeping their business going. However, Mrs. Wong's responses indicated that the notion of freedom or autonomy (*ziyou*) did not seem to be the only explanation for keeping their business, since entrepreneurial freedom did not fully encapsulate the meaning and intention of her work as a migrant boss. Having observed and studied the dismantlement of the urban villages, I took the future dismantlement of the fabric market, along with the closing of the Wongs' factory, as the worst-case scenario for the migrant couple. Upon reflection, however, it seemed that the Wongs would rather move out of the Zhaocun garment district and try their luck at an entirely different business venture than give up their hope or potential opportunity for entrepreneurial success by taking up stable employment as wage workers. After all, migrant entrepreneurship offered the Wongs not only the possibilities of economic "freedom" from waged labor but also an emergent sense of entrepreneurial and cosmopolitan self that connected to the worlds of export commodities, transnational clients, and fast money.

The economic plight brought by COVID-19 made clear that the Wongs' small-scale, family-owned *jiagongchang* in the urban villages was their only connection to the possibilities of worldliness, financial security, social mobility. Laboring in the delipidated urban villages paradoxically facilitated a platform for the Wongs to extend their productive capacities to the global markets. Their hopes for accumulation, along with their aspirations for worldliness and entrepreneurship, were tied squarely to their engagement as bosses across the fast fashion supply chains. Otherwise, their hopes for social mobility and personal advancement would have been cut off from their livelihoods in Guangzhou, forcing them to return to their hometown (Guigang) and to limit their desires and aspirations. And yet, their very participation in the transnational supply chains of fast fashion as migrant bosses left them more exploited and isolated than before.

Although they had been able to sustain their transnational business across the fast fashion supply chain, the Wongs learned that not every transnational supply chain guaranteed the same profits and rewards. The unevenness of the global supply chains, which became exacerbated during the pandemic, left the Wongs in a paradoxical dilemma. Even though their profits fell, their rents increased, and their working hours lengthened, their financial returns were barely enough to keep them on a treadmill of stalled mobility. For them, staying on the treadmill of long hours for little pay in the hope of converting their exclusion as migrants into possibilities that lay beyond China's borders meant more than any economic return. Indeed, the fuchsia-colored dresses that were destined for the wholesale markets in West Africa represented an extension of the Wongs' desires to expand their aspirations for entrepreneurship to the outside world. Yet the fulfillment of their aspirations depended on economic and political forces that remained entirely outside their control. The Wongs' mixed sense of regret, deferment, and stalled mobility resulted from the global pandemic and the pending demolition of the urban villages, which had immediate effects on their participation in the transnational supply chains for fast fashion.

When I departed the Wongs' *jiagongchang* that day, I suggested to Mrs. Wong that we could perhaps see each other again later in the week, when she needed to buy groceries or go out for a walk. Mrs. Wong regretfully admitted that she hardly went out for walks since they had moved into their new workshop. The tight deadlines and long working hours made it difficult for her to schedule a meeting in advance. Yet, as she explained her work situation to me, I sensed a degree of loneliness and isolation in her voice. Before we departed, Mrs. Wong assured me, "Meet us again in Guangzhou or in Guigang. You are family to us now. We may be apart, but in our hearts, you are our family!"

COMMON PROSPERITY AND CHINA'S GLOBAL ASPIRATIONS
AS THE NEXT FRONTIER OF CAPITALIST ACCUMULATION

From a broader perspective, a critical aspect of the Wongs' conditions of uncertainty and stalled mobility stemmed from the Chinese state's emphasis on the domestic market as the next site for capitalist accumulation, which took place at the time of my fieldwork and writing in 2021. This move was part of a broader set of policies toward national self-strengthening and exercise of tighter state control over the economic life of its people in the face of a series of global financial crises and subsequent growing tensions with trading partners, particularly the United States.[1] The global Silk Road and the Belt and Road Initiative, for instance, sought to alleviate inflationary pressures and the risks of over-accumulation within China's domestic borders by investing in heavy industries and infrastructural projects in countries across the Global South (Winter 2019; A. Chong and Pham 2020; Rojas and Rofel 2022). Meanwhile, local governments across the nation created economic initiatives to upgrade manufacturing sectors from the Made in China model of low-cost mass manufacture to the *Created in China* model of technological and design innovation, following Beijing's Made in China 2025 industrial upgrading policy (Keane 2011; Wei et al. 2017; Agarwala and Chaudhary 2021). The mushrooming of innovative parks, alongside the mass mobilization of surveillance technologies in cities and border regions across China (Keane 2011; Liang and Wang 2020; Byler 2021; Tabanelli 2021) attested to the prioritization of the domestic economy as the next frontier of capitalist technological accumulation.

The emergence of the COVID-19 pandemic hastened these movements. From 2020 to 2021, for instance, while the rest of the world struggled to control the COVID virus, China, under the policy of zero-COVID, successfully warded off localized infections across most of the country and focused on maintaining manufacturing and economic productivity through its reliance on the continued growth of domestic consumer markets. On my visits to Guangzhou's wholesale markets for fast fashion, including the Xi Fang Hang market, in the summer of 2021, nearly every stall was owned and operated by Chinese locals and migrants from the nation's countryside. Many fashion stalls displayed their operations online via WeChat, Xiaohongshu (Little Red Book), and Douyin (or TikTok) to connect to consumer markets across lower-tiered cities and rural regions across China.

While observers of China misleadingly describe these economic and political developments as an example of China's moment of "de-globalization" or isolation, this move, I suggest, was instead a response to global economic developments. Campaigns to expand and upgrade domestic markets served as attempts to avoid, or ward off, the possibility of what economists have described as global secular stagnation, a long-term period of little to no economic growth, as experienced by Japan since the early 2000s (Hansen 1939; Krugman 2014; Summers 2018; Hillenbrand 2023). To be sure, major economic events that unfolded in China over the past few years—including the fall of the Evergrande real estate corporation, rising unemployment among college graduates, resistance against the 996 work system, rising inflation, and the decline of the working-age population—stoked the fires of anxiety and uncertainty about China's economic future. The condition of stalled mobility, which I have described at length in this book, encapsulates the treadmill-like experiences of labor and productivity among migrant bosses and laborers who do not benefit from long-term and meaningful accumulation.

China's turn to domestic markets thus held the promise of accelerated growth, even if that hope was short-lived. While the domestic consumer markets absorbed the inventory of China-made goods, even as global supply chains were being disrupted by the global pandemic, the central state asserted an even tighter grip over market activities, particularly on the exchange and speculation of private capital. The central state's call for common prosperity aimed to narrow the widening wealth gap and income inequalities across various class segments in China. By bringing attention to the politics of distribution, the central state sought to curb the unbridled expansion of speculative capital among private investors and local state agents. In 2021, for example, the central government in Beijing enacted tax and data-sharing regulations on the internet giants Alibaba (an e-commerce company) and Di Di (a ride-hailing app). The refusal of the central government to provide emergency funds to the failing real estate giant Evergrande attested to the reprioritization of distribution of public goods over the relentless pursuit and expansion of private capital in China.

The policy of common prosperity specified the role of the central state in *curbing the excesses* of the expansion and accumulation of private capital, but it fell short in defining its role as a *benefactor in providing welfare* to its people under the banner of egalitarianism. The politics of distribution continued to privilege global market forces as the primary mechanisms with which to redistribute wealth, providing access to capital and determining wages and incomes for citizens of various class segments. Consequently, the crushing effects of unequal or inadequate distribution of welfare and public goods was borne by China's migrant populations and other vulnerable groups. This was especially the case throughout 2022, when the Omicron variant spread across Chinese cities, leading to a series of strict lockdowns and other zero-COVID measures in cities and towns across China. These measures were accompanied by the mass build-up of health surveillance technologies, snap citywide lockdowns, continuous testing, centralized quarantines, forced evictions, and violent policing. Many migrants were evicted and left to sleep on the streets, while others lost their jobs and were sent to *fangacang* (centralized quarantines). Still others were forced to live and work in universities or export factories for 16–24 hours a day in a strictly enforced closed-loop system, where students, teachers, and workers were not allowed to leave the school or factory premises.

IMMOBILITY IN THE URBAN VILLAGES

The lockdowns of Zhaocun village and other urban villages in Guangzhou in November 2022 demonstrated the detrimental effects of this widening social inequality across China and the world's supply chains. On the evening of the November 2022 protests, with which I began this book, images and videos of migrant laborers gathering in the streets went viral across social media. Observers, including bloggers and pundits, shared short documentaries and analyses that elaborated on the difficult conditions of the migrants' lives in the urban villages. Some of these observers explained that the migrants' concerns and demands highlighted their growing sense of distrust toward the village landlords. According to one video blogger, migrants asserted the following demands: (1) for residents to be allowed to take the COVID tests by the front doors of their apartments, instead of requiring them to stand in line downstairs (by staying in their homes, migrants minimized the risks of cross-infection); (2) for the government to distribute food and essential goods directly to individual residences and not through village landlords, who, at the time of the protests, were widely distrusted by migrant laborers; and (3) for the government to announce the final date of the lockdown so that migrants could resume business as soon as possible (N. W. 2023). These demands, though seemingly pragmatic and reasonable, ultimately revealed to the public the deepening tensions that brewed beneath the surface of everyday labor and life in the urban villages.

These tensions had been exacerbated by the institution of grid management, an urban planning technique that was used nationwide to enforce

COVID prevention policies and other bureaucratic requirements. Following the directives of grid management, numerous security checkpoints were established across Chinese cities to govern and regulate the movement of people, and presumably viruses, across spatial grids (Xiang 2021a). These security checkpoints constituted the important human component of this complex network of grid management via face-to-face encounters. The checkpoints were equipped with body temperature scanners, which closely resembled metal detectors, as well as with bodyguards, whose jobs were to gather people's temperatures, check their QR health codes, and ultimately grant or deny them permission to pass through. However, because these checkpoints were set up primarily in the entryways of residential compounds, commercial buildings, and along the perimeters of the urban villages, the infrastructural landscapes of apartment buildings, roads, and urban zones determined the spatial size and population density of the "grid."

Within each grid, neighborhood committees (jiuweihui) were also tasked with carrying out regular testing requirements and the distribution of food, medicine, and other essential items necessary for the everyday nourishment and life for those who resided within the grid. Many of these committees were composed of village landlords and employees of third-party property management corporations as well as resident volunteers of apartment compounds or residential neighborhoods. Most of these members were local Cantonese-speaking residents. In the case of the urban villages, an entire district or subdistrict might constitute a spatial grid, which included hundreds or even thousands of migrant laborers living outside of the purview of the village committee and the municipal government. As members of the "floating population" (according to the hukou policy of population control) living under the radar of state enforcement within informal neighborhoods such as the urban villages, migrants had limited mobility and protection from police harassment and systemic discrimination. Most migrant residents were not formally registered, so village committees had no way of knowing how many people lived in a flat or an apartment.

Consequently, hundreds, if not thousands, of migrant laborers fell between the gaps of the bureaucratic grid management system that regulated and oversaw the distribution of food and other essential items that were critical during periods of strict lockdowns. Across social media, migrants under quarantine in the urban villages complained about inconsistent, substandard, and inadequate food supplies. One migrant stated that deliveries by the government were patchy and inadequate (Women on a Swing 2022). One migrant complained that on the days when he did receive food, he was provided only with instant noodles, canned food, and instant rice, which was not enough for his family of four people. Volunteers from village committees, who were tasked with delivering medicine, were grossly understaffed. Some attempted to navigate the complex maze of narrow alleyways to find addresses to which they needed to deliver the supplies, but many simply gave up or could not find the recipient(s). Consequently, online orders for daily essential items, including medicines for non-COVID illnesses—medicines were necessary to compensate for the inadequate food and supplies provided by the government—could not reach their intended (migrant) recipients. Thus, even though migrant residents in Zhaocun and in other urban villages were organized into spatial grids, the maze-like, zigzag layout of the urban villages, compounded by the invisible status of the migrant residents, left large swaths of the migrant population unaccounted for, exposing the problems of grid management in urban villages that had never been able to easily fit into formalized "grids."

Failures to deliver public goods exposed not only the problems of urban management but, more importantly, the negligence and lack of will to address the needs of the migrant population. Many migrants believed that village landlords became de facto middlemen who received the provisions through their village collectives before redistributing them to their migrant tenants. Some landlords were rumored to have hoarded supplies for themselves, while others were believed to have resold the goods to migrant residents at inflated prices. For the most part, migrants did not know definitively whether food and supplies were sent from the village committee or directly from the municipal government. Such a lack of communication and transparency exacerbated the inequalities that existed long before the pandemic. The lack of logistic channels through which migrants could air their concerns and grievances intensified their struggles.

Before the COVID-19 lockdowns, the ability of *jiagongchang* to sustain the just-in-time delivery of low-cost fast fashions lay precisely in the mobility of people, commodities, and capital, which floated into and out of the urban villages. For the migrant laborers, being physically mobile yielded a limited sense of freedom, agency, and control over the day-to-day rhythms of labor and livelihood. Becoming "boss" was even seen by some as an emblem of masculinity, as an embodiment of the pioneering and risk-taking entrepreneur. Having the ability to be mobile, even in a very limited sense, eased, if not outright obscured, the exploitative effects of low-cost mass manufacturing across the global supply chains. Yet, as soon as the lockdowns immobilized the daily activities of the *jiagongchang* and the physical mobility of the migrant laborers, the crushing effects of extraction and exploitation came to the surface and became palpable, eventually leading to mass unrest.

With the introduction of strict lockdowns in the urban villages, the state's biopolitical and necropolitical policies of grid management determined the possibilities for migrants' life projects, which hinged not only on the ability to live, but also the ability to be physically and subjectively mobile so as to claim for themselves the ability to dictate the terms of their exploited labor. Migrants fought for the ability to survive the precarious conditions of their work lives in the city, which they sutured together by moving from one low-paying job to another to ease the exploitative effects of the global supply chains. Indeed, migrants who labored over sewing machines in the *jiagongchang* over the course of my ethnographic research often found comfort from the monotony of their industrial tasks by hopping from one job to another or by temporarily returning to their families in their home villages. They frequently shuttled between their home villages and the urban villages of Guangzhou. The trip was a form of relief from their tedious labor in the urban villages.

LAYERS OF EXPLOITATION; MOMENTS OF
MIGRATORY LIFE AND DEATH

The practice of grid management, a key aspect of China's zero-COVID policy, thus exposed the contradictions of labor and capital in Guangzhou's manufacturing hub. These contradictions became apparent when the mobility of migrants, commodities, and capital that are necessary for supply chain capitalism ground to a halt. More specifically, it revealed the tensions and inequalities between village landlords and migrant laborers, which sustained the supply chains of fast fashion manufacture. The November 2022 unrest among migrant laborers in Zhaocun laid bare preexisting social inequalities between migrant laborers and village landlords, upon which the global supply chains for low-cost mass manufacturing depended.

The unrest of November 2022 was not an isolated event. It was part of a string of past collective actions among migrants who needed to assert their claims to dignified labor and livelihood in Guangzhou. For example, one such collective action included public protests against the large-scale confiscation of pedicab bikes by local officials in 2015. Pedicab deliveries of raw materials for garment mass manufacture provided a source of livelihood for many itinerant migrants. In a second example, in 2017, large-scale protests erupted in Zhaocun and neighboring villages against a local real estate developer that was engaged in negotiations with the village committees over the transfer of villagers' use-rights to the land. The developer and village landlords intended to demolish the apartments and industrial sites that migrants' livelihoods depended on. Migrant protests worked to stop the profit-seeking practices of developers and village landlords.

The lockdowns in Zhaocun and other urban villages in 2022, as well as other events, exposed the historical layers of extraction and exploitation under which the migrant population in the urban villages lived and worked. The overlay of *hukou* policy that denied migrants' claims to state welfare onto the global supply chains that exploited migrants' labor and exposed them to rent-seeking villagers, compounded by the techniques of grid management, which cut off their main sources of economic survival during the lockdowns, ultimately exposed the market cycles of continuous extraction and exploitation in the urban villages. These cycles had intensified over the several decades since the introduction of market reforms. They also exposed the inequalities of wealth and political power between migrant laborers and the village landlords.

TRANSNATIONAL TRANSIENCY AND IMMOBILITY

Similarly, transnational migrants faced struggles and vulnerabilities as Chinese rural migrants when they encountered economic downturns or when the supply chains no longer needed them. Experiences of market instabilities, evictions, and racial discrimination related to the COVID-19 pandemic intensified the precarious conditions that migrant bosses already faced in their struggle for decent labor and livelihood across the global fast fashion supply chains in Guangzhou. As I described in chapter 5, West African migrants, who lived in urban villages outside of Zhaocun, were first subject to mandatory testing and forced quarantine in 2020. These strict requirements were likely fueled by widespread racist and xenophobic beliefs among local authorities and residents (Cezne and Visser 2023). African migrants were ultimately evicted from their homes when the Chinese village landlords preferred to rent their apartments to Chinese tenants. Consequently, African migrants were left to sleep on the streets without any official documentation or state-sponsored protections (Burke 2020; Castillo 2020a; Vincent 2020). Such mistreatment targeted African migrants, while other foreign groups were spared, demonstrating the precarious conditions African migrant bosses faced in China amid the COVID-19 pandemic.

By then, many South Korean and *Chaoxianzu* (Korean Chinese) bosses in Guangzhou had already moved their garment factories and wholesale businesses to Southeast Asia—including Cambodia, Thailand, and Vietnam—where they continued to follow the transnational flows of capital. Even though they were spared from COVID-related state surveillance and regulation in China, they were still subject to global economic downturns and large-scale disruptions to the transnational supply chains that occurred during the height of the pandemic. Many logistics agents and wholesalers in Guangzhou faced a dramatic decrease in the number of production orders they received from their long-standing corporate clients. To keep their businesses afloat while commodity chains around the globe stood at a standstill, jobbers had to quickly pivot their businesses by exporting medicine and other medical supplies to countries across Africa and Southeast Asia.

A long durée perspective on the historical emergence of the urban villages, as well as a look into the socioeconomic struggles of China's migrant populations (transnational and domestic) since the introduction of market reforms in the late 1970s, shows how the country's zero-COVID policy exposed the relations of capitalist extraction and exploitation upon which the global supply chains in Guangzhou's urban villages are anchored. The stifling of economic activity for the sake of COVID prevention in Guangzhou's urban villages did not (re)introduce any Maoist-era forms of state governance. Instead, it uncovered the dynamics of exploitation and extraction upon which the supply chains of fast fashion depended. The precarious conditions of labor and livelihood of migrant laborers in China, as this book has demonstrated, existed long before the start of the pandemic. Current policies of community-based health and security have merely brought them into public light.

The protests in Guangzhou's urban villages revealed the ripple effects of social inequality across the chains of exploitation and extraction among the transnational and domestic migrant populations. Indeed, the chains of low-cost commodity manufacture and exchange in Guangzhou articulate precisely with the chains of exploitation and extraction from village landlords to migrant bosses to temporary piecework laborers in the urban villages. Across the intermediary links of subcontracted labor along Guangzhou's fast fashion supply chains, migrant bosses become exposed to the accumulative dictates of those who occupy positions of relative power, including village landlords; local, competing bosses; and police officers. Indeed, migrants' personal ambitions to achieve entrepreneurial wealth and autonomy leave them vulnerable to extraction, exploitation, and extortion by these competing agents. In response to these conditions, as I have shown, migrant bosses devise ways to confront, evade, and comply with such acts of violence and exclusion, exercising novel and original practices of labor, flexible appropriation, and market exchange. Such encounters reveal how broader structures of power, social hierarchy, and inequality rub uneasily against the personal and individualistic desires and ambitions of migrants who transgress not only national and rural-urban boundaries but also the labor/capital divide.

PROSPECTS FOR THE ENTREPRECARIAT

The ethnographic sketches in this book tell a distinctive story of China's postsocialist transformation as the country intensifies its participation in the worlds' fast fashion supply chains. To be sure, the rise of the entreprecariat, along with the dilemmas and paradoxes of bosshood in China, must be analyzed within the contexts of China's postsocialist transformation and transnational capitalism. At the same time, however, the narratives that I present reveal a bigger snapshot of a kind of capitalist transformation that has emerged upon the global stage, one in which indefinite economic growth, productivity, and accumulation can no longer be taken for granted. For this reason, the experiences of migrant bosshood resonate with migrant laborers who work across transnational commodity chains around the globe. Indeed, mass media reports and popular critiques about fast fashion's damage to the environment, its effects on climate change, its production of waste, and its exploitative treatment of workers around the globe have sparked global uncertainties and debates about the future of sustainable consumption and sustainable growth.

Although this book focuses on the practices of migrant bosshood in China, my ethnographic analyses echo people's experiences of migration and labor across the globe. Conditions of subcontracting, as exemplified by laborers across the transnational supply chains of fast fashion, have minimized the power of unionized labor in determining the terms of employment contracts upon which worker protections, rights, and benefits are defined and enforced. At the same time, subcontracting has also transformed the terms by which the state confers certain rights and protections to its people based on a social contract. The large-scale retrenchment of the welfare state, accompanied by the expansion of market interests via the rise of the multinational corporation (MNCs), leaves millions of individuals vulnerable to the fluctuations of market supply and demand characteristic of transnational capitalism. As my book shows, the structural organization of global supply chains via transnational subcontracting signifies more than MNCs' attempts to pass on the costs of labor, environmental harm, and financial risks to migrant bosses. Global supply chains also serve as chains of accumulation, through which small-scale migrant bosses individually compete and collaborate for profit margins in the hope of achieving financial wealth and stability despite encountering the profit-seeking interests of local landlords, uniformed officers, and state agents. In spite their aspirations and hard work, their dreams of entrepreneurial freedom often fail to come to fruition. Instead, the structural vulnerability of these migrant bosses and workers becomes ever more apparent, as evidenced by the Rana Plaza building collapse in Bangladesh in 2013, the ongoing experiences of forced labor in the borderlands of central Asia, the suffering of black lung victims in China and Sudan, and the economic hardships among garbage collectors in Brazil and factory women in Mexico's maquiladoras.

Migrants' experiences of bosshood across various parts of the globe demonstrate that precarious accumulation leaves them with just enough return on their labor, hope, and personal investments to stay on track toward entrepreneurship. Yet, their returns are not enough to forge a concrete pathway toward meaningful fulfillment of their aspirations and desires. While the current literature in economic anthropology tends to conceptualize risk in terms of "big" events such as crises, bankruptcy, tragedy, accidents, and collapse, this book illustrates how everyday practices of migrant bosshood are shaped by historically specific conditions of labor and livelihood. Domestic and transnational migrants in postsocialist China engage in capitalist accumulation in ways that blur the boundaries of mobility/immobility and freedom/unfreedom. In effect, the blurring of these boundaries keeps the migrants continuously striving for promises of a better life, but the practices of accumulation across the supply chains fail to deliver on those promises.

The paradoxes, dilemmas, and tensions encapsulated by the figure of the migrant boss in the era of global fast fashion thus critically unveil the disjuncture between widening structural inequalities and the deepening of migrants' intersubjective desires and aspirations for capitalist accumulation. In China, this is particularly true in light of the unmaking of the peasant classes, who once were the vanguard of the Maoist Revolution. Indeed, it can be argued that the symbol of the peasant in China and elsewhere has now been replaced by the figure of the migrant boss. The retrenchment of state protection and security that would otherwise serve as social safety nets for meaningful accumulation, mobility, and autonomy leave the fulfillment of entrepreneurial desires and aspirations anchored upon capitalistic accumulation in ways that expose migrants to a stalling or a deferment of those ambitions. The historical and structural contexts of postsocialist capitalist accumulation in China, through which migrants or other individuals construct these entrepreneurial ambitions and pursue them, are thus significant in how our understandings of hope, desire, and optimism often get in the way of realizing alternative possibilities of meaningful life, labor, and personhood.

Notes

1   Other studies have documented how fast fashion production exposes Chinese workers to danger and poses serious health risks. For example, migrant workers work in sweatshops, live in crowded dormitories, and are exposed to harmful chemicals and molecules such as silica dust and lead. Mothers have no access to childcare. Above all, fast fashion in China has been linked to human trafficking, including forced labor trafficking (Simpson 2020).

2   Social scientists and anthropologists have characterized "just in time" production as exemplary of the post-Fordist condition. See Appadurai 1996; Bauman 2000; Harvey 1990; Tsing 2009; Muehlebach 2011; Hoffman 2011; Appel 2019; Rofel and Yanagisako 2018. These works emphasize the reproductive features of "just in time" production of the current political economy, or what Karl Marx (1857) calls "concrete abstractions." They may also be approached as what Susan Narotzky and Gavin Smith (2006) describe as the social ensemble of labor and material production that "condition(s) the possibilities of social reproduction" (5). Other works on futurity, time/space compression, and flexible accumulation approach "just in time" production as a singular logic, characterized by either the temporal dimensions of speed and flexibility or the dilemmas of the present in relation to the past and future (Harvey 1990).

3   Focused on consumption, theorists of fashion and material culture have aptly conceptualized fashion as a generative dreamworld of capitalist desire and aspiration (Wilson 1985; Horning 2011), elaborating on clothing and adornment as intersubjective and embodied experiences that intersect gendered, racial, sexual, religious, nationalistic, and ethnic identifications. While some anthropologists, for example, have demonstrated that certain veiling practices within the worlds of global Islamic fashion enable women to feel more pious and modern at the same time, thus emphasizing the fantasies and religiosities that certain adornment practices generate, other scholars underscore the anxieties,

alienation, and violence often associated with clothing (Woodward 2005; Jones 2007; Woodward and Miller 2007). Highlighting fast fashion, Rob Horning (2011) concludes, the multiplication of new looks through shorter production cycles perpetuates consumers' desires for constant shopping. For him, the globally recognized fast fashion chain, Forever 21, serves what it purports to deliver; that is, never-ending desires among its targeted female consumers to achieve or maintain perpetual youth through constant shopping (Horning 2011).

4 Capitalist accumulation, as Karl Marx (1885) informs us, requires a certain degree of "fixity," or stability, in both dimensions of time and space in order for capital to grow. In contrast, in the world of contemporary fast fashion, spatial fixity and temporal stability are no longer the primary strategies of accumulation, particularly for the financially vulnerable migrant populations. Rather, the ongoing circulation of people, commodities, and money through migration, commodity speculation, and the unregulated redistribution of wealth have become channels through which regulatory authority governs the distribution of profit and through which Guangzhou's migrant populations anchor their entrepreneurial dreams and desires across the supply chains for fast fashion.

5 Jonathan Nitzan and Shimshon Bichler (2009) describe this dynamic as differential accumulation.

6 As David Harvey (1990) notes in his analysis of the postmodern condition: "Indeed, learning to play the volatility right is now just as important as accelerating turnover time. This means either being highly adaptable and fast-moving in response to market shift or masterminding the volatility" (286–87). Furthermore, he writes, "Within this matrix of (modern and post-modern) relations, there is never one fixed configuration, but a swaying back and forth between centralization and decentralization, between authority and deconstruction, between hierarchy and anarchy, between permanence and flexibility" (339). As such, this book explores these complex and contradictory dynamics of autonomy and control, as experienced by migrant laborers and entrepreneurs in Guangzhou.

7 Some anthropological studies have analyzed the generative aspects of forms of life and livelihood among people who labor outside of formal waged labor (Guyer 2004; Millar 2018; Tsing 2009; Bear 2014). These works have tended to focus on how people engage alternative forms of value, practices of labor, cosmological orderings, and ritualistic performances in face of privatization, rising debt, and the large-scale retreat of state welfare. They also tend to highlight how ordinary people create spaces of dignity, desire, and hope for themselves that cannot be easily subsumed by the structural demands of capitalism. For these scholars, the creation of capitalist relations and the reproduction of

market value critically depend on noncapitalistic relations, as exemplified by gift-giving relations, kinship, cosmology, ritual, and hope within spaces *outside* of capitalism from which to territorialize and accumulate productive and reproductive labor and surplus value. These ethnographies emphasize contingency over structural conditions of transnational capitalism as the primary determinant in the creation and reproduction of life, labor, and value.

8   As Judith Butler (2009) points out, "precarity" is distinguished from "precariousness" in that precarity describes a generalized condition of human sociality, whereas precariousness refers to a condition of dependence and mutual vulnerability in a human relationship. See Melinda Hinkson 2017 for an elaboration of these concepts.

9   There are varying structures of real estate ownership among different classes of rural and urban citizens in China, ranging from full ownership of property or land among urban citizens (with the implicit understanding that property in China belongs to the central government and is "leased" to the owner for seventy years); possession of use-rights over formerly agricultural land among wealthy peasant landlords who are rural citizens; and no or insecure access to property ownership of urban land and housing among migrants based on their rural statuses in the cities. Low-end housing projects set up by the state are an exception to this general structure, since they enable migrants to gain access to affordable housing in the cities. But these projects are often left incomplete and unfinished, sometimes even unlivable, leaving migrants in the cities even more precarious and vulnerable to financial losses and instability.

10   More recently, precarity's origins in work and employment have been expanded to more generalized conditions of uncertainty, permeating various aspects of social life outside the contexts of labor and economy (Neilson and Rossiter 2005; Butler 2006; Rofel 2007; Allison 2013; Anagnost et al. 2013; Amin and Thrift 2016; Richaud and Amin 2020).

11   For more on the specific dynamics of class and labor in relation to rural-to-urban migration in China, see Solinger 1995, 1999; Pun 2005; Pun and Smith 2007; Swider 2015; Evans 2020; Hillenbrand 2023.

12   Butollo (2014), Lüthje et al. (2013), Lüthje (2019), and Gereffi et al. (2022) further discuss industrial development and upgrading across transnational commodity chains in China.

13   While some scholars have questioned whether China's market reforms can be appropriately described as neoliberal, I join the interdisciplinary scholars of labor, migration, and urbanization in China who have analyzed at length the widening socioeconomic inequalities, rising unemployment, and growing discontentment that migrant groups have experienced since the opening of Deng Xiaoping's market reforms in 1978 (Solinger 1999; L. Zhang 2002; Pun 2005; Pun and Smith 2007; Siu

2007; Yan 2008; Swider 2015; I. Pang 2019; Evans 2020; Ling 2020; Y. Zhan 2022; Hillenbrand 2023).

14 These class groups include the so-called flexi-precariat classes, including independent subcontractors, contract workers, and part-time employees, whose conditions of temporary and part-time labor leave them pendulating between the roles of a full-time employee and a self-employed entrepreneur (Hillenbrand 2023).

15 The disproportionate focus on precarity/precariousness in liberal democracies in the Global North has compelled some observers to critique the Eurocentric tendencies that remain implicit in these concepts. Scholars of Africa and Latin America have argued that these regions of world have never witnessed the economic growth and stabilities associated with Fordist economies of the Global North and that unemployment and informal/contingent labor, along with associated conditions of economic uncertainty and vulnerability, have long been the defining characteristics of life and livelihoods in these places (Neilson and Rossiter 2005; Mezzadra and Neilson 2012; Munck 2013; C. K. Lee 2018; I. Pang 2019; Driessen 2019; H.-M. L. Liu 2023).

16 Anthropological studies have addressed precarity and precariousness as analytical lenses through which to view the ways people interpret their social worlds. By using ethnography as a mode of interpretive sensibility (Narotzky and Smith 2006), these studies underscore a pervasive condition of livelihood and labor that reinforces and is produced by the uneven effects of privatization, globalization, and flexible accumulation (Tsing 2009; Narotzky and Smith 2006; Millar 2018). Taking practices of the everyday, or ordinary affects as the central object of inquiry, these scholars bear witness to the uncertainty and nostalgic yearning that exemplify the post-Fordist condition.

17 Through their market participation in the chains of fast fashion manufacture and exchange, migrant bosses engage in ongoing speculation about what aspects of the supply chain they can control, manage, and manipulate. They are not passive subjects in the processes of capital accumulation.

18 Much like the Cameroonian market boys and other intermediaries (the population *flottante*) that collectively form the basis of Janet Roitman's (2005) study of the unregulated economy in Central Africa, market participants across the fast fashion supply chains in Guangzhou bring together various conflicting appropriations of economic concepts, including price and quality. Together, these contestations question the foundational distribution of profit and wealth, thus shedding light on the dynamics of economic regulation, state surveillance, market exclusion, social inequality across supply chains.

19 The large-scale suppression of protests, the discourse of *suzhi* (human quality), and the social credit system are other contemporary examples

of the ways in which neoliberal market mechanisms intersect with and enhance the authoritarian governance of the central state in China (Hillenbrand 2023).

20 Anthropologists and geographers who have written extensively on globalization, commodity chains, and transnational labor regimes have also acknowledged that acts of laboring across the global supply chains invariably entail various projects of global scaling (Friedberg 2004; Chalfin 2004; Tsing 2009; West 2012; Rofel and Yanagisako 2018; Litzinger 2013; J. Chan et al. 2020). Scaling or scale-making is the cultural and discursive framing of place-based practices, resources, meanings, and symbols, which make capitalist accumulation possible. While urban geographers have tended to highlight spatiotemporal dimensions of capital accumulation and labor flows, anthropologists have underscored various practices of world-making, which are contingently made through worldly encounters and other cross-cultural relations of mobility exchange (Faier 2009; M. Zhan 2009; Tsing 2009; J. Chu 2010; Faier and Rofel 2014; Rofel and Yanagisako 2018).

21 Some scholars highlight the role of contingency in the making and remaking of socioeconomic life; their conceptual framing of possibility remains embedded within larger structural dynamics of power, regulation, and social reproduction. For instance, John Halloway (2010) describes contradictions of global capitalism as "cracks" or emergent openings that reveal potential alternative lives and livelihoods to capitalist relations.

22 Such ethnographic moments, as I argue, are key to revealing the cracks and fissures that mar the seemingly seamless flows of commodity, objects, and people around the globe. They are particularly significant since the "just in time" delivery of post-Fordist forms of mass manufacture, along with contemporary practices of subcontracted labor, have increasingly collapsed the boundaries that once defined spaces inside and outside of capitalism. The conceptual vocabulary and categorical frameworks that strive to imagine the possibility of life outside of capitalism, such as resistance, disavowal, and revolution, take on different meanings and valences in dissimilar contexts. This is particularly true across the fast fashion supply chains in Guangzhou, where the categorical boundaries between formal/informal as well as waged/nonwaged labor are continuously challenged through everyday practices.

CHAPTER 1. MADE IN CHINA, JUST IN TIME

1 Other anthropologists have drawn from Karl Polanyi's idea of economic ideologies as embedded within particular social relationships. For example, Chris Hann et al. (2001) emphasize the contextual specificities of "actually existing socialism," a term introduced by German social scientist

Rudolf Bahro (1978). They argue that the ushering in of capitalist consumption to China and the former Soviet Union has failed to completely obliterate the nostalgia for the socialist past among those who yearn for the return of the public sector and for particular entitlements that socialist governments provided. Hann et al. therefore conceive postsocialism as a historicizing concept that conveys the specific ethical and moral dimensions among various groups of people experiencing broad socio-political transformations.

Daphne Berdahl (1999), by contrast, views social change as physical and metaphorical landscapes of transition, whereby large-scale structures of transition articulate with local and individual phenomena. Berdahl situates the postsocialist landscape as social processes for reflecting and constituting depictions of rapid change in apparent stability of place. She therefore conceptualizes the postsocialist transition as encounters that intersect extra-local economic, political, and social processes with individual lives.

2 To be sure, urban villages are not exclusive to the Pearl River Delta region. Scholars and observers have written about urban villages in Beijing, Chongqing, Hangzhou, Qingdao, Wenzhou, and Lanzhou just to name a few. For a more comprehensive study, see Al 2014. Moreover, scholars of India have also used the term *urban villages* to refer to poor, slum-like communities in urban areas. Though they, too, focus on the problems of rapid urbanization, problems related to poverty, migration, and urban development are place-based and vary by historical context. As a case in point, see Nidhi Batra, "Village in the City—New Slums? China's and India's Approach," Terra Urban, December 5, 2012, http://terraurban.wordpress.com/tag/urban-village/. Interestingly, "urban village" has also been used to describe pockets of small-scale, gentrified communities across the developed world (Sharma 2012). As part of so-called localization projects, urban planners design low-density housing that purports to retain sustainability, community solidarity, and collective engagement. On the one hand, while the shared use of the term signifies common concerns in regard to urbanization and environmental degradation, the appropriation of it by urban planners in the developed world merely glosses over the problem of class and inequality. In China and India, urban villages are visible testaments to income disparities. See Jian and Tan 1950; Y. Liu 1950; Qian 1951; Lu 1991; Ren 1991; Zheng 1991; Choi 2006; and A. Chong and Pham 2020 for further studies on Guangzhou's urban villages.

3 China's market reforms in the early 1980s included the establishment of town and village enterprises as well as the creation of tax-free industrial zones across the Pearl River Delta region. The discursive conjuring of China's so-called workshops of the world has thus historically been

made possible precisely through the spatial reordering of migratory life and labor in and around these zones and urban cores. In fact, not far from the garment district upon which this ethnographic project is based, a state-sponsored zone called TIT Creative Industry Park occupies a red-brick factory warehouse that dates back to the Maoist period during the 1950s. Inspired by the success of the high-end 798 art zone in Beijing, Guangzhou's TIT Creative Industry Park celebrates contemporary fashion, art, and design by featuring fashion by high-end local designers who authenticate local Guangdong-based sensibilities with globally recognized, high-end fashion brands.

4   Through their mutual collaborations, whether they are short-term or long-term, they perform the critical work of what Hirokazu Miyazaki (2013) describes as spatiotemporal arbitrage, that is, the exploitation of the gaps and differentials between space and timeframes so as to create surplus value.

5   While the *trabalhador* worker associated with stable income and employment benefits remains a figure of respect and aspiration among the *catadores* (informal waste collectors) in Brazil, as Kathleen Millar (2018) points out, the Maoist figure of the worker, or *gongren*, as the vanguard of the communist revolution is no longer held in the same regard by Chinese rural migrants. After all, far fewer rural citizens received the full spectrum of state welfare and benefits as the urban citizens had received during the Maoist period. Rather, rural migrants engage in the present-day struggle to shed their identities as factory workers in pursuit of self-employment through small-scale entrepreneurship both as a last resort and as a means of staking a certain degree of risk in hopes of attaining upward social mobility, material wealth, and economic security.

6   As Anna Tsing (2015) writes, "Concentration of wealth is possible because value produced in unplanned patches is appropriated for capital" (5). In the case of Guangzhou's fast fashion sector, such "patchy" forms of accumulation are key to sustaining the global supply chains of fast fashion, particularly among migrant subcontractors who labor within unregulated, nonformalized sectors of the economy. I draw inspiration from this concept to further elaborate on the conditions of precariousness that migrant bosses encounter in their attempts to accumulate capital.

7   As Laura Bear (2014) writes in her analysis of capitalist temporalities, time serves as both a structural dynamic and a source of contingent livelihood. Time serves both as a structural determinant and a cultural resource that may be manipulated and reconfigured. As ethnographic accounts in this book show, people labor in and of time (Bear 2014).

8   As Michael Taussig (2012) claims, "Scarcity is not the mark of so-called primitive society but instead of so-called affluent society, where, as the

craze to consume spreads ever wider, enabling capitalist growth, so does the feeling that one never has enough, combined with the even greater feeling of having to consume more" (22). By perpetuating the fuel of consumerist desires into the indefinite future, commodity scarcity evokes and reproduces mass consumerist desires as an end goal.

9   Citing Walter Benjamin's (2002) notes on fashion from *The Arcades Project*, Michael Taussig (2012) explains that the cycles of fashion styles and trends reflect the ritualistic metaphors of life and death, whereby the shorter shelf-life or relevancy of a particular style (its quick death) ensures the creation or (or rebirth) of another style that in turn sustains the reproduction of so-called newness. These market cycles, in turn, necessitate a temporal reordering of consumer desires through the subjective constructions of scarcity and excess. Consumer desires have become increasingly fickle, as volatility pervades other realms of social life, including labor processes, production techniques, and leisure preferences (Harvey 1990). The dual effects of disposability and instantaneity pervading all areas of social life echo what Marshall Berman (1988) described, "All that is solid melts into air."

10   Elizabeth Wilson (1985) writes, "[Capitalism] manufactures dreams and images as well as things, and fashion is as much a part of the dream world of capitalism as of its economy" (14).

11   This statistic does not account for the number of undocumented migrants from Africa who illegally entered China or remained in the country past their visa expiration date. Although population numbers are difficult to confirm, another 50,000 migrants from Africa are estimated to live in the area (Mathews 2011; Bodomo 2012).

12   According to Roberto Castillo (2016), African traders in Guangzhou may be broadly categorized by the following, based on their migration histories and trajectories in China: (1) the more established, (2) the itinerant and semi-settled, and (3) the newly arrived.

13   Susana Narotzky and Gavin Smith (2006) elaborate further by writing, "Hegemony works through the payoffs of active collusion. Collusion arises in which participation in the social project promises to empower those recognized as legitimate members through the intensified productivity of the overall corporate politic. . . . Power then, far from being about restriction and restraint, might be made to appear to rest in their opposites" (25).

CHAPTER 2. STALLED MOBILITY

1   Anthropologists have cogently pointed out the important ways in which belonging, obligations, and social reproduction are critically shaped by the spatiotemporal dimensions through which households

are conceived. These aspects, as scholars have pointed out, challenge the dichotomy between public and private as well as formal/informal domains. As anthropologist Elizabeth Deluca (2017) writes, "Households are objects of government and market expertise. Knowledge about individual and aggregate households forms the basis for social entitlements and access to financial instruments, imposing particular understandings of family and deservingness while shaping daily life in ways that are gendered and racialized." For example, she elaborates, "The scale of the household is formed through finance, law, and policy, systems that rely not only on the notion of the abstract individual but also on the nuclear family, familial obligations, and the domestic realm" (See also Guyer 1986; Yanagisako and Delaney 1995).

In the case of the *jiagongchang*, household workshops in Guangzhou challenge assumptions of the household that attribute to it exclusively as private, stable, and noneconomic forms of reproductive labor. *Jiagongchang* emerge at the confluence of the following two distinct, yet interlocking, forms of household: (1), the construction of self-contained units of privatized land by villagers as enforced by the household responsibility system, and (2), the enduring legacy of the *hukou* household registration system, which continues to administratively categorize citizens as either rural or urban citizens.

2   Specifically, Michael Piore and Charles Sabel (1986) describe the following dimensions of industrial organization and labor as exemplary of flexible specialization: One, individual workshops are spatially and temporally fragmented such that each workshop carries out one specialized task along the supply chain. Mass manufacture based on low volumes responds flexibly to changes to production cycles. Two, such division of tasks along horizontal lines is assumed to promote skilled labor, worker collaboration, and variation of labor practices, thereby reducing monotony of tasks, worker alienation, trust, and interdependence. Third, though spatially fragmented, individual workshops specializing in a particular task are linked along a production chain that responds quickly and flexibly to changing volumes and to various types of goods while maintaining productivity and efficiency.

3   These anthropological works have shed light on the social relationships and types of personhood that drive various forces of production and profit-making activities in an age of flexible production. While these studies have underscored unequal relations of power in the everyday operation of industrial workshops, they have tended to downplay how the spatial and temporal aspects of commodity mass production in home-based factories blur the categorical boundaries between worker and entrepreneur in an era of transnational subcontracting. Indeed, though the spatial fluidity of the home-based factory allows the speedy movement of people, commodities, and capital to float in and out of

the factory space, the temporal demands of the production process limit migrant factory owners from adequately disciplining their hired workers and controlling the rhythms of the assembly line. The ethnographic analyses that I present in the following sections add to this literature on kin-based industrial relations and transnational capitalism by examining how the movement of factory spaces into home-based workshops within the context of transnational fast fashion production and exchange shapes people's engagements with export manufacturing in post-socialist China.

4   Additionally, sociologist John Tomaney (1994), for instance, has argued that Piore and Sabel have overemphasized the so-called revitalization of craft work as a historically unique break from Taylorist and Fordist forms of mass manufacture. Rather, he contends that flexible specialization, namely the integration of segmented elements of the production process into a coordinated and continuous flow, has merely intensified older forms of labor exploitation and managerial control. The intensification of preexisting forms of worker exploitation and control, as Tomaney argues, is deeply embedded in specific histories and geographies of industrial organization and practice.

5   Contrary to the assertions of some social scientists who claim that large-scale manufacturers are more able to deliver different kinds of products more quickly and efficiently (Appelbaum 2008; J. Chan et al. 2013), the 2014 protests at the Yue Yuen factory in southern China, where much of the world's athletic footwear is manufactured, have revealed the numerous small-scale subcontractors upon which this giant producer relies in order to meet its transnational orders (Hobbes 2015). This case, as Hobbes argues, emphasize the importance of small-scale production sites in supporting the transnational supply chains for fashion garments, shoes, and accessories.

6   Michael Hardt and Antonio Negri draw from Gilles Deleuze's (1992) "Postscript on the Societies of Control." In his piece, Deleuze describes the reorganization of societies in the postwar period from disciplinary societies based on spaces of enclosure to control societies that operate through certain information technologies. These instruments of control uphold hegemonic notions of freedom and individuality while enacting practices of neoliberal governmentality.

7   The kanban approach also perfects the subjective image of "the organization man," a combination of the worker/manager in its most masculine and idealized form (Whyte 1956). The organization man embodies the epitome of the corporate worker, a predecessor of today's white-collar worker. This figure finds the promise of economic security, social mobility, and high standards of living through the protection of large institutions, whether the government, the corporation, the university, or the labor union.

8   Moishe Postone (1982, 1993) elaborates on the intensification of exploitation and control by analyzing the temporal dynamics of labor and industrial production in the post–Cold War era. He argues that the segmented and intensified use of advanced technologies in industrial production generates what he calls a treadmill effect, whereby overall productivity is increased (as measured by commodity units per every labor hour) yet the margin of profit on every unit of commodity made is increasingly low. This is because overall productivity within a given industry gradually rises with the introduction of new technologies, yet workers using mixed methods of older and newer forms of production must compete to sustain the overall levels of enhanced productivity. In effect, labor becomes intensified for most workers, while industry-wide returns for every commodity unit produced are reduced. Postone's treadmill effect in the post-Fordist era (as dominated by state capitalism) thus challenges the emancipatory potential that Piore and Sabel celebrate in their theories of flexible specialization.

9   As anthropologists (Cairoli 2011; Thomas 2009; Park 2012; Krause 2018) studying the transnational garment industry have shown, factory women's practices of mutual nurture and care include forms of social labor that cannot be easily categorized as capitalistic, yet they are paradoxically complicit with labor discipline along with its exploitative effects. Home-based industrial workshops, for instance, depend on the family as the primary agents of production and capital accumulation, thereby mapping entrepreneurial desires, risks, and exploitation onto kin relations. Within the home-based factory workshops in Guangzhou, the overlapping realms of the household and industrial spaces thus color the everyday desires and losses that migrant entrepreneurs and garment workers in the city's low-cost fashion industry encounter.

10   Scholars who have examined neoliberal governmentality underscore the processes of turning organizations and persons into self-activating agents through various normalizing processes. As Elizabeth Dunn (2004) shows in her case study of a factory undergoing privatization in postsocialist Poland, employees are identified and categorized as "bundles of qualities" (118). Audit cultures in these workplaces are cultivated by requiring employees to constantly perform self-evaluations such that each worker is accountable for her performance. These evaluations effectively become tools of self-discipline. See Marilyn Strathern 2000 for an anthropological theorization of audit cultures.

11   Along a similar vein, in his study on a South Korean–operated garment factory in northern China, Jaesok Kim (2013) shows how structures of class power and inequality within various levels of management and labor are inflected and made complicated by constructions of South Korean, Han Chinese, and Korean Chinese inter-ethnic identities on the shop floor. In the case of the Nawon factory, as Kim points out, relative

class mobility raised the social status of the Korean Chinese minority while intensifying the animosity among Han Chinese wage workers toward their Korean Chinese managers. Though both contexts illustrate the inter-ethnic dynamics between South Korean managers and Chinese workers, the rounds of negotiation between the Wongs and Mr. Liu reveal the fluidity through which these class and ethnic constructions are constantly challenged and remade.

CHAPTER 3. SURVEILLANCE AND REGULATION IN THE *SHENFEN* (IDENTIFICATION) ECONOMY

1   In his study of Xiaobei and Dengfeng urban villages, Guangzhi Huang (2020) notes that various units of law enforcement regularly patrolled the areas. Some of these units included the Armed Police (a division of the military), the Special Unit Police, and the Urban Administration (*chengguan*). While these units represent the formal units of law enforcement, I contend that there are other security forces hired privately by local landlords and business owners in the urban villages. Oftentimes, during their encounters with police, migrants (African and rural Chinese) do not know the branch of law enforcement the officers represent.

2   Mark Seigel (2018) further argues that the police is the quintessential incarnation of state power. The police, as he explains, is broad reaching so that it may carry out the functions of state governance. Its power is inherently legitimate. He writes, "The power to govern *is* the police power; the police refract the power of the state . . . Police realize—they make real—the core of the power of the state" (10).

3   Historically, the police force in China has been deeply entangled with other law enforcement agencies legitimated by the court as well as by other Party and governmental organs. Aimed to protect the Party-state from its "enemies," the police force enjoys broad a range of powers that include interrogation, investigation, and detention of the people (Han 2010). According to Michael Dutton (2005), the police force was created in the 1920s to protect the Chinese Communist Party (CCP) when the Nationalist Party split from the Party and began to massacre masses of Communists and other sympathizers (see also Han 2010).

4   Michael Dutton (1998) and Li Zhang (2001) documented at length the policing of rural migrants in Zhejiang Village in Beijing, before the migrant community was demolished in the name of tackling crime.

5   Police power, as Michel Foucault (1975) argues, is infinite. In his essay "Critique of Violence," Walter Benjamin (1986) adds that police power "is formless, like its nowhere-tangible, all-pervasive, ghostly presence in the life of civilized states" (287).

6　The racialized practices of policing and extortion that I elaborate in this chapter echo in many ways what Kedron Thomas (2016) has observed in the informal garment sector in the Guatemalan Highlands. Such regulatory practices by the police and other uniformed officials have pushed Mayan garment workers further underground, leading market participants to build an ethnos of solidarity and secrecy in their attempts to dodge violence and regulation by the Guatemalan state.

7　While the cultural and historical reasons for the negative construction and the discrimination fall outside the scope of this book, several scholars have written extensively on this topic (see Lan 2016a, 2016b; Castillo 2020; Huang 2020). According to Shanshan Lan (2016a), nationality, alongside English-language proficiency, class belonging, and economic status, complicate rankings and meanings placed along the color line in China.

8　To further illustrate my point, G. Huang (2020) cites a news article published in the state-sponsored *Southern Metropolis Daily* (Qiu and Wu 2016), touting the successful gentrification of Xiaobei and Dengfeng urban villages in attempts to showcase the "uplift" and market value of its private properties. In the article, the journalist highlights the successful regulation over informal and possibly illegal activities by citing regular door-to-door police inspections of its residents. Furthermore, the article emphasizes that the properties attract white foreigners (represented by white Europeans and white Americans), not only black Africans, using race to demonstrate developmental progress and property value.

9　For a more extensive elaboration of the history of anti-Blackness, race, and racial constructions in China, see Sautman 1994; Sullivan 1994; Wyatt 2009; Cheng 2011; Shih 2013; Dikotter 2015; Lan 2016b; and G. Huang 2020.

10　Other negative perceptions of African migrants by Chinese netizens on the internet, as Lan (2016b) states, are colored by China's developmental aid to African governments, China's stringent immigration policies, the sexualization of African bodies (including the demonization of African masculinity), and popular narratives of the so-called African threat in Guangzhou.

11　Anthropologist Shanshan Lan (2016b), in her ethnographic study of Chinese-African race relations in Xiaobei, notes similar practices of detainment and release by the Guangzhou police. She adds that this pattern of intimidation and policing results from the local government's lack of resources. In her interview with a local official in Guangzhou, the official states, "The police only make arrests before some major events. Most of the time, they turn a blind eye to the many undocumented Africans on the street. For those who got arrested, they were locked up for several days and then released. Repatriation costs money, so the only solution is to turn them loose again" (19).

12 Evaluations of low-quality counterfeits fall within a spectrum of product quality based on grades (from lowest, A, to highest quality, AAA) as in so-called real fakes or simply "good or high-quality samples" (*ban*).

13 Dong Han (2010) elaborates that, legally speaking, anybody can be considered *san fei*, or the "three withouts," if they do not possess the necessary IDs and documents at the moment of police encounter. In essence, *san fei* refers to the moment of encounter when a migrant is stopped by the police and cannot produce the necessary paperwork to avoid detention.

14 Dong Han (2010) notes that the rates of crime committed by rural migrants in China are generally overestimated. Zhao and Kipnis (2000) further argue that most crimes by rural migrants are nonviolent, petty crimes driven by destitution and marginalization.

15 Just as commodities are subject to assessment and control, however, *suzhi* discourses subject migrants to evaluative criteria according to distinctions of high and low as well as to categories of possession (Kipnis 2006). The term acquires discursive power by reconstructing personhood as possessive individuals (Strathern 2018), that is, individuals who can acquire certain qualities or characteristics through consumption, education, childhood nurture, and skills acquisition—resources that remain beyond the reach of rural migrants in the cities (Anagnost 2004). Through qualities of civility, self-discipline, and modernity, *suzhi* links the concepts of market value and the language of economic (under) development with interiorized reconstructions of the self (Yan 2008).

16 The racialized criminalization of migratory groups in Guangzhou may be thought of as part of what Michel Foucault (1975) describes as a carceral network, which encompasses the "mechanisms, technologies, and knowledge systems" that serve the carceral state.

17 As Dylan Rodriguez (2019) writes, carcerality is a logic of power that operate across multiple spatial scales of institutional confinement such prisons, police, reservations, segregated cities, etc.

CHAPTER 4. SPECULATIVE REAL ESTATE AND FLEXIBLE APPROPRIATION

1 In this chapter, I use the roles of wholesalers and migrant bosses interchangeably.

2 The site of the Xi Fang Hang market was the birthplace of what scholars describe as the globally recognized Canton Trade System in Guangzhou (Perdue 2009). From approximately 1700 to 1842, Guangzhou was a vital center of the Canton Trade System, which served markets to the Middle East, Europe, and the Americas during the Qing dynasty. This maritime

network was founded upon the administrative and shipping infrastructure that was already built nearly a thousand years prior, when Arab and Persian traders had lived in the city's foreign quarters and exchanged silk and spices during the eighth century (Perdue 2009). Situated at the head of the Pearl River, Guangzhou (historically named Canton by early British colonial traders) featured the Canton Trade System during the sixteenth and seventeenth centuries. Through its geographic proximity to the South China Sea, Guangzhou flourished as a vital confluence of commercial and cultural exchange among Chinese traders and Euro-American seafarers. China's southern coastline, sampans, rivers, and steamboats attested to Guangzhou's historic orientation to the world through its maritime history.

3   In her book *Friction* (2005), Anna Tsing describes "friction" as the tensions and contradictions that emerge through moments of cultural misunderstanding and awkward engagement. Capitalist exchanges operate through universal categories, which, as Tsing highlights, remain localized and contested. Creativity within the realm of fast fashion may be seen as one of these universal categories. Once put into action, its essential definition becomes blurred and ambiguous.

4   Christina Moon (2016) writes that fast fashion reflects the highly volatile and precarious nature of global fashion markets. Consumers, whose finicky tastes quickly shift and change, now demand a wider variety of design trends, at cheaper prices.

5   As Walter Benjamin (1969) argues, technologies of mechanical reproduction become the hallmark of modernity as these technologies privilege the copy over the so-called authentic or original works of art. Using moving images of film as an example, Benjamin argues that the aura of a work of art diminishes through processes of cutting, segmenting, and inserting images via technologies of mechanical reproduction. Indeed, Benjamin's essay underscores a shift in the modern period in what counts as a work of art amidst the proliferation of techniques of reproducibility. The shift from poiesis (poetry and philosophical thinking) to techne (know-how in craft and art), as Benjamin argues, signals a reconfiguration in the ways a work of art is critiqued and evaluated, as objects and images are decontextualized and recontextualized in divergent spatiotemporal realms. The transformation in the relation between art and criticism, as Andrew Benjamin (2006) asserts, is ultimately a transformation in the relationship between time and object.

6   Walter Benjamin (2002) also argues that in fashion, what is constant is temporal change. By cyclically resurrecting past elements and remaking them in the present moment (*die Aktuelle*), fashion becomes a marker of constant change and movement. Fashion thus defines itself through ongoing practices of making and marking time as objects constantly shift

into and out of categories of the "old" and the "new" as well as of "fashion" and "nonfashion." In citing the example of a dress ruffle, Andrew Benjamin (2006) writes, "The ruffle, in being transitory, is engendered by the conception of change generated by the idealist conception of the idea" (27).

7 As Rob Horning (2011) observes, the comparative advantage of fast fashion companies lies in speed, not brand recognition, garment durability, or reputable design. Fast fashion thus derives its competitive edge by mobilizing time, space, and object into relations of value creation and distribution. As the cycles of fast fashion demonstrate, the flexible accumulation of commodities and capital is achieved through the everyday practices of temporalization, spatialization, and reappropriation of objects as they cycle into and out of fashion.

8 In fact, physical altercations within the market spaces are so frequent that market participants there uphold informal codes of conduct. One rule forbids shoppers from obstructing the displays of the tightly packed stalls. I learned of this unsaid rule from one of my first visits there, during which I was waiting for a friend to complete a transaction nearby and a young saleswoman physically pushed me out of the way because I was momentarily obstructing her clothing displays.

9 Such speedy acts of reappropriation along the chains of fast fashion commodities enable the flexible accumulation of money and capital by constantly remaking temporalities and spaces. These processes, I contend, produce uneven market spaces and temporalities for the sale of fast fashion, yet they are key elements in the recreation of surplus value along the supply chains.

10 This insight has been made possible by the guidance of Sylvia Yanagisako (personal communication 2020).

11 An example of this is the "Made in Italy" label in the realms of high fashion and ready-to-wear. In these stylistic worlds, authentic "fashion" remains geographically rooted to place-based identifications and proximate locations (Reinach 2015; Yanagisako 2018).

CHAPTER 5. TRANSNATIONAL MIGRANT BOSSHOOD

1 Other state-sanctioned religious organizations include the following: (1) the Chinese Taoist Association, (2) the Buddhist Association of China, and (3) the Islamic Association of China.

2 The cultural and physical border that separates China and South Korea highlights the work of the *Chaoxianzu*'s gendered longing as these market intermediaries wait for their fate to run its predestined course. In her study of Korean Chinese couples in Yanbian, June Hee Kwon (2015,

2023) cogently describes what she calls "the work of waiting" among the *Chaoxianzu* who remain in China while their partners have migrated to South Korea to pursue better economic opportunities. In her insightful ethnography, she explores the affective dimensions of love and marriage among couples who become physically and emotionally separated by the border between China and Korea. She demonstrates how the Korean Chinese experiences of the border exist not only across spatial dimensions but also across affective and temporal divides. By demonstrating how acts of waiting for their loved one's return engender conditions of vulnerability and circulations of care, Kwon shows how these acts are not merely passive. Waiting, as she argues, serves as a form of affective labor. That is, they are affective deferrals amidst vulnerable socioeconomic conditions, constituting a form of value production. Suspended between the present and their potential and anticipated future, the Korean Chinese practices of waiting become provisional ways of "making sense of the present" (Kwon 2015).

3   At the time, this multinational conglomerate signed a deal to provide land for a US missile defense system, Terminal High-Altitude Area Defense (THAAD), apparently under pressure from North Korea.

CONCLUSION

1   While some scholars suggested that the tightening of state control over the domestic economy slowly began as early as the 2008 Beijing Olympics under President Hu Jintao (Shirk 2022), these dynamics intensified in recent years, particularly since the start of the COVID-19 pandemic.

References

Adkins, Lisa. 2009. "Sociological Futures: From Clock Time to Event Time." *Sociological Research Online* 14 (4): 88–92.

Agarwala, Nitin, and Rana D. Chaudhary. 2021. "'Made in China 2025': Poised for Success?" *India Quarterly* 77 (3): 424–61.

Al, Stefan. 2014. *Villages in the City: A Guide to South China's Informal Settlements.* Hong Kong: Hong Kong University Press.

Alexander, Peter, and Anita Chan. 2004. "Does China Have an Apartheid Pass System?" *Journal of Ethnic and Migration Studies* 30 (4): 609–29.

Allison, Anne 1994. *Nightwork: Sexuality, Pleasure, and Corporate Masculinity in a Tokyo Hostess Club.* Chicago: University of Chicago Press.

Allison, Anne. 2013. *Precarious Japan.* Durham, NC: Duke University Press.

Alvi, Anjum. 2013. "Concealment and Revealment: The Muslim Veil in Context." *Current Anthropology* 54 (2): 177–99.

Amin, Ash, ed. 1994. *Post-Fordism: A Reader.* Hoboken, NJ: Wiley-Blackwell.

Amin, Ash, and Nigel Thrift. 2016. *Seeing Like a City.* Cambridge: Polity Press.

Anagnost, Ann 1997. *National Past-Times: Narrative, Representation, and Power in Modern China.* Durham, NC: Duke University Press.

Anagnost, Ann. 2004. "The Corporeal Politics of Quality (*Suzhi*)." *Public Culture* 16 (2): 189–208.

Anagnost, Ann. 2008. "From 'Class' to 'Social Strata': Grasping the Social Totality in Reform-Era China." *Third World Quarterly* 29 (3): 497–519.

Anagnost, Ann, Andrea Arai, and Hai Ren. 2013. *Global Futures in East Asia: Youth, Nation, and the New Economy in Uncertain Times.* Stanford, CA: Stanford University Press.

Andreas, Joel, and Shaohua Zhan. 2015. "Hukou and Land: Market Reform and Rural Displacement in China." *Journal of Peasant Studies* 43 (4): 798–827.

Appadurai, Arjun. 1996. *Modernity at Large: Cultural Dimensions of Globalization.* Minneapolis: University of Minnesota Press.

Appel, Hannah. 2019. *The Licit Life of Capitalism: US Oil in Equatorial Guinea.* Durham, NC: Duke University Press.

Appelbaum, Richard. 2008. "Giant Transnational Contractors in East Asia: Emergent Trends in Global Supply Chains." *Competition and Change* 12 (1): 69–87.

Arrighi, Giovanni. 2007. *Adam Smith in Beijing: Lineages of the Twenty-First Century*. New York: Verso.

Bach, Jonathan. 2010. "'They Come In Peasants and Leave Citizens': Urban Villages and the Making of Shenzhen, China." *Cultural Anthropology* 25 (3): 421–58.

Bahro, Rudolf. 1978. *The Alternative in Eastern Europe*. New York: Penguin-Random House.

Bair, Jennifer, and Marion Werner. 2011. "The Place of Disarticulations: Global Commodity Production in La Laguna, Mexico." *Environment and Planning A: Economy and Space* 43 (5): 998–1015.

Barme, Geremie. 1996. *Shades of Mao: The Posthumous Cult of the Great Leader*. New York: Routledge.

Bauman, Zygmunt. 2000. *Liquid Modernity*. Cambridge: Polity Press.

Bear, Laura. 2014. "Doubt, Conflict, Mediation: The Anthropology of Modern Time." *Journal of the Royal Anthropological Institute* 20 (1): 3–30.

Bear, Laura, Karen Ho, Anna Lowenhaupt Tsing, and Sylvia Yanagisako. 2015. "Gens: A Feminist Manifesto for the Study of Capitalism." *Society for Cultural Anthropology: Theorizing the Contemporary*, March 30. https://culanth.org /fieldsights/gens-a-feminist-manifesto-for-the-study-of-capitalism.

Beech, Hannah. 2012. "A Nigerian Dies in China—and Racial Tensions Heat Up." *Time Magazine*, June 20. https://world.time.com/2012/06/20/a-nigerian -dies-in-china-and-racial-tensions-heat-up/.

Benjamin, Andrew. 2006. *Style and Time: Essays on the Politics of Appearance*. Evanston, IL: Northwestern University Press.

Benjamin, Walter. 1969. "The Work of Art in the Age of Mechanical Reproduction." In *Illuminations*, edited by Hannah Arendt, translated by Harry Zohn. New York: Schocken.

Benjamin, Walter. 1986. *Reflections: Essays, Aphorisms, Autobiographical Writings*. New York: Schocken.

Benjamin, Walter. 2002. *The Arcades Project*. Cambridge, MA: Belknap Press.

Berdahl, Daphne. 1999. *Where the World Ended: Re-Unification and Identity in the German Borderland*. Berkeley: University of California Press.

Berger, John. 2008. *Ways of Seeing*. New York: Penguin Classic.

Berlant, Lauren. 2011. *Cruel Optimism*. Durham, NC: Duke University Press.

Berlinger, Joshua. 2018. "Beijing's Crackdown on Religion Clouds Holiday Season for China's Faithful." *CNN World*, December 26. https://www.cnn.com/2018 /12/26/asia/china-christian-crackdown-christmas-intl/index.html.

Berman, Marshall. 1988. *All That Is Solid Melts into Air: The Experience of Modernity*. New York: Penguin.

Biehl, João. 2013. *Vita: Life in a Zone of Social Abandonment*. Berkeley: University of California Press.

Bodomo, Adams. 2012. *Africans in China: A Sociocultural Study and Its Implications for Africa-China Relations*. New York: Cambria Press.

Bolchover, Joshua. 2018. "Palimpsest Urbanism." *e-flux Architecture*, January. https://www.e-flux.com/architecture/urban-village/169801/palimpsest-urbanism/.

Branigan, Tania. 2012. "Africans in China Protest After Death of Expat." *The Guardian*, June 19. https://www.theguardian.com/world/2012/jun/19/foreigners-protest-china-death-expat.

Bravo, Lauren. 2020. *How To Break Up with Fast Fashion: A Guilt-Free Guide to Changing the Way You Shop—For Good*. London: Hachette UK.

Breznitz, Dan, and Michael Murphree. 2011. *Run of the Red Queen: Government, Innovation, Globalization, and Economic Growth in China*. New Haven, CT: Yale University Press.

Burke, Jason. 2020. "China Fails to Stop Racism Against Africans Over COVID-19." *The Guardian*, April 27. https://www.theguardian.com/world/2020/apr/27/china-fails-to-stop-racism-against-africans-over-covid-19.

Butler, Judith. 2006. *Precarious Life: The Powers of Mourning and Violence*. London: Verso.

Butler, Judith. 2009. *Frames of War: When Is Life Grievable?* New York: Verso.

Butollo, Florian. 2014. *The End of Cheap Labour? Industrial Transformation and "Social Upgrading" in China*. Frankfurt: Campus Verlag.

Buyandelgeriyn, Manduhai. 2007. "Post-Post-Transition Theories: Walking on Multiple Paths." *Annual Review of Anthropology* 37: 235–50.

Byler, Darren. 2021. *In the Camps: China's High-Tech Penal Colony*. New York: Columbia University Press.

Cairoli, Laetitia M. 2011. *Girls of the Factory: A Year with the Garment Workers of Morocco*. Gainesville: University Press of Florida.

Carling, Jørgen, and Heidi Østbø Haugen. 2020. "Circumstantial Migration: How Gambian Journeys to China Enrich Migration Theory." *Journal of Ethnic and Migration Studies* 47 (12): 2778–95.

Castillo, Roberto. 2016. "'Homing' Guangzhou: Emplacement, Belonging and Precarity Among Africans in China." *International Journal of Cultural Studies* 19 (3): 287–306.

Castillo, Roberto. 2018. "What 'Blackface' Tells Us About China's Patronising Attitude Towards Africa." *The Conversation*, March 6. https://theconversation.com/what-blackface-tells-us-about-chinas-patronising-attitude-towards-africa-92449.

Castillo, Roberto. 2020a. "Africans in Guangzhou Are on Edge, After Many Are Left Homeless Amid Rising Xenophobia as China Fights a Second Wave of Coronavirus." *Africans in China*, April 16. https://africansinchina.net/2020/04/16/news-reports-africans-in-guangzhou-are-on-edge-after-many-are-left-homeless-amid-rising-xenophobia-as-china-fights-a-second-wave-of-coronavirus/.

Castillo, Roberto. 2020b. "'Race' and 'Racism' in Contemporary Africa-China Relations Research: Approaches, Controversies and Reflections." *Inter-Asia Cultural Studies* 21 (3): 310–36.

Cezne, Eric, and Roos Visser. 2023. "Why Race Matters in Africa-China Relations." *LSE* (blog), June 27. https://blogs.lse.ac.uk/africaatlse/2023/06/27/why-race-matters-in-africa-china-relations/.

Chalfin, Brenda. 2004. *Shea Butter Republic: State Power, Global Markets, and the Making of an Indigenous Commodity*. New York: Routledge.

Chan, Chris King-chi, Éric Florence, and Jack Linchuan Qiu. 2021. "Precarity, Platforms, and Agency: The Multiplication of Chinese Labour." *China Perspectives* 2021 (1): 3–7.

Chan, Jenny, Ngai Pun, and Mark Selden. 2013. "The Politics of Global Production: Apple, Foxconn and China's New Working Class." *New Technology, Work and Employment* 28 (2): 100–115. https://doi.org/10.1111/ntwe.12008.

Chan, Jenny, Mark Selden, and Ngai Pun. 2020. *Dying for an iPhone: Apple, Foxconn, and the Lives of China's Workers*. Chicago: Haymarket Books.

Chang, Leslie T. 2009. *Factory Girls: From Village to City in a Changing China*. New York: Random House.

Cheng, Yinghong. 2011. "From Campus Racism to Cyber Racism: Discourse of Race and Chinese Nationalism." *China Quarterly* 207: 561–79.

Choi, Jingshan. 2006. 城市正规经济与非正规经济的联系——以广州中大布匹市场及其周边的制衣行业为例 [The connection between urban formal economy and informal economy——Taking Guangzhou zhongda cloth city as an example]. MA thesis, Department of Human Geography, Sun Yatsen University, Guangzhou.

Chong, Alan, and Quang Minh Pham. 2020. *Critical Reflections on China's Belt and Road Initiative*. London: Palgrave Macmillan.

Chong, Gao. 2006. "The Making of Migrant Entrepreneurs in Contemporary China: An Ethnographic Study of Garment Producers in Suburban Guangzhou." PhD diss., Department of Sociology, University of Hong Kong.

Chu, Julie. 2010. *Cosmologies of Credit: Transnational Mobility and the Politics of Destination in China*. Durham, NC: Duke University Press.

Chu, Nellie. 2016. "The Emergence of 'Craft' and Migrant Entrepreneurship Along the Global Commodity Chains for Fast Fashion in Southern China." *Journal of Modern Craft* 9 (2): 193–213.

Chu, Nellie. 2019. "Cartographic Imaginaries of Fast Fashion in Guangzhou, China." In *Fashion and Beauty in the Time of Asia*, edited by S. Heijin Lee, Christina H. Moon, and Thuy Linh Nguyen Tu, 242–68. New York: New York University Press.

Chu, Nellie. 2022. "Tu Er Dai Peasant Landlords and the Infrastructures of Accumulation in Guangzhou's Urban Villages." *positions: asia critique* 30 (3): 479–99.

Chu, Nellie, Ralph Litzinger, Mengqi Wang, and Qian Zhu. 2022. "Guest Editors' Introduction." In "The Urban In-Between." Special issue, *positions: asia critique* 30 (3): 411–27.

Chua, Charmaine. 2018. "Logistical Violence, Logistical Vulnerabilities." *Historical Materialism* 24 (3): 167–82.

Chua, Charmaine. 2020. "Abolition Is a Constant Struggle: Five Lessons from Minneapolis." *Theory and Event Supplement* 23 (4): 127–47.

Chuang, Julia. 2020. *Beneath the China Boom: Labor, Citizenship, and the Making of a Rural Land Market*. Berkeley: University of California Press.

Chumley, Lily. 2016. *Creativity Class: Art School and Culture Work in Postsocialist China*. Princeton, NJ: Princeton University Press.

Cline, Elizabeth L. 2013. *Overdressed: The Shockingly High Cost of Cheap Fashion*. New York: Portfolio.

Comaroff, Jean, and John Comaroff. 2006. *Law and Disorder in the Postcolony*. Chicago: University of Chicago Press.

Coombe, Rosemary. 1998. *The Cultural Life of Intellectual Properties: Authorship, Appropriation, and the Law*. Durham, NC: Duke University Press.

Daxue Consulting. 2019. "China's Luxury Industry," White Paper, August. https://daxueconsulting.com/fashion-luxury-in-china/.

Day, Alexander. 2013. *The Peasant in Postsocialist China: History, Politics, and Capitalism*. Cambridge: Cambridge University Press.

Deleuze, Gilles. 1992. "Postscript on the Societies of Control." *October* 59: 3–7.

DeLuca, Elizabeth. 2017. "The Household." *Society for Cultural Anthropology: Member Voices*, August 4. https://culanth.org/fieldsights/series/the-household.

Diederich, Manon. 2013. "Maneuvering Through the Spaces of Everyday Life: Transnational Experiences of African Women in Guangzhou, China." Master's thesis, Department of Geography, University of Cologne.

Dikotter, Frank. 2015. *The Discourse of Race in Modern China*. Oxford: Oxford University Press.

Dirlik, Arif. 1989. "Postsocialism? Reflections on 'Socialism with Chinese Characteristics.'" *Bulletin of Concerned Asian Scholars* 21 (1): 33–44.

Driessen, Miriam. 2019. *Tales of Hope, Tales of Bitterness: Chinese Road Builders in Ethiopia*. Hong Kong: Hong Kong University Press.

Du, Ming. 2023. "Unpacking the Black Box of China's State Capitalism." *German Law Journal* 24 (1): 125–50.

Dunn, Elizabeth. 2004. *Privatizing Poland: Baby Food, Big Business, and the Remaking of Labor*. Ithaca, NY: Cornell University Press.

Dutton, Michael. 1998. *Streetlife China*. Cambridge: Cambridge University Press.

Dutton, Michael. 2005. *Policing Chinese Politics: A History*. Durham, NC: Duke University Press.

Elyachar, Julia. 2005. *Markets of Dispossession: NGOs, National Development, and the State in Cairo*. Durham, NC: Duke University Press.

English, Bonnie. 2013. *A Cultural History of Fashion in the 20th and 21st Centuries: From Catwalk to Sidewalk*. London: Bloomsbury.

Evans, Harriet. 2020. *Beijing from Below: Stores of Marginal Lives in the Capital's Center*. Durham, NC: Duke University Press.

Faier, Lieba. 2009. *Intimate Encounters: Filipina Women and the Remaking of Rural Japan*. Berkeley: University of California Press.

Faier, Lieba, and Lisa Rofel. 2014. "Ethnographies of Encounter." *Annual Review of Anthropology* 43: 363–77.

Fan, Lulu, and Boy Luethje. 2019. "Taobao Villages: Rural E-Commerce and Low-End Manufacturing in China." *East-West Wire*, July 31. https://www.jstor.org/stable/resrep25001.

Federici, Silvia. 1975. *Wages Against Housework*. Bristol: Falling Wall Press.

Finkelstein, Maura. 2019. *The Archive of Loss: Lively Ruination in Mill Land Mumbai*. Durham, NC: Duke University Press.

Florence, Eric. 2006. "Debates and Classification Struggles Regarding the Representation of Migrants Workers." *China Perspectives* 65 (May/June): 1–21. https://journals.openedition.org/chinaperspectives/629.

Foucault, Michel. 1975. *Discipline and Punish: The Birth of the Prison*. New York: Vintage.

Freeman, Carla. 2014. *Entrepreneurial Selves: Neoliberal Respectability and the Making of a Caribbean Middle Class*. Durham, NC: Duke University Press.

Friedberg, Susanne. 2004. *French Beans and Food Scares: Culture and Commerce in an Anxious Age*. Oxford: Oxford University Press.

Friedman, Eli. 2014. *The Insurgency Trap: Labor Politics in Post-Socialist China*. Ithaca, NY: Cornell University Press.

Friedman, Eli, and Lee, C. K. 2010. "Remaking the World of Chinese Labour: A 30-Year Retrospective." *British Journal of Industrial Relations* 48 (3): 507–33.

Gaetano, Arianne, and Tamara Jacka, eds. 2004. *On the Move: Women and Rural-to-Urban Migration in Contemporary China*. New York: Columbia University Press.

Gereffi, Gary, Penny Bamber, and Karina Fernandez-Stark. 2022. *China's New Development Strategies: Upgrading from Above and from Below in Global Value Chains*. Shanghai: Palgrave Macmillan.

Gibson-Graham, J. K. 2006a. *The End of Capitalism (As We Knew It): A Feminist Critique of Political Economy*. Minneapolis: University of Minnesota Press.

Gibson-Graham, J. K. 2006b. *A Postcapitalist Politics*. Minneapolis: University of Minnesota Press.

Guyer, Jane. 1984. *Family and Farm in Southern Cameroon*. Cambridge: Cambridge University Press.

Guyer, Jane. 2004. *Marginal Gains: Monetary Transactions in Atlantic Africa*. Chicago: University of Chicago Press.

Guyer, Jane, Laray Denzer, and Adigun Agbaje. 2002. *Money Struggles and City Life: Devaluation in Ibadan and Other Urban Centers in Southern Nigeria*. Portsmouth, NH: Heinemann.

Halloway, John. 2010. *Crack Capitalism*. London: Pluto Press.

Han, Dong. 2010. "Policing and Racialization of Rural Migrant Workers in Chinese Cities." *Ethnic and Racial Studies* 33 (4): 593–610.

Hann, Chris, Caroline Humphrey, and Katherine Verdery. 2001. "Introduction: Postsocialism as a Topic of Anthropological Investigation." In *Postsocialism:*

Ideals, Ideologies and Practices in Eurasia, edited by C. M. Hann, 1–28. London: Routledge.

Hansen, Alvin H. 1939. "Economic Progress and Declining Population Growth." *American Economic Review* 29 (1): 1–15.

Hao, Feng. 2016. "Will China's 'Taobao Villages' Spur a Rural Revolution?" *China-File*, May 31. https://www.chinafile.com/media/will-chinas-taobao-villages-spur-rural-revolution.

Haraway, Donna. 1988. "Situated Knowledges: The Science Question in Feminism and the Privilege of Partial Perspective." *Feminist Studies* 14 (3): 575–99.

Hardt, Michael, and Antonio Negri. 2000. *Empire*. Cambridge, MA: Harvard University Press.

Harvey, David. 1982. *The Limits to Capital*. Chicago: University of Chicago Press.

Harvey, David. 1987. "Flexible Accumulation Through Urbanization: Reflections on 'Post-Modernism' in the American City." *Antipode* 19 (3): 260–86.

Harvey, David. 1990. *The Condition of Postmodernity: An Enquiry into the Origins of Cultural Change*. Hoboken, NJ: Wiley-Blackwell.

Harvey, David. 2001. *Spaces of Capital: Towards a Critical Geography*. Oxford: Routledge.

Harvey, David. 2005. *A Brief History of Neoliberalism*. Oxford: Oxford University Press.

Haugen, Heidi Østbø. 2012. "Nigerians in China: A Second State of Immobility." *International Migration* 50 (2): 65–80.

Haugen, Heidi Østbø. 2013. "African Pentecostal Migrants in China: Marginalization and the Alternative Geography of a Mission Theology." *African Studies Review* 56 (1): 81–102.

Haugen, Heidi Østbø. 2018. "Petty Commodities, Serious Business: The Governance of Fashion Jewellery Chains Between China and Ghana." *Global Networks* 18 (2): 307–25.

Haynes, Naomi. 2013. "On the Potentials and Problems of Pentecostal Exchange." *American Anthropologist* 115 (1): 85–95.

Hayward, Jane, and Małgorzata Jakimów. 2022. "Who Makes the City? Beijing's Urban Villages as Sites of Ideological Contestation." *positions: asia critique* 30 (3): 455–77.

Heila Sha (Saheira Haliel). 2020. "Transnational Marriage in Yiwu, China: Trade, Settlement and Mobility." *Journal of Ethnic and Migration Studies* 46 (11): 2326–45.

Hendrickson, Hildi, ed. 1996. *Clothing and Difference: Embodied Identities in Colonial and Post-Colonial Africa*. Durham, NC: Duke University Press.

Hernandez, Javier C. 2018. "As China Cracks Down on Churches, Christians Declare 'We Will Not Forfeit Our Faith.'" *New York Times*, December 25. https://www.nytimes.com/2018/12/25/world/asia/china-christmas-church-crackdown.html.

Hertz, Ellen. 1998. *The Trading Crowd: An Ethnography of the Shanghai Stock Market*. Cambridge: Cambridge University Press.

Hillenbrand, Margaret. 2023. *On the Edge: Feeling Precarious in China*. New York: Columbia University Press.

Hinkson, Melinda, 2017. "Precarious Placemaking." *Annual Review of Anthropology* 46: 49–64. https://doi.org/10.1146/annurev-anthro-102116041624.

Ho, Karen. 2009. *Liquidated: An Ethnography of Wall Street*. Durham, NC: Duke University Press.

Hobbes, Michael. 2015. "The Myth of the Ethical Shopper." *Huffington Post: Highline*. Accessed December 21, 2024. https://highline.huffingtonpost.com/articles /en/the-myth-of-the-ethical-shopper/.

Hochschild, Arlie. 1985. *The Managed Heart: Commericalization of Human Feeling*. Berkeley: University of California Press.

Hochschild, Arlie. 2012. *The Second Shift: Working Families and the Revolution at Home*. New York: Penguin.

Hoffman, Daniel. 2011. "Violence, Just in Time: War and Work in Contemporary West Africa." *Cultural Anthropology* 26 (1): 34–57.

Horkheimer, Max, and Theodor W. Adorno. 2002. *Dialectic of Enlightenment*. Edited by Gunzelin Schmid Noerr. Translated by Edmund Jephcott. Stanford, CA: Stanford University Press.

Horning, Rob. 2011. "The Accidental Bricoleurs." *n+1*, June 3. https://nplusonemag .com/online-only/online-only/the-accidental-bricoleurs.

Hsing, You-Tien. 2010. *The Great Urban Transformation: Politics of Land and Property in China*. Oxford: Oxford University Press.

Hsiung, Ping-Chun. 1996. *Living Rooms as Factories: Class, Gender, and the Satellite Factory System*. Philadelphia: Temple University Press.

Huang, Erin Y. 2021. "Ocean Media: Digital South China Sea and Gilles Deleuze's Desert Islands." *Verge: Studies in Global Asias* 7 (2): 177–203.

Huang, Guangzhi. 2019. "Policing Blacks in Guangzhou: How Public Security Constructs Africans as *Sanfei*." *Modern China* 45 (2): 171–200.

Huang, Guangzhi. 2020. "Conflating Blackness and Rurality: Urban Politics and Social Control of Africans in Guangzhou, China." *Journal of Contemporary Eastern Asia* 19 (2): 148–68.

Huang, Philip C. C., Gao Yuan, and Yusheng Peng. 2012. "Capitalization Without Proletarianization in China's Agricultural Development." *Modern China* 38 (2): 139–73.

Humphrey, Caroline. 2002. *The Unmaking of Soviet Life: Everyday Economies After Socialism*. Ithaca, NY: Cornell University Press.

Hung, Ho Fung. 2009. *China and the Transformation of Global Capitalism*. Baltimore, MD: Johns Hopkins University Press.

Huynh, Tu. 2015. "A 'Wild West' of Trade? African Women and Men and the Gendering of Globalisation from Below in Guangzhou." *Identities* 23 (5): 501–18.

Ibañez-Tirado, Diana, and Magnus Marsden. 2020. "Trade 'Outside the Law': Uzbek and Afghan Transnational Merchants Between Yiwu and South-Central Asia." *Central Asian Survey* 39 (1): 135–54.

Jameson, Fredric. 1990. *Postmodernism, or, The Cultural Logic of Late Capitalism*. Durham, NC: Duke University Press.

Jessop, Bob. 2004. "Spatial Fixes, Temporal Fixes, and Spatio-Temporal Fixes." Department of Sociology, Lancaster University, UK, June 27, 2004. https://www.lancaster.ac.uk/fass/resources/sociology-online-papers/papers/jessop-spatio-temporal-fixes.pdf.

Jian, Muzhen, and Wenhuan Tan. 1950. "Lujiang Ertong Jiating Jiaoyang Diaocha" (鸷江儿童家庭教养调查) [Lujiang's children education surveys]. Bachelor's thesis, Department of Sociology, Lingnan University.

Jones, Carla. 2007. "Fashion and Faith in Urban Indonesia." *Fashion Theory* 11 (2/3): 211–32.

Keane, Michael. 2006. "From Made in China to Created in China." *International Journal of Cultural Studies* 9 (3): 285–96.

Kim, Jaesok. 2013. *Chinese Labor in a Korean Factory: Class, Ethnicity, and Productivity on the Shop Floor in Globalizing China.* Stanford, CA: Stanford University Press.

Kipnis, Andrew. 2006. "Suzhi: A Keyword Approach." *China Quarterly* 186: 295–313.

Kirton, David. 2020. "China: COVID-19 Discrimination Against Africans: Forced Quarantines, Evictions, Refused Services in Guangzhou." Human Rights Watch, April 13, 2020. https://www.hrw.org/news/2020/05/05/china-covid-19-discrimination-against-africans.

Klein, Naomi. 2000. *No Logo: Taking Aim at the Brand Bullies.* Toronto: Knopf Canada.

Kohnert, Dirk. 2022. "African Migrants Plight in China: Afrophobia Impedes China's Race for Africa's Resources and Markets." MPRA Paper No. 111346. MPRA: Munich Personal RePEc Archive, January 2. https://mpra.ub.uni-muenchen.de/111346/1/MPRA_paper_111346.pdf.

Kornbluh, Anna. 2024. *Immediacy: Or, The Style of Too Late Capitalism.* New York: Verso.

Krause, Elizabeth. 2018. *Tight Knit: Global Families and the Social Life of Fast Fashion.* Chicago: University of Chicago Press.

Krugman, Paul. 2014. "What Secular Stagnation Isn't." *New York Times Blog*, January 27. https://archive.nytimes.com/krugman.blogs.nytimes.com/2014/10/27/what-secular-stagnation-isnt/.

Kuruvilla, Sarosh, Ching Kwan Lee, and Mary E. Gallagher. 2011. *From Iron Rice Bowl to Informalization: Markets, Workers, and the State in a Changing China.* Ithaca, NY: Cornell University Press.

Kwon, June Hee. 2015. "The Work of Waiting: Love and Money in Korean Chinese Transnational Migration." *Cultural Anthropology* 30 (3): 477–500.

Kwon, June Hee. 2023. *Borderland Dreams: The Transnational Lives of Korean Chinese Workers.* Durham, NC: Duke University Press.

Lam, Tong. 2019. "Futures and Ruins: The Politics, Aesthetics, and Temporality of Infrastructure." *Made in China Journal* 4 (2): 78–83.

Lam, Tong. 2020. "The Dark Side of the Miracle: Spectacular and Precarious Accumulation in an Urban Village Under Siege." *positions: asia critique* 30 (3): 523–47.

Lan, Shanshan. 2015. "State Regulation of Undocumented African Migrants in China: A Multi-Scalar Analysis." *Journal of Asian and African Studies* 50 (3): 289–304.

Lan, Shanshan. 2016a. "The Shifting Meanings of Race in China: A Case Study of the African Diaspora Communities in Guangzhou." *City and Society* 28 (3): 298–318.

Lan, Shanshan. 2016b. "Between Mobility and Immobility: Undocumented African Migrants Living in the Shadow of the Chinese State." In *Mobility, Sociability and Well-Being of Urban Living*, edited by Donggen Wang and Shenjing He, 3–21. Princeton, NJ: Springer Publishing.

Lan, Shanshan. 2017. "'China Gives and China Takes': African Traders and the Nondocumenting States." *Focaal: Journal of Global and Historical Anthropology* 77: 50–62. https://doi.org/10.3167/fcl.2017.770105.

Lee, Ching Kwan. 1998. *Gender and the South China Miracle: Two Worlds of Factory Women*. Berkeley: University of California Press.

Lee, Ching Kwan. 2018. *The Specter of Global China: Politics, Labor, and Foreign Investment in Africa*. Chicago: University of Chicago Press.

Lee, S. Heijin, Christina H. Moon, and Thuy Linh Nguyen Tu. 2019. *Fashion and Beauty in the Time of Asia*. New York: New York University Press.

Lefebvre, Henri. 1992. *The Production of Space*. Hoboken, NJ: Wiley-Blackwell.

Li, Mengfeiyang, Wei Kang, and Zongru Yang. 2022. "The Impacts of the Africans in Guangzhou." In *Proceedings of the 2022 6th International Seminar on Education, Management and Social Sciences (ISEMSS 2022)*, edited by Ghaffar Ali, Mehmet Cüneyt Birkök, and Intakhab Alam Khan, 921–27. Paris: Atlantis Press. https://doi.org/10.2991/978-2-494069-31-2_107.

Li, Zhigang, Michal Lyons, and Alison Brown. 2012. "China's 'Chocolate City': An Ethnic Enclave in a Changing Landscape. "*African Diaspora* 5 (1): 51–72.

Li, Zhigang, Laurence J. C. Ma, and Desheng Xue. 2009. "An African Enclave in China: The Making of a New Transnational Urban Space." *Eurasian Geography and Economics* 50 (6): 699–719.

Liang, Sisi, and Qingfang Wang. 2020. "Cultural and Creative Industries and Urban (Re)Development in China." *Journal of Planning Literature* 35 (1): 54–70.

Liao, Yu, and Junfu Zhang. 2020. "Hukou Status, Housing Tenure Choice and Wealth Accumulation in Urban China." IZA Discussion Paper No. 13836. IZA Institute of Labor Economics. http://dx.doi.org/10.2139/ssrn.3726438.

Liebman, Benjamin, and Curtis Milhaupt. 2015. *Regulating the Visible Hand? The Institutional Implications of Chinese State Capitalism*. Oxford: Oxford University Press.

Lim, May. 2015. "From Farmers to Entrepreneurs: China's 'Taobao Village.'" *McGill International Review*, March 29. https://www.mironline.ca/from-farmers-to-entrepreneurs-chinas-taobao-village/.

Lin, Kevin. 2019. "New Sites of Struggle in a Changing China." *Socialist Worker*, September 3. https://socialistworker.co.uk/socialist-review-archive/new-sites-struggle-changing-china/.

Lin, Yi-Chieh Jessica. 2011. *Fake Stuff: China and the Rise of Counterfeit Goods*. London: Routledge.

Ling, Minhua. 2020. *The Inconvenient Generation: Migrant Youth Coming of Age on Shanghai's Edge*. Stanford, CA: Stanford University Press.

Lipovetsky, Gilles. 2002. *The Empire of Fashion: Dressing Modern Democracy*. Princeton, NJ: Princeton University Press.

Litzinger, Ralph. 2013. "The Labor Question in China: Apple and Beyond." *South Atlantic Quarterly* 112 (1): 172–78.

Liu, Huwy-Min Lucia. 2023. *Governing Death, Making Persons: The New Chinese Way of Death*. Ithaca, NY: Cornell University Press.

Liu, Xin. 2000. *In One's Own Shadow: An Ethnographic Account of the Condition of Post-Reform Rural China*. Berkeley: University of California Press.

Liu, Xin. 2002. *The Otherness of Self: A Genealogy of Self in Contemporary China*. Ann Arbor: University of Michigan Press.

Liu, Yaoquan. 1950. "Lujiangcun de Quanli Jiegou" (鹭江村的权力结构) [The power structure of Lujiang Village]. Bachelor's thesis, Department of Sociology, Lingnan University.

Lorusso, Silvio. 2020. *Entreprecariat: Everyone Is an Entrepreneur. Nobody Is Safe*. Eindhoven: Onomatopee Projects.

Lu, Xueren. 1991. "Lujiangcun Laodongli Jiegou jiqi Bianqian" (鹭江村劳动 力结构及其变迁) [Lujiang Village's labor force structure and its changes]. PhD diss., Department of Sociology, Zhongshan University.

Lüthje, Boy. 2019. "Platform Capitalism 'Made in China'? Intelligent Manufacturing, Taobao Villages and the Restructuring of Work." *Science, Technology and Society* 24 (2): 199–217.

Lüthje, Boy, Siqi Luo, and Hao Zhang. 2013. *Beyond the Iron Rice Bowl: Regimes of Production and Industrial Relations in China*. Frankfurt: Campus Verlag.

Luvaas, Brent. 2012. *DIY Style, Fashion, Music and Global Digital Cultures*. New York: Bloomsbury Academic Press.

Marx, Karl. 1857. *Grundrisse: Foundations of the Critique of Political Economy*. London: Pelican Books.

Marx, Karl. (1885) 1959. *Das Kapital, a Critique of Political Economy*. Chicago: H. Regnery.

Mason, Matt. 2008. *The Pirate's Dilemma: How Youth Culture Is Reinventing Capitalism*. New York: Free Press.

Mathews, Gordon. 2011. *Ghetto at the Center of the World: Chungking Mansions, Hong Kong*. Chicago: University of Chicago Press.

Mathews, Gordon, Linessa Dan Lin, and Yang Yang. 2015. *The World in Guangzhou: Africans and Other Foreigners in South China's Global Marketplace*. Chicago: University of Chicago Press.

Mauldin, Joshua T. 2020. "Law, Religion, and Society in China: A Contested Terrain." *Journal of Law and Religion* 35 (1): 102–12.

Mezzadra, Sandro, and Brett Neilson. 2012. "Between Inclusion and Exclusion: On the Topography of Global Space and Borders." *Theory, Culture and Society* 29 (4–5): 58–75.

Mezzadri, Alessandra, and Lulu Fan. 2018. "'Classes of Labour' at the Margins of Global Commodity Chains in India and China." *Development and Change* 49: 1034–63. https://doi.org/10.1111/dech.12412.

Millar, Kathleen. 2018. *Reclaiming the Discarded: Life and Labor on Rio's Garbage Dump.* Durham, NC: Duke University Press.

Miller, Daniel. 2009. *Stuff.* Cambridge: Polity Press.

Minney, Safia. 2017. *Slave to Fashion.* Oxford: New Internationalist Publications.

Mitchell, Timothy. 1991. *Colonising Egypt.* Berkeley: University of California Press.

Mitchell, Timothy. 1999. "Society, Economy, and the State Effect." In *State/Culture: State-Formation after the Cultural Turn,* edited by George Steinmetz. Ithaca, NY: Cornell University Press.

Miyazaki, Hirokazu. 2013. *Arbitraging Japan: Dreams of Capitalism at the End of Finance.* Berkeley: University of California Press.

Moon, Christina. 2014. "The Secret World of Fast Fashion." *Pacific Standard,* March 17. https://psmag.com/economics/secret-world-slow-road-korea-los -angeles-behind-fast-fashion-73956/.

Moon, Christina. 2016. "Times, Tempos, and the Rhythm of Fast Fashion in Los Angeles and Seoul." In *Fashion and Beauty in the Time of Asia,* edited by Heijin Lee, Christina Moon, and Thuy Linh Tu, 269–82. New York: New York University Press.

Moon, Christina. 2020. *Labor and Creativity in New York's Global Fashion Industry.* London: Routledge.

Muehlebach, Andrea. 2011. "On Affective Labor in Post-Fordist Italy." *Cultural Anthropology* 26 (1): 59–82. https://doi.org/10.1111/j.1548-1360.2010.01080.x.

Munck, Ronaldo. 2013. "The Precariat: A View from the South." *Third World Quarterly* 34 (5): 747–62.

Nakassis, Constantine V. 2013. "Brands and Their Surfeits." *Cultural Anthropology* 28 (1): 111–26. https://doi.org/10.1111/j.1548-1360.2012.01176.x.

Narotzky, Susana, and Gavin Smith. 2006. *Immediate Struggles: People, Power, and Place in Rural Spain.* Berkeley: University of California Press.

Neilson, Brett, and Ned Rossiter. 2005. "From Precarity to Precariousness and Back Again: Labour, Life and Unstable Networks." *Fibreculture Journal* (Issue 5), December 1. http://five.fibreculturejournal.org/fcj-022-from-precarity -to-precariousness-and-back-again-labour-life-and-unstable-networks/.

Neilson, Brett, and Ned Rossiter. 2008. "Precarity as a Political Concept, or, Fordism as Exception." *Theory, Culture and Society* 25 (7–8): 51–72.

Nguyen, Mimi Thi. 2015. "The Hoodie as Sign, Screen, Expectation, and Force." *Signs: Journal of Women in Culture and Society* 40 (4): 791–816.

Nguyen, Minh, Phill Wilcox, and Jake Lin. 2024. "Guest Editors' Introduction." In "The Good Life in Late-Socialist Asia: Aspirations, Politics, and Possibilities." Special issue, *positions asia critique* 32 (1): 1–25.

Nitzan, Jonathan, and Shimshon Bichler. 2009. *Capital as Power: A Study of Order and Creorder.* London: Routledge.

Nordstrom, Carolyn. 2007. *Global Outlaws: Crime, Money, and Power in the Contemporary World*. Berkeley: University of California Press.

N. W. 2023. "In Fear of Spatiotemporal Overlap: Coping with the Infrastructure of Zero-COVID." HAU: *Journal of Ethnographic Theory* 13 (2): 288–91.

O'Donnell, Mary Ann. 2013. "Laying Siege to the Villages: Lessons from Shenzhen." *OpenDemocracy*, March 28. https://www.opendemocracy.net/en /opensecurity/laying-siege-to-villages-lessons-from-shenzhen.

O'Donnell, Mary Ann, Winnie Wong, and Jonathan Bach. 2017. *Learning from Shenzhen: China's Post-Mao Experiment from Special Zone to Model City*. Chicago: University of Chicago Press.

Olander, Eric. 2016. "China Was Once a Hot Destination for African Migrants, Not Any More." *China File*, January 12. https://www.chinafile.com/china-africa -project/china-was-once-hot-destination-african-migrants-not-any-more.

Omni, Michael, and Howard Winant. 1994. *Racial Formation in the United States: From the 1960s to the 1990s*. London: Routledge.

Ong, Aihwa. 2006. *Neoliberalism as Exception: Mutations in Citizenship and Sovereignty*. Durham, NC: Duke University Press.

Ong, Aihwa, and Stephan J. Collier. 2004. *Global Assemblages: Technology, Politics, and Ethics as Anthropological Problems*. Hoboken, NJ: Wiley-Blackwell.

Ong, Aihwa, and Li Zhang. 2008. *Privatizing China: Socialism from Afar*. Ithaca, NY: Cornell University Press.

Osella, Filippo. 2022. "The Unbearable Lightness of Trust: Trade, Conviviality, and the Life-World of Indian Export Agents in Yiwu, China." *Modern Asian Studies* 56 (4): 1222–52.

Ou, Tzu-Chi. 2022. "Low-End Accumulation: Spatial Transformation and Social Stratification in a Beijing Urban Village." *positions: asia critique* 30 (3): 619–40.

Pang, Irene. 2019. "The Legal Construction of Precarity: Lessons from the Construction Sectors in Beijing and Delhi." *Critical Sociology* 45 (4–5): 549–64.

Pang, Laikwan. 2012. *Creativity and Its Discontents: China's Creative Industries and Intellectual Property Rights Offenses*. Durham, NC: Duke University Press.

Park, Seo Young. 2012. "Stitching the Fabric of Family: Time, Work, and Intimacy in Seoul's Tongdaemun Market." *Journal of Korean Studies* 17 (2): 383–406.

Park, Seo Young. 2021. *Stitching the 24-Hour City: Life, Labor, and the Problem of Speed in Seoul*. Ithaca, NY: Cornell University Press.

Peirce, Charles Sanders. 1955. *Philosophical Writings of Peirce*. Edited by Justus Buchler. New York: Dover Press.

Perdue, Peter. 2009. "Rise and Fall of the Canton Trade System—III: Canton and Hong Kong." MIT Visualizing Cultures. https://visualizingcultures.mit.edu /rise_fall_canton_01/pdf/cw03_essay.pdf.

Piore, Michael, and Charles Sabel. 1986. *The Second Industrial Divide: Possibilities for Prosperity*. New York: Basic Books.

Postone, Moishe. 1982. "Critical Pessimism and the Limits of Traditional Marxism." *Theory and Society* 11 (5): 617–58.

Postone, Moishe. 1993. *Time, Labor, and Social Domination: A Reinterpretation of Marx's Critical Theory*. Cambridge: Cambridge University Press.

Prieto, Nancy. 1997. *Beautiful Flowers of the Maquiladora: Life Histories of Women Workers in Tijuana*. Austin: University of Texas Press.

Pun, Ngai. 2005. *Made in China: Women Factory Workers in a Global Workplace*. Durham, NC: Duke University Press.

Pun, Ngai. 2012. "Gender and Class: Women's Working Lives in a Dormitory Labor Regime in China." *International Labor and Working Class History* 81: 178–81.

Pun, Ngai, and Jenny Chan. 2012. "Global Capital, the State, and Chinese Workers: The Foxconn Experience." *Modern China* 38 (4): 383–410.

Pun, Ngai, and Chris Smith. 2007. "Putting Transnational Labour Process in Its Place: The Dormitory Labour Regime in Post-Socialist China." *Work, Employment and Society* 21 (1): 27–45.

Qian, Chuwen. 1951. "Lujiangcun Yule Huodong de Yanjiu" (鹭江村娱乐活动的研究) [Research on recreational activities in Lujiang Village]. Bachelor's thesis, Department of Sociology, Lingnan University.

Qiu, P., and G. Wu. 2016. "Yuexiuqu zhengzhi chengzhongcun liuluan xiri zangluan dengfengcun gaizao bian lvyouqu" [Yuexiu District dealt with six disorderly phenomena, dirty and chaotic Dengfeng Village of yesterday transformed into tourist spot]. *Southern Metropolis Daily*, March 9.

Raustiala, Kal, and Christopher Sprigman. 2006. "The Piracy Paradox: Innovation and Intellectual Property in Fashion Design." *Virginia Law Review* 92 (8): 1687–777.

Reinach, Simona Segre. 2005. "China and Italy: Fast Fashion versus Prêt à Porter. Towards a New Culture of Fashion." *Fashion Theory* 9 (1): 43–56.

Ren, Gaoyu. 1991. "Jinjiao Nongcun de Chengshihua—Guangzhoushi Haizhuqu Lujiangcun Chengshihua Yanjiu" (近郊农村的城市化——广州市海珠区鹭江村城市化研究) [Urbanization of suburban rural areas—Research on the urbanization of Lujiang Village, Haizhu District, Guangzhou City]. In *Zhujiang Saojiaozhou Jizhen yu Jumin—Shehuixue de Shequ Yanjiu* (珠江三角洲集镇与居民—社会学的社区研究) [Market towns and residents in the Pearl River Delta—Sociological community research], edited by He Zhaofa, 138–57. Guangzhou: Huanan Ligong Daxue Chubanshe (广州: 南理工大学出版社) [Nanjing University of Technology Press].

Richaud, Lisa, and Ash Amin. 2020. "Life Amidst Rubble: Migrant Mental Health and the Management of Subjectivity in Urban China." *Public Culture* 32 (1): 77–106.

Rodriguez, Dylan. 2019. "Abolition as Praxis of Human Being: A Foreword." *Harvard Law Review* 132 (6). https://harvardlawreview.org/print/vol-132/abolition-as-praxis-of-human-being-a-foreword/.

Rofel, Lisa. 1999. *Other Modernities: Gendered Yearnings in China After Socialism*. Berkeley: University of California Press.

Rofel, Lisa. 2007. *Desiring China: Experiments in Neoliberalism, Sexuality, and Public Culture*. Durham, NC: Duke University Press.

Rofel, Lisa, and Sylvia Yanagisako. 2018. *Fabricating Transnational Capitalism: A Collaborative Ethnography of Italian-Chinese Global Fashion*. Durham, NC: Duke University Press.

Roitman, Janet. 2005. *Fiscal Disobedience: An Anthropology of Economic Regulation in Central Africa*. Princeton, NJ: Princeton University Press.

Rojas, Carlos, and Ralph A. Litzinger, eds. 2016. *Ghost Protocol: Development and Displacement in Global China*. Durham, NC: Duke University Press.

Rojas, Carlos, and Lisa Rofel. 2022. *New World Orderings: China and the Global South*. Durham, NC: Duke University Press.

Şaul, Mahir, and Michaela Pelican. 2014. "Global African Entrepreneurs: A New Research Perspective on Contemporary African Migration." *Urban Anthropology and Studies of Cultural Systems and World Economic Development* 43 (1/2/3): 1–16. http://www.jstor.org/stable/24643106.

Sautman, Barry. 1994. "Anti-Black Racism in Post-Mao China." *China Quarterly* 138: 413–37.

Schumpeter, Joseph. 1994. *Capitalism, Socialism, and Democracy*. London: Routledge.

Seigel, Mark. 2018. "Violence Work: Policing and Power." *Race and Class* 59 (4): 15–33. https://doi.org/10.1177/0306396817752617.

Sharma, Tarun. 2012. "Urban Villages of the Developed and Developing World." ThisBigCity, October 24. http://thisbigcity.net/urban-villages-of-the-developed-and-developing-world/.

Shih, Shu-Mei. 2013. "Race and Revolution: Blackness in China's Long Twentieth Century." PMLA/*Publications of the Modern Language Association of America* 128 (1): 156–62.

Shingō, Shigeo. 1989. *A Study of the Toyota Production System: From an Industrial Engineering Viewpoint*. Translated by Andrew P. Dillon. London: Routledge.

Shirk, Susan L. 2022. *Overreach: How China Derailed Its Peaceful Rise*. Oxford: Oxford University Press.

Siegle, Lucy. 2011. *To Die For: Is Fashion Wearing Out the World?* Notting Hill: Fourth Estate Publishing.

Simpson, Hannah. 2020. "Fast Fashion in China: A Humanitarian Issue." *Borgen Magazine*, October 14. https://www.borgenmagazine.com/fast-fashion-in-china/.

Siu, Helen. 2007. "Grounding Displacement: Uncivil Urban Spaces in Post-Reform South China." *American Ethnologist* 34 (2): 329–50.

Smart, Alan, and Li Zhang. 2006. "From Mountains and the Fields: The Urban Transition in the Anthropology of China." *China Information* 20 (3): 481–518.

Smith, Chris, and Pun Ngai. 2018. "Class and Precarity: An Unhappy Coupling in China's Working-Class Formation." *Work, Employment and Society* 32 (3): 599–615.

Solinger, Dorothy. 1995. "The Floating Population in the Cities: Changes for Assimilation?" In *Urban Spaces in Contemporary China: The Potential for Autonomy and Community in Post-Mao China*, edited by Deborah Davis. Cambridge: Woodrow Wilson Center Press and Cambridge University Press.

Solinger, Dorothy. 1999. *Contesting Citizenship in Urban China: Peasant Migrants, the State, and the Logic of the Market*. Berkeley: University of California Press.

Solinger, Dorothy. 2022. *Poverty and Pacification: The Chinese State Abandons the Old Working Class*. Blue Ridge Summit, PA: Rowman and Littlefield.

Sontag, Susan. 2001. *On Photography*. London: Picador.

Standing, Guy. 2011. *The Precariat: The New Dangerous Class*. New York: Bloomsbury.

Steffen, Megan. 2022. "The Fruits of Demolition: Generative Neglect in Zhengzhou's Urban Villages." *positions: asia critique* 30 (3): 571–94.

Strathern, Marilyn. 2000. *Audit Cultures: Anthropological Studies in Accountability, Ethics and the Academy*. London: Routledge.

Strathern, Marilyn. 2018. "Persons and Partible Persons." In *Schools and Styles of Anthropological Theory*, edited by Matei Candea. London: Routledge.

Sullivan, Michael J. 1994. "The 1988–89 Nanjing Anti-African Protests: Racial Nationalism or National Racism?" *China Quarterly* 138: 438–57.

Summers, Lawrence H. 2018. "Secular Stagnation and Macroeconomic Policy." *IMF Economic Review* 66: 226–50.

Swider, Sarah. 2015. *Building China: Informal Work and the New Precariat*. Ithaca, NY: Cornell University Press.

Tabanelli, Vania. 2021. "Science Parks and Their Role in China's Economy." *European Guanxi*, January 27. https://www.europeanguanxi.com/post/science-parks-and-their-role-in-china-s-economy.

Tally, Robert T. 1996. "Jameson's Project of Cognitive Mapping: A Critical Engagement." In *Social Cartography: Mapping Ways of Seeing Social and Educational Change*, edited by Rolland G. Paulston, 399–416. New York: Garland Publishing.

Taussig, Michael. 1983. *The Devil and Commodity Fetishism in South America*. Chapel Hill: University of North Carolina Press.

Taussig, Michael. 2012. *Beauty and the Beast*. Chicago: University of Chicago Press.

Taylor, Frederick Winslow. 1997. *The Principles of Scientific Management*. Garden City, NY: Dover Publications.

The F Team. 2021. *F**k Fast Fashion: 101 Ways to Change How You Shop and Help Save the Planet*. London: Trapeze Books.

Thomas, Dana. 2019. *Fashionopolis*. New York: Penguin.

Thomas, Kedron. 2009. "Structural Adjustment, Spatial Imaginaries, and 'Piracy' in Guatemala's Apparel Industry." *Anthropology of Work Review* 30 (1): 1–10.

Thomas, Kedron. 2016. *Regulating Style: Intellectual Property Law and the Business of Fashion in Guatemala*. Berkeley: University of California Press.

Tomaney, John. 1994. "A New Paradigm of Work Organization and Technology?" In *Post-Fordism: A Reader*, edited by Ash Amin, 157–94. Hoboken, NJ: Wiley-Blackwell.

Tsianos, Vassilis, and Dimitris Papadopoulos. 2006. "Precarity: A Savage Journey to the Heart of Embodied Capitalism." *Transversal Texts*, October. https://transversal.at/transversal/1106/tsianos-papadopoulos/en.

Tsing, Anna. 2005. *Friction: An Ethnography of Global Connection*. Princeton, NJ: Princeton University Press.

Tsing, Anna. 2009. "Supply Chains and the Human Condition." *Rethinking Marxism* 21 (2): 148–76.

Tsing, Anna. 2015. *The Mushroom at the End of the World: On the Possibility of Life in Capitalist Ruins*. Princeton, NJ: Princeton University Press.

Vann, Elizabeth. 2008. "The Limits of Authenticity in Vietnamese Consumer Markets." *American Anthropologist* 108 (2): 286–96.

Veblen, Thorstein. 1904. *The Theory of Business Enterprise*. New Brunswick, NJ: Transaction Books.

Verdery, Katherine. 1996. *What Was Socialism and What Comes Next?* Princeton, NJ: Princeton University Press.

Verdery, Katherine. 2003. *The Vanishing Hectare: Property and Value in Postsocialist Transylvania*. Ithaca, NY: Cornell University Press.

Vincent, Danny. 2020. "Africans in China: We Face Coronavirus Discrimination." BBC, April 16. https://www.bbc.com/news/world-africa-52309414.

Wang, Amber. 2023. "China's Christian Groups Told to Ensure 'Strict' Oversight of Religion as Communist Party Controls Tighten." *South China Morning Post*, December 24. https://www.scmp.com/news/china/politics/article/3246162 /chinas-christian-groups-told-ensure-strict-oversight-religion-communist -party-controls-tighten.

Wang, Hui, and Rebecca E. Karl. 2004. "The Year 1989 and the Historical Roots of Neoliberalism in China." *positions: east asia cultures critique* 12 (1): 7–70.

Wang, Qianni, and Ge Shifan. 2020. "How One Obscure Word Captures Urban China's Unhappiness." *Sixth Tone*, January 4. https://www.sixthtone.com /news/1006391.

Wang, Zhi'an. 2022. "Wang Sir's News Talk: 'Riot' in Kangle Village, Guangzhou." YouTube, uploaded November 16, 2002. https://www.youtube.com/watch?v =oP_ky5S8K5c.

Watson, Rubie. 1994. *Memory, History, and Opposition under State Socialism*. Santa Fe, NM: School for Advanced Research Press.

Weber, Isabella. 2018a. "China's Escape from the 'Big Bang': The 1980s Price Reform Debate in Historical Perspective." *Apollo—University of Cambridge Repository*. https://doi.org/10.17863/CAM.18824.

Weber, Isabella. 2018b. "China and Neoliberalism: Moving Beyond the China Is/ Is Not Neoliberal Dichotomy." *The SAGE Handbook of Neoliberalism*, edited by Damien Cahill, Melinda Cooper, Martjn Konings, and David Primrose, 219–33. Los Angeles: SAGE Reference.

Weber, Isabella. 2020. "Origins of China's Contested Relation with Neoliberalism: Economics, the World Bank, and Milton Friedman at the Dawn of Reform." *Global Perspectives* 1 (1): 12271. https://doi.org/10.1525/gp.2020.12271.

Weber, Isabella. 2021. *How China Escaped Shock Therapy: The Market Reform Debate*. New York: Routledge.

Weber, Max. (1904) 2002. *The Protestant Ethic and the Spirit of Capitalism*. London: Routledge.

Wei, Shang-Jin, Zhuan Xie, and Xiaobo Zhang. 2017. "From 'Made in China' to 'Innovated in China': Necessity, Prospect, and Challenges." *Journal of Economic Perspectives* 31 (1): 49–70.

Weller, Robert. 2012. "Responsive Authoritarianism and Blind-Eye Governance in China." In *Socialism Vanquished, Socialism Challenged: Eastern Europe and China 1989–2009*, edited by Nina Bandelj and Dorothy J. Solinger, 83–102. Oxford: Oxford University Press.

West, Paige. 2012. *From Modern Production to Imagined Primitive: The World of Coffee from Papua New Guinea*. Durham, NC: Duke University Press.

Whyte, William. 1956. *The Organization Man*. Philadelphia: University of Pennsylvania Press.

Wielander, Gerda. 2018. "Chinese Dreams of Happiness: What Are the Chances?" *Made in China Journal*, November 24. https://madeinchinajournal.com/2018/11/24/chinese-dreams-of-happiness-what-are-the-chances/.

Wilczak, Jessica. 2018. "'Clean, Safe, and Orderly': Migrants, Race and City Image in Global Guangzhou." *Asian and Pacific Migration Journal* 27 (1): 55–79.

Williams, Raymond. 2014. "From Preface to Film" (UK, 1954). In *Film Manifestos and Global Cinema Cultures: A Critical Anthology*, edited by Scott MacKenzie, 607–13. Berkeley: University of California Press.

Wilson, Elizabeth. 1985. *Adorned in Dreams*. Berkeley: University of California Press.

Winter, Tim. 2019. *Geocultural Power: China's Quest to Revive the Silk Roads for the Twenty-First Century*. Chicago: University of Chicago Press.

Women on a Swing (荡秋千的妇女). 2022. "困在城中村的人, 在等待希望/广州康乐村封控纪实" [People trapped in urban villages are waiting for hope/Guangzhou Kangle Village sealed record]. WeChat post, 20 November. https://archive.ph/mu1C7#selection-103.14-103.48.

Woodward, Sophie. 2005. "Looking Good: Feeling Right: Aesthetics of the Self." In *Clothing as Material Culture*, edited by Susanne Küchler and Daniel Miller, 21–40. New York: Berg.

Woodward, Sophie, and Daniel Miller. 2007. "Manifesto for a Study of Denim." *Social Anthropology/Anthropologie Sociale* 15 (3): 335–51. https://doi.org/10.1111/j.0964-0282.2007.00024.x.

Wyatt, Don J. 2009. *The Blacks of Premodern China*. Philadelphia: University of Pennsylvania Press.

Xiang, Biao. 2021a. "Grid Reaction: Comparing Mobility Restrictions During COVID-19 and SARS." *MoLab Inventory of Mobilities and Socioeconomic Changes*, January. https://doi.org/10.48509/molab.5217.

Xiang, Biao. 2021b. "Suspension: Seeking Agency for Change in the Hypermobile World." *Pacific Affairs* 94 (2): 233–50.

Yan, Hairong. 2008. *New Masters, New Servants: Migration, Development, and Women Workers in China*. Durham, NC: Duke University Press.

Yanagisako, Sylvia. 2002. *Producing Culture and Capital: Family Firms in Italy*. Princeton, NJ: Princeton University Press.

Yanagisako, Sylvia. 2018. "Reconfiguring Labour Value and the Capital/Labour Relation in Italian Global Fashion." *Journal of the Royal Anthropological Institute* 24 (S1): 47–60.

Yanagisako, Sylvia, and Carol Delaney, eds. 1995. *Naturalizing Power: Essays in Feminist Cultural Analysis*. London: Routledge.

Zhan, Mei. 2009. *Other-Worldly: Making Chinese Medicine Through Transnational Frames*. Durham, NC: Duke University Press.

Zhan, Yang. 2015. "'My Life Is Elsewhere': Social Exclusion and Rural Migrants' Consumption of Homeownership in Contemporary China." *Dialectical Anthropology* 39 (4): 405–22.

Zhan, Yang. 2022. "When It Is Dark in the East, It Is Light in the West: Lifelong Venturing and Accelerated Temporality in Beijing's Urban Villages." *positions: asia critique* 30 (3): 595–617.

Zhang, Hong. 2021. "Builders from China: From Third-World Solidarity to Globalised State Capitalism." *Made in China Journal*, December 1. https://madeinchinajournal.com/2021/12/01/builders-from-china-from-third-world-solidarity-to-globalised-state-capitalism/.

Zhang, Li. 2002. *Strangers in the City: Reconfigurations of Space, Power, and Social Networks Within China's Floating Population*. Stanford, CA: Stanford University Press.

Zhang, Xia. 2008. "Ziyou (Freedom), Occupational Choice, and Labor: Bangbang in Chongqing, People's Republic of China." *International Labor and Working-Class History* 73: 65–84.

Zhao, Shukai, and Andrew Kipnis. 2000. "Criminality and the Policing of Migrant Workers." *China Journal* 43: 101–10.

Zheng, Deben. 1991. "Chengjiao Renkou de Shehui Liudong Yanjiu—Yige Guangzhou Chengjiao Nongcun de Ge'an Fenxi" (城郊人口的社会流动研—一个广州城郊农村的个案分析) [Research on the social mobility of suburban population—A case study of Guangzhou's suburban rural areas]. In *Zhujiang Saojiaozhou Jizhen yu Jumin—Shehuixue de Shequ Yanjiu* (珠江三角洲集与居民——社会学的社区研究) [Communities and residents in the Pearl River delta—Community research in sociology], edited by He Zhaofa, 119–37. Guangzhou: Huanan Ligong Daxue Chubanshe (广州:华南理工大学出版社) [South China University of Technology Press].

Index

Page numbers in italics refer to figures.

evangelical entrepreneurship, 176, 177–78

Evergrande real estate corporation, 205

exploitation, 211, 225n8; accumulation, 28; by clients, 65, 86–92, 142–43, 188, 200, 201–2; fee collections, 21, 29, 42, 102–3, 108–9, 121, 133–34, 148; of female workers, 67; of migrant laborers, 35; mutual nurture, 80–82, 225n9; in production process, 224n4

extortion, 31; bribery, 109–12, 116, 125, 128, 131, 146–48, 184; customs inspection, 173–74; distribution of supplies during COVID-19, 207–8; human trafficking, 215n1; racialized practices of, 227n6; *shenfen* economy (identification economy), 29; Xi Fang Hang market, 29, 131, 132

extraction, 29, 54, 131, 211

factories: closures, 192, 201–2; household spaces, 222n1, 225n9; inter-ethnic identities, 225n11; personal narratives on factory labor, 96–97

faith-based accumulation, 51, 166, 169–70

family: abuse, 79; as agents of production, 5, 80–82, 225n9; biological reproductive family, 8; childcare, 61–62, 78, 79, 215n1; household formation, 222n1; parents, 62, 70, 215n1; separations, 38, 39, 179, 230n2; support of, 31, 62

fashion showrooms, 142, *143*

fashion trends, 135, 137–38

fast fashion markets: logistics, 155–58, 162, 178–79, 184, 210–11; temporality of, 26, 41–43, 66–67, 75, 155, 156–58, 207–8, 221n4

fast fashion supply chains, 25–26, 49, 212; categories of boundaries of, 77–78, 219n22; commodity exchanges, 32–35, 213; exclusion from, 58–59; flipping (*chao huo*), 29, 41, 136, 151–52, 159, 230n9; Made in China model, 8, 45; "patchy" accumulation, 42, 129, 221n6; pricing, 43–44, 221n8; sociality, 77–78, 206; speed to market delivery, 43–45, 56,

137–39, 151, 221n8; supply chain capitalism (Tsing), 25; transnational supply chains, 65–66. See also boss/bosshood; *contractor headings*

fee collections, 21, 29, 42, 102–3, 108–9, 121, 133–34, 148

financial crises, 142–44, 150

flexible appropriation, 142, 152–54, 159, 161; design copying, 135–37; flipping (*chao huo*), 29, 41, 134, 136, 151–52, 159, 230n9; inert inventory, 155–56; just-in-time manufacture, 28, 63, 67–69, 77–78, 79–86, 108, 124–25, 215n2, 219n20, 219n22, 223n2; raw materials, access to, 6, 22, 57, 138–39, 159, 200; retagging of garments, 29, 134, 151–52

flexible specialization, 67–68, 223n2, 224n4, 225n8

flipping (*chao huo*), 29, 41, 136, 151–52, 159, 230n9

floating population (*liudong renkou*), 7–8, 35, 39, 119–20

food distribution during pandemic, 207–8

forced labor trafficking, 215n1

Fordism, 2, 12, 24, 25, 41, 63, 78, 218n15, 218n16; flexible specialization and craft-based production, 67–68, 223n2; Taylorism, 68, 78, 224n4; tensions between contingency and control, 68–69, 224n6; wage work, 6, 16–17, 38–39, 63–64, 66, 73, 96–97

Fordist factories, 12; exploitation in, 66; migrant labor in, 40; women in, 62, 66–67

Forever 21 (retail chain), 56

Foucault, Michel, 226n5, 228n16

freedom, 2, 8, 16, 28, 39–41, 58–59, 62–64, 202, 224n6

free market enterprise, 18–20, 21

"friction" (Tsing), 229n3

gift-giving relations, 216n7

Global Pentecostal Living Faith Fellowship (GPLFF), 168–70, 176–78

policing of, 35; pride in workmanship, 166; religious tolerance, 177, 195; street vendors, 46–47; surveillance, 41; vulnerability of, 35, 96–98

migrants: access to mobility, 26; accumulation, 18–19; agency, 26; ages of, 73; aspirations of, 15–16; autonomy of, 39, 41; capital accumulation, 22; cash-based policing of, 108–9; challenges, 10–11; collective actions of, 209–10; commercial opportunities, 32–33; cross-cultural collaborations, 47; documentation checks, 7–8, 35, 39, 52, 54, 107, 113, 115–16, 119–20, 195, 228nn13–14; entrepreneurial aspirations of, 41–42; exclusion of, 39; exploitation of, 7, 13, 53; extraction of, 13; as floating population (*liudong renkou*), 7–8, 35, 39, 119–20; freedom felt by, 58–59; harassment of, 115; intimidation of, 109–10; languages of, 55, 57, 60, 94, 181, 191, 227n7; low-wage labor, 7; media images of, 105; performances of personhood, 47; personal dignity, 216n7; police harassment of, 109; protests, 128; risk, 64–65; rural migrants, 7–9, 35, 39, 47, 82–84, 104–5, 119, 164, 219n5; sanctions, 7; social status of, 9; state-sponsored benefits, 6–7, 8; street vendors (*zou gui*), 46–47, 51–53, 104–5, 108, 116–17, 156, *157*; temporary employment, 26, 28, 41, 66, 71, 73, 75, 82–84, 200, 221n4

migrant tenants: exploitation of, 35

migrant wholesalers in Xi Fang Hang market: treatment of, 131

migrant workers: exploitation by bosses, 65; kin-based relations, 78; as noncitizens, 9; police intimidation, 108; stalled mobility, 18–21, 28, 30, 62–66, 74, 197–99, 202–5

migration, *chuang* (breaking out), 13, 180; government regulation of, 35; out-migration of South Korean migrants, 58, 192–93, 195, 231n3; of peasants, 6–7; personal experiences of, 18; restrictions on, 6–7; sanctions, 6–7; transnational

migrants, 13. See also *hukou* household registration system

migratory entrapment, 64

migratory labor: mobility, 19

migratory sociality, 79–80

migratory venturing, 63

Millar, Kathleen, 219n5

Miyazaki, Hirokazu, 221n4

MNCs (multinational corporations), 213

mobility, 28, 213; boycott of Korean consumer goods, 192–93, 231n3; class mobility, 225n11; cross-border trading, 184; delivery men, 46, 50; disease-related lockdowns, 2, 176, 206–8, 209; entrepreneurial deferment, 74; of ethnic groups, 58–59, 192–93, 195, 210, 231n3; floating population (*liudong renkou*), 7–8, 35, 39, 119–20; grid management, 206–7, 209; Guangdong Act, 115; ID checks, 7–8, 35, 39, 52, 107, 113, 115–16, 119–20, 228nn13–14; inter-ethnic dynamics in *jiagongchang*, 88–95, 225n11; job-hopping, strategies of, 26, 41, 221n4; language proficiency, 55, 57, 60, 89, 94, 181, 184, 191–92, 227n7; logistics of, 155–58, 162, 178–79, 184, 210–11; migratory sociality, 79–80; networks, 30, 35, 49, 51–53, 57, 71, 163, 179, 184, 186, 191–92; out-migrations, 30, 58–59, 162–63, 168, 192–93, 195, 210–11, 231n3; pedicabs, 6, 46, 128, 139, 209–10; personal safety, 121–22; traffic patrols, 107–8; wage labor, 6, 16–17, 38–39, 64–66, 73, 96–97. *See also* COVID-19 pandemic; surveillance

Moon, Christina, 229n4

Mr. Liu (South Korean representative), 88–95, 225n11

multinational corporations, 56–58, 87–90

NAFTA (North American Free Trade Agreement), 179

Nancy (migrant entrepreneur), 121–22

Narotzky, Susana, 215n2, 222n13

negotiation strategies, 86–94

Negri, Antonio, 68–69, 224n6

subcontracting practices, 219n22; appeal of, 73–74; corporate oversight, 87–88; craft-based production, 43, 66–68, 223nn2–3, 224n4; prices impacted by, 44–45

subcontractors, 218n14; entrepreneurship of, 56, 188; mobility of, 62–63; personal narratives, 88–95, 225n11; risks of, 3, 10–11, 26–27, 43, 87–88, 559; roles of, 12, 16, 22, 44–45, 224n5. *See also* boss/boss-hood; *jiagongchang* (household assembly workshops); *Wong headings*

Sun (jobber), 181–83, 184

Sunyuanli (urban village), 36

Sunyuanli district, 42, 54–55, 99, 117, 127, 196

supply chain capitalism (Tsing), 25

surveillance, 28, 30, 100, 103, 105, 204; Christian congregations, 168–69; COVID-19 pandemic, 164, 205–7, 209; in factories, 41; fast fashion supply chains, 29, 87–88; gaps in, 116; racialization of migrants, 110–12, 113–14, 115, 117–18, 227n11; of religious congregations, 164, 168–69, 177, 195; *shenfen* economy (iden-tification economy), 100–102; traffic patrols, 107–8; visual tools of, 101; in Xi Fang Hang market, 131, 146

surveillance technologies, 204

suspension (*xuanfu*), strategies of, 20, 41, 221n4

suzhi (human quality), 55, 102, 118–21, 218n19, 228n15

Sylvianne (Senegalese trader), 99–100, 112–13, 123–24, 127, 162

Taobao villages, 1, 45

Taussig, Michael, 221n8, 222n9

taxation, 156, 184, 220n3

Taylorism, 68, 78, 224n4

temporary employment, 26, 28, 41, 66, 71, 73, 75, 82–84, 200, 207–8, 221n4

tensions between contingency and control, 68–69, 224n6

tensions between mobility and fixity, 68–69, 224n6

THAAD anti-ballistic missile system, 58, 192–93, 195, 231n3

third-party agents, 26

Thomas (pastor), 169, 171–72, 175–78

Thomas, Kedron, 227n6

Tianmall, 1, 45

Tina (migrant entrepreneur), 162–64, 181, 184, 185

TIT Creative Industry Park, 220n3

Tiyuxilu, 54

Tomaney, John, 224n4

Toyota Production System, 67

trabalhador workers, 221n5

traders: as brokers, 53

trade shows, 187

traffic patrols, 107–8

transitionology, 33

translational capitalism, 26

transnational capitalism, 24; precarity, 16

transnational mobility: cross-cultural dynamics, 49–50

treadmill effect, 205, 225n8

Tsing, Anna, 24, 42, 221n6, 229n3

tu er dai (peasant landlords), 10, 29, 34–35, 36, 42, 102–3

TVEs (township and village enterprises), 12–13

underground churches, 168–69, 194, 195

undocumented migrants, 6–7, 222n11

United States, 58, 163, 185, 187–90, 192–93, 195, 231n3

unmarried female migrants, 62, 67

unsold merchandise, 156–58

urban villages: construction of, 36; defined, 220n2; Sanyuanli district, 42, 54–55, 99, 117, 127, 196. *See also* Guangzhou; *jiagongchang* (household assembly work-shops); Xiaobei; Zhaocun

Verdery, Katherine, 34

wage labor, 6, 16–17, 38–39, 64–66, 73, 96–97

wealth distribution, 216n4, 218n18

www.ingramcontent.com/pod-product-compliance
Lightning Source LLC
Chambersburg PA
CBHW032345280326
41935CB00008B/463